Performing Noncitizenship

Performing Noncitizenship

Asylum Seekers in Australian Theatre, Film and Activism

Emma Cox

ANTHEM PRESS

Anthem Press
An imprint of Wimbledon Publishing Company
www.anthempress.com

This edition first published in UK and USA 2015
by ANTHEM PRESS
75–76 Blackfriars Road, London SE1 8HA, UK
or PO Box 9779, London SW19 7ZG, UK
and
244 Madison Ave #116, New York, NY 10016, USA

British Library Cataloguing-in-Publication Data
A catalogue record for this book is available from the British Library.

Library of Congress Cataloging-in-Publication Data
Cox, Emma.
Performing noncitizenship : asylum seekers in Australian theatre,
film and activism / Emma Cox.
pages cm
Includes bibliographical references and index.
ISBN 978-1-78308-400-5 (hardback : alk. paper) – ISBN 978-1-78308-401-2
(paperback : alk. paper) – ISBN 978-1-78308-402-9 (pdf ebook)
1. Marginality, Social–Australia. 2. Culture conflict–Australia.
3. Political refugees–Australia. 4. Refugees–Australia. I. Title.
HN843.5.C69 2015
303.60994–dc23
2015003284

ISBN-13: 978 1 78308 400 5 (Hbk)
ISBN-10: 1 78308 400 6 (Hbk)

ISBN-13: 978 1 78308 401 2 (Pbk)
ISBN-10: 1 78308 401 4 (Pbk)

This title is also available as an ebook.

CONTENTS

ACKNOWLEDGEMENTS

A number of people generously provided information, texts and other research materials, or critical insight during the period that this project has been in development and I extend my gratitude to each of them: Mohsen Soltany Zand; Victoria Carless; Ben Eltham; Linda Jaivin; Rosie Scott; Catherine Simmonds; Leah Mercer; Rand Hazou; David Williams; Paul Dwyer; Alison Jeffers; David Farrier; Jacqueline Lo; Helen Gilbert; Katharine Ellis; Christine Bacon; Linda Anchell; Susan Metcalfe; Helen Leeder; Don Reid; Sam Watson; Robbie Thorpe (Djuran Bunjileenee). The book could not have been completed without the library and archive resources of the Refugee Council Archive, University of East London; the Refugee Claimants Support Centre, Brisbane; the Australian National University; the National Library of Australia; the University of Cambridge; and especially Royal Holloway, University of London. I am grateful for funding support provided by the Australian National University and Royal Holloway.

Warm thanks to Andrew Sofer and my peer respondents at the Mellon School of Theater and Performance Research, Harvard University, for their incisive and constructive feedback on the work-in-progress. I also acknowledge the three anonymous peer reviewers of this book, whose thoughtful reports prompted new dimensions in my analysis.

Particular acknowledgement is due to Shahin Shafaei, Towfiq Al-Qady, Majid Shokor and Ardeshir Gholipour for sharing their time, knowledge and good humour, and for their willingness to remember the difficult past.

Earlier versions of material in chapters three and five have appeared in *Moving Worlds: A Journal of Transcultural Writings* (2012) and *Australian Studies* (2011), respectively, and I thank the editors and anonymous reviewers of both journals. Every effort has been made to trace copyright holders and to obtain their permission for the use of the images in this book.

Boundless thanks, as ever, to Anne and Graham Cox and above all to Jaya Savige.

INTRODUCTION:
FRAMING NONCITIZENSHIP

The decisive activity of biopower in our time consists in the production
not of life or death, but rather of a mutable and virtually infinite survival.

—Giorgio Agamben, *Remnants of Auschwitz*

In the early morning of 16 April 2009, a small Indonesian fishing vessel that
had been intercepted the previous day by an Australian Navy patrol exploded,
causing the drowning of five of the forty-seven asylum seekers on board and
injuring dozens more. A coronial inquest in 2010 found that 'a passenger or
passengers deliberately ignited petrol' in an attempt to ensure that the boat,
designated SIEV 36,[1] would not be returned to Indonesia (Cavanagh 5). The
explosion occurred near Ashmore Reef in the Indian Ocean; thirteen seriously
injured people were evacuated directly to the city of Darwin for urgent burns
treatment, while twenty-nine were transported to AED Oil's Front Puffin rig
in the Timor Sea before being taken to detention centres. While the injured
thirteen were entitled access to Australia's refugee determination and appeals
procedures, the remaining twenty-nine were not, having first arrived at an
excised offshore place.[2] The oil rig stands outside Australia's migration zone
under the terms of legislation devised in response to the *Tampa* scandal
of August 2001, when the Australian government refused to permit the
Norwegian container ship MV *Tampa* and its human cargo of 438 rescued
asylum seekers entry into Australian waters. That escalation point in policy
and mood on unauthorized asylum seekers, concurrent with the tightening
of security measures worldwide amid the shockwaves of 9/11, continues to
inflect Australia's combative engagement with 'irregular' noncitizens. The
control by disavowal over the bodies of the asylum seekers taken to the oil rig
can be traced to the instrumentalization of lives at sea that prevailed during
the *Tampa* incident eight years earlier.

It is just such lines of articulation that map the territory of this book. With reference to theatre, film and activism that has been engaged in the portrayal or participation of asylum seekers and refugees post-*Tampa*, I make the case that this work has been informed by and indeed contributed to the consolidation of noncitizenship as a cornerstone idea in contemporary Australian political and social organisation. That is not to say that practitioners or activists privilege the interests of citizens—certainly, as far as aims and intentions are concerned, they do nothing of the sort—but rather, that in the foregrounding of unauthorized asylum seekers as subjects and unauthorized arrival as an engagement against which Australians may be pitted as political and ethical actors, noncitizenship emerges as a concept with a peculiar, contradictory purchase. In a climate where asylum is heavily overdetermined (that is, readily conscripted for divergent ends by political leaders and mainstream media outlets, as well as a proliferation of cultural commentators), it seems less helpful to assume that performance, film or activism that advocates asylum seekers' rights to hospitality and political community will enact (or even *aim* to enact) interventions, much less emancipatory ends. In some moments, capacities or environments such work may do so, but its implications in terms of power and participation are complex and often contradictory. For one thing, by foregrounding stakes in asylum debates, creative and activist work can reiterate a politics of delineation, further entrenching distinctions artists and activists might hope to breach. As Judith Butler notes in *Bodies That Matter* in the context of gender, 'naming is at once the setting of a boundary, and also the repeated inculcation of a norm' (8). Similarly, the identification of asylum as a category subject to artistic and political representation, regardless of the emancipatory ideals of that representation, does not merely *describe* but is also *generative* of the category.

To a certain extent, this is always already the predicament or compact of artistic and cultural work that is targeted to a cause or condition, and it need not mean that politically counter-discursive or inclusive goals for theatre, film or activism are attenuated. Insightful and important work has been written on theatre and citizenship in the context of public participation (Wiles) and on how far performance may function as radical intervention (Kershaw) or intersect with and energize practices of social inclusion (Nicholson). But there has been little attention paid to theatre and performance's implicatedness in how irregular noncitizenship has been taken up in Western neoliberal democracies as a diagnosis for the ills of a precarious social and economic status quo. A core purpose of this book is to identify and illuminate the increasing power and leverage of irregular noncitizenship as an idea. In its interest in the ways representations of asylum seekers in Australia are informed by and inform identity politics amongst those who make up the majority of audiences and spectators for this work—that is: citizens, or those who already belong—*Performing Noncitizenship* differs in its primary orientation from recent cognate studies of asylum seeker and refugee representation in theatre, film and literature, which are broadly concerned with transformations at the nexus between refugee and host or with how the imaginative bonds of membership within national communities may be extended (Woolley, Balfour, Jeffers 2012). This study traces the contours of a politically potent compound category: Australian noncitizenship. Those two words depend on one another to generate a very particular meaning. Australian noncitizenship has been reified as a direct consequence of asylum seeker-related public discourse since 2001 to the extent that it has become impossible to imagine what Australia *means* without it.

While this book's discussion has obvious and significant resonances with global contexts of asylum and creative practices in host nations, discourse and representation in Australia are framed by a unique set of contingencies. Unlike so-called illegals or failed asylum seekers in the UK, *clandestino/a* in Italy, *sans-papiers* in France or illegal aliens and DREAMers in the US, Australian noncitizenship as it pertains to undocumented or unlawful asylum seekers has been successfully constructed as a contained (or containable) and administratively accounted-for category. This is largely the result of sophisticated and expensive technologies of immigration detention and deterrence enacted within a distinctive context of island-continent geography—'fortress Australia', as it is sometimes known. The overwhelming majority of the irregular asylum seeker population (which should not be confused with the generally depoliticized humanitarian quota entrants who arrive with protection visas) is either held in high-security detention camps or, more rarely, in community-style detention. While significant numbers of irregular or undocumented noncitizens in other economically developed nations navigate ambiguous quasi-lives within the territorial borders of the places they would seek refuge, existing in a vulnerable zone between visibility and invisibility, asylum seekers who have not obtained refugee status in Australia *cannot* directly contribute in any meaningful sense to Australian society. Australian noncitizenship is not, in terms of civic life, a condition that generates practical ambiguity or tension between the public sphere and the clandestine sphere. From this, two points should be drawn: one, that Australian borders have taken on a near-totemic power as a site of inoculation from outside, and two, that modes of appearance and representation other than in civic life take on a more prominent role in shaping conversations about what 'illegal' noncitizenship is.

Constructed in and through the practices that order their emplacement, Australian noncitizens are made recognizable en masse to the extent that (and in moments when) they are classed as *not acting within the law*. Such practices are on the one hand bureaucratic and forcible—they are, for instance, the technologies of deterrence and territorial excision that fuelled the distress cited as a cause for one or more asylum seekers to set fire to a boat in 2009—and they are also social. Sara Ahmed identifies a particular mode of sociality that constructs belonging relative to its other, arguing that it is 'relationships of social antagonism that produce the stranger as a figure in the first place' (79). While Ahmed's discussion encompasses the social construction of the stranger in public or civic spaces, I want to draw a distinction in the context at hand between instrumental sociality and civic sociality. Australian noncitizens are excluded from civic life, but they enter into instrumental social relations upon encountering citizens as people-at-work: Navy personnel, immigration authorities, detention guards and other detention centre employees, health professionals and so on. One of the key strategies or modes in Australian theatre, film and activism on this issue has been to bring the sociality of asylum into civic spaces via imagination and representation. Here, the depotentiated stranger can be figured in terms of sympathetic sociality. What we tend to see, then, is the stranger whose difference provokes hospitality, or the stranger who isn't that different after all, or the stranger who offers a context for redefining the familiar or the stranger who is permitted to tell his or her own story to those who choose, and are not compelled by their profession, to listen. The common denominator that can begin to emerge here is a universalized relation that Ahmed would recognize as stranger-ness, if not 'stranger fetishism' (9). This is perhaps a risk inherent to cultural production that is configured, in part, for political awareness and social change.

The works discussed in this book—theatrical productions, performance art and installation, documentary films and activist practice—are selected and understood in their capacity as performative engagements, and they all raise questions about embodiment or appearance and the politics and affects of representation, but they constitute a coherent body of work less for generic or aesthetic reasons than because their primary raison d'être can be traced in a direct line of descent to the precipitously swift way in which asylum was concretized in the Australian collective consciousness after 2001. As far as governmental responses to asylum within a Western neoliberal democracy—undoubtedly one of today's most fraught international engagements—are concerned, Australia has set out an exemplary series of policy innovations. A hot-button issue following the momentous domestic and global events that inaugurated the twenty-first century, asylum is now more divisive in Australia than it has ever been. News media typically fleshes out the noncitizen via reports of their most disturbing 'characteristic' behaviours: rioting, self-harm and suicide in overcrowded detention centres, as well as tragic deaths at sea following the wrecks of overloaded people-smuggling boats. All this stems from the policies that delineate Australian noncitizenship most starkly, that is, the laws and logistics of detention, maritime deterrence and resettlement. Australia has had in place a policy of mandatory immigration detention for all unauthorized asylum seekers since the passing of the Migration Amendment Act 1992. The most drastic and controversial *geopolitik* was spearheaded by the Liberal–National conservative coalition under John Howard's leadership (1996–2007), particularly in the years 2001–2005. Notwithstanding a brief softening of policy during the first year of the most recent Labor government (2007–2013),[3] punitive response to asylum seekers has become normalized and is now a bipartisan federal strategy. In the first half of 2013, the nation's onshore and offshore detention centres and transit accommodations peaked at almost nine thousand people, including some sixteen hundred children under eighteen.[4] This was more than double the previous peak in the years 2000–2001. Labor Prime Ministers Kevin Rudd (2007–2010, 2013) and Julia Gillard (2010–2013) remained under intense pressure from an opposition that took every opportunity to remind the electorate of the government's failure to 'stop the boats'. Toward the end of his second, brief prime ministership in 2013, Rudd announced that no asylum seekers arriving by boat would be given the opportunity to be resettled in Australia, even if they were found to be refugees. Less than a fortnight after its election victory in September 2013, the conservative Tony Abbott Liberal–National government inaugurated 'Operation Sovereign Borders', led by Lieutenant General of the Australian Army Angus Campbell, involving the forcible return of people-smuggling boats to Indonesia and other setting-off points, thereby reiterating a semantic drift several years in the making, which sees the work of corralling noncitizenship as a military operation.[5]

For political philosopher Giorgio Agamben, the militarization of sovereignty is epitomized in the modern nation state. He characterizes the concentration camp as inaugurating and exemplifying what has come to be a permanent 'state of exception', a concept developed from Carl Schmitt to describe the suspension of normal law and process in exceptional circumstances and applied to exceptional human lives.[6] Agamben explains that in the camp as it emerged during the Second World War, what 'was essentially a temporal suspension of the state of law, acquires a permanent spatial arrangement that, as such, remains constantly outside the normal state of law' (*Means* 39). Agamben is clear that statehood is not just *characterized* by its spatio-temporal capture of its own organizational exception, but is *defined* by it. With reference to US biopower since 9/11, he argues that 'the voluntary creation of a permanent state of emergency (though perhaps not declared in the technical sense) has become one of the essential practices of contemporary states, including so-called democratic ones' (*State* 2). A state of exception or emergency is, then—ostensibly in spite of itself—a permanent condition of ambiguity between biological human life and human life under the law, and is in this ambiguity that contemporary sovereign nations are demarcated and invested with biopolitical power. As far as concerns the peculiar duality of irregular noncitizenship as a necessary component of Australian citizenship that I seek to trace in this book, Agamben's conception of the 'topological structure' of the state of exception is constructive:

> *Being-outside, and yet belonging*: this is the topological structure of the state of exception, and only because the sovereign, who decides on the exception, is, in truth, logically defined in his being by the exception, can he too be defined by the oxymoron *ecstasy-belonging*. (*State* 35, italics in original)

From this we can derive a framework for understanding Australian noncitizenship as having ideological, temporal and topological bases. We may also perceive that Agamben is setting out here the corollary of the idea that exceptional bodies are held outside the nation: the sovereign authority's 'ecstasy'—in the etymological sense, its capacity to *stand outside itself*—derives from its being empowered to determine the exceptions to its own rules. Agamben's invocation of 'ecstasy' here is adroit, signifying as it does the sovereign as its own arbiter, enthralled by itself.

Of the structure of the exception, Agamben explains that it is not merely a zone or set of spatial arrangements subjected to the removal of the rule of law, but exists in a constitutive relation to the rule, characterized by suspension or abandonment: '[h]ere what is outside is included not simply by means of an interdiction or an internment, but rather by means of the suspension of the juridical order's validity—by letting the juridical order, that is, withdraw from the exception and abandon it' (*Homo* 18). This relational structure of abandonment and the zone of indistinction that it generates is what Agamben also refers to as 'the ban' (*Homo* 25). In *Postcolonial Asylum: Seeking Sanctuary Before the Law*, his study of asylum regimes and cultural production in the UK and Australia, David Farrier deftly sets out the implications of Agamben's ban in the context of the phenomenology and materiality of both asylum seeker and citizen; as he argues, 'the ban that subjects asylum seekers to the inclusive-exclusive relationship is replicated in the citizen's declaration of "we": one excludes by retaining the abandoned subject in the grip of the law's censure; the other includes by referring to those who fall outside the definition of the collective' (18). Farrier's observation offers an indirect but nevertheless sharp explanation for just how it is that performances of Australian noncitizenship have so much to say about what it looks and feels like to be Australian in the twenty-first century.

Australian sovereign power is imbricated in year-on-year policy measures but also exceeds them, articulating to bigger issues, such as globalization and global economics, international relations and security, as well as more deeply rooted ideas. Like noncitizenship, which is both a legislative ontology and a subjective condition of exclusion, ideas embedded in sovereignty as a mode of knowledge and power, including belonging, national identity, culture and heritage, engage both dispassionate and passionate human faculties. This is crucial to my discussion, which speaks to the need to chart a politics of emotion in and through creative and activist work. Agamben rejects relational creativity or agency as components by which the belonging of the citizen is cohered and reiterated as/in a community, asserting, '[t]he understanding of the Hobbesian mythologeme in terms of *contract* instead of *ban* condemned democracy to impotence every time it had to confront the problem of sovereign power and has also rendered modern democracy constitutionally incapable of truly thinking a politics freed from the form of the State' (*Homo* 65, italics in original). By dismissing the concept as well as the affective work of the social contract, Agamben perhaps underestimates the emotional textures of belonging as an affect whose interstitial contagiousness can confound a direct relationship to nationhood. It is in the interstices of affective belonging that the citizen's 'we', which Farrier rightly identifies as necessary for delineating the 'they' of the noncitizen, may (momentarily?) belie its own delineation. The qualification to this, which *Performing Noncitizenship* tries to map, is how robust the contagions of affect may be both inside and outside the time-space of the theatre, or the cinema, or a protest, or a personal encounter.

A critical tendency, detectable in Agamben, to distrust emotion (or at least, to doubt its creative or resistant potential), implies particular assumptions about what emotion is and what it does politically. Surveying research on emotions in sociology (the discipline outside the natural sciences that has dominated work on affect) over the last three or four decades, Jochen Kleres notes that one of the main challenges faced by sociologists, and more recently by humanities scholars, is of reckoning with the valorization of psycho-biological or neuroscientific accounts of emotion. A related challenge is that of deconstructing assumptions that scientific method operates independently of emotion; as Kleres argues, '[t]he emphasis on the internal logic of the scientific method—objectivity, the dispassionate operator—fails to convince when one considers that emotions are not reducible to neurochemicals, but are only real in the sense that they are experienced within the context of sociality and more specifically of unfolding lives' (15). Certainly, as far as this book is concerned, attention to the affective consequences of artistic and activist work illuminates the work's impact within communities or social networks, as well as its relationship to the hard materiality of protection and resettlement practices.

Paying attention to the politics of emotion is crucial to perceiving noncitizenship as an idea whose conditions of possibility are simultaneously legislative and affective. These categories seem to be mutually constitutive, but artistic and activist practice trades most of all on the latter. An individual's feelings about nationhood, security and belonging are constructed through a constellation of emotional responses (to places, people, events, ideas, discourses, senses) and theatre, film and activism are currencies with which these forms of knowledge are rehearsed, tested or reoriented. The types of emotions generated across cultures via the work I examine include shame, pity, fascination, exoticization and aversion as well as the more genial (and probably expected) feelings of compassion, empathy and hope; in this sense, cross-cultural affect constitutes, as I show, an ambivalent engagement. Indeed, outside the sphere of artistic and activist practice, the emotional consequences of cross-cultural contact can be decidedly unconvivial. Ghassan Hage has demonstrated how affect and affective practice can operate in the context of exclusionary nationalism. For Hage, writing about former Australian Prime Minister Howard's tenure, the affective pull of nationhood is epitomized by the xenophobic figures of the worried citizen or paranoid nationalist (*Against* 3). In an era when 'worried' citizens of economically developed nations perceive asylum seekers and refugees by indirect yet vivid means—through government discourse, media reports and the idea of a defendable national interest—theatre, film and activism of the kind examined here can offer spaces for other perceptions and knowledges. At the same time, the projects included in this book raise difficult questions about whether they serve the interests of asylum seekers as comprehensively as they consolidate alternative visions of ethical Australianness—in other words, the interests of the already 'converted'.

Until quite recently, scholarly work on asylum seekers and refugees has been largely the domain of social and political scientists, mental health researchers, economists, historians and international law experts. Over the last five to ten years, humanities scholars have turned their attention to debates relating to forced migration and associated issues of multiculturalism, cosmopolitanism and global interconnection. While grounded in the humanities, *Performing Noncitizenship* employs an interdisciplinary approach, engaging with scholarly, government, legislative, journalistic and non-specialist discourse, as well as my own interviews and correspondences with artists and activists from refugee and non-refugee backgrounds. The purpose of this book is not to construct anything resembling an archive of work that has responded to asylum politics since 2001; rather, it seeks through 'thick' description of selected theatre, film and activism to elucidate these as sites of representation (stories, images, ideas, discourses and so on) and as sites of social practice that are generative of, and not just reflective of, the ways that identities manifest in the spaces between groups separated-in-proximity by demarcations of national community.

The Structure of this Book

Each chapter of *Performing Noncitizenship* raises a particular set of critical and theoretical concerns, responsive to the particular modality of performance, film or activism under discussion. In chapter one, I map what I call a 'politics of innocence' in four theatrical productions about asylum seekers and refugees that employed various truth-telling techniques, chiefly verbatim theatre and non-naturalistic autobiography. As a consequence of the bureaucratic nexus in which the identifying tags asylum seeker and refugee are enmeshed—whereby, as Alison Jeffers argues in *Refugees, Theatre and Crisis: Performing Global Identities*, UN Refugee Convention frameworks necessitate *conventional* performances of refugee selfhood (17)—refugee innocence is often glossed with the presumption of innocence upheld in many criminal law jurisdictions. This chapter applies pressure to the concept of innocence, seeking to reconcile the legal presumption of innocence in criminal contexts, the moral structures of belief of and in asylum seekers and Hannah Arendt's conception of political innocence in *The Origins of Totalitarianism*. I make the case that as exceptional subjects who exist outside the frames of both criminal justice and civic life, Australian noncitizens activate *neither* a legal presumption of innocence *nor* a preemptive presumption of non-innocence (such as is activated by civic surveillance technologies, for instance). The theatrical representation of asylum, I argue, enters the aporia that opens up here, applying preemptive moral belief in the innocence of the noncitizen; but while the legal presumption of innocence serves individuals accused of crimes well, in its moral form it serves characters in theatrical performance less so, reducing rather than producing possibilities for complex, nuanced response. This chapter investigates how—or to put it more pointedly, how well—the four productions under discussion reproduced and found ways to exceed innocence, while still insisting that if certain rights (most pertinently, to habeas corpus, legislative appeal and non-refoulement) accrue to personhood, not citizenship, then their removal or deprivation must be a violation acted upon an innocent subject.

The productions analysed in this chapter span a period from 2004–2010. *Through the Wire* (2004) was a verbatim play devised and directed by Australian Ros Horin and presented in Melbourne, Canberra and regional New South Wales. The play's mode of presentation was documentary realism and its aim was to collapse distinctions between asylum seekers and their representation. In *Through the Wire*, the characters of three asylum seekers, based upon actual people and their testimonies, were played by Australian actors, while a fourth performed as himself. A very different verbatim piece, *CMI (A Certain Maritime Incident)* (2004), problematized its truth-telling capacity to a far greater extent. It was devised and performed by members of innovative Sydney-based theatre company version 1.0, utilizing Hansard transcripts of the 2002 Senate Select Committee on A Certain Maritime Incident, which dealt with the notorious 'children overboard' affair of the previous year, a political scandal involving government misrepresentation of a sea rescue, and the SIEV X tragedy (the X signifies that the boat was unintercepted), in which 353 asylum seekers lost their lives. Expressionistic approaches to history and narrative were to the fore in the other two works discussed in this chaper. *Nothing But Nothing: One Refugee's Story* (2005), was written and performed in Brisbane by Iraqi refugee Towfiq Al-Qady and supported by the advocacy collective Actors for Refugees. Al-Qady's piece interwove his own life history and those of his loved ones and the other asylum seekers with whom he was transported to Australia in a poetic, stream-of-consciousness narrative. *Journey of Asylum—Waiting* (2010) was devised by Catherine Simmonds and members of the Asylum Seeker Resource Centre in Melbourne and consisted of a series of vignettes based upon refugees' experiences, from daily realities in their homelands to uneasy resettlement in Australia. This chapter's analysis generates questions relating to memory, translation, agency, empathy and belief as they apply to the representation of real people and the communities of which they are part.

In the second chapter I consider the intimate territoriality of the home in two theatre productions that employed techniques of farce, satire and the absurd. With reference to Michel Foucault's concept of the heterotopia, I contend that even as it galvanizes the territoriality of Australian authorities, the condition of noncitizenship maps a border space that is simultaneously inside and outside the 'home' of the nation. This chapter interrogates the meanings and implications of this condition of in-betweenness via a discussion of *The Rainbow Dark* (2006) by Victoria Carless and Ben Eltham's *The Pacific Solution* (2006). By scaling political manoeuvres down to the domestic sphere via farce and absurdism, both Carless's and Eltham's plays crystallized the banal attitudes and impulses that can underpin the act of suspending another person's liberty. In both plays, asylum-seeking strangers are, surreally, locked into cupboards. My discussion applies Henri Bergson's *Laughter: An Essay on the Meaning of the Comic* as a framework for identifying where comedy lies in the midst of horrific abuse of refugees. It also considers Gaston Bachelard's lyrical reading of how we inhabit intimate domestic spaces, particularly the way cellars can represent the intensified emotional life of a house's inhabitants. The political implications of refugee comedy as it is theorized in this chapter foreground the subversiveness of comedy as a mode, and also chime with Agamben's concept in *Means Without End: Notes on Politics* of how the extrajudicial detention zone enacts a simultaneous exclusion and inclusion, that 'it is not simply an external space. According to the etymological meaning of the term *exception* (*ex-capere*), what is being excluded in the camp is *captured outside*, that is, it is included by virtue of its very exclusion' (40). The two plays' comedic fabulations of a domestic-carceral zone seem to offer an imaginative distillation of Agamben's concept of the paradoxical capture inside. Ultimately, I argue that Carless's and Eltham's domestic heterotopias generate spaces (both literally and figuratively) for interrogating and destabilizing noncitizenship even as they require the coherence of noncitizenship as a category in order to make any sense as critiques.

Documentary film has, over the last decade, been one of the most prominent and widely circulated modes of representing asylum stories in Australia. In the third chapter, I examine two feature-length documentary films, *Letters to Ali* (2004), written and directed by Clara Law and co-written by Eddie L. C. Fong, and *Hope* (2007), directed by Steve Thomas. The result of relationships of care and collaboration that developed between filmmakers and subjects, citizens and noncitizens, both documentary projects articulate ambivalently to the empowering affective practice of hope, in Ghassan Hage's sense, and to a mode of moral victimhood that requires the perpetual suffering of the asylum seeker. Both films frame noncitizenship in terms of territorial zones—borderscapes that manifest in the desert interior and the vast ocean, and even further afield, in Indonesia. While in Law's film the eponymous teenage Afghan asylum seeker, Ali, remains unseen, a phantom protagonist, Iraqi woman Amal Basry's self-representation in *Hope* consolidates her position as a public advocate for and voice by proxy of the asylum seekers who drowned in the 2001 sinking of the SIEV X. This chapter considers whose interests are served when the epistolary fragments of an unseen Ali and Basry's own bold testimony become signifiers of national asylum seeker policy, figured into a larger counter-discursive, counter-memorializing project. An important part of this signification process is the self-positioning of the asylum advocate-cum-filmmaker, whose political and personal attachments dictate the terms of cross-cultural engagement, marking out in the process out an imagined community of like-minded Australian citizens.

In chapter four I investigate the capacity of theatre, performance and activism to engage directly with the most contentious aspect of Australian asylum politics, extrajudicial detention, and in particular its starkest consequence: self-injury. In *Homo Sacer: Sovereign Power and Bare Life*, Agamben observes that the incarceration of people who are excluded from political participation or belonging represents the exacting, paradigmatic power of twentieth- and twenty-first century sovereignty to produce *homo sacer*, or 'bare life'. Developing Arendt's ideas, set out in *The Origins of Totalitarianism* and *The Human Condition*, on the right to have rights and on state violence, and simultaneously investigating the banned or expelled man under ancient Roman law, Agamben develops the concept of the *homo sacer* in the context of life divested of political significance (most crucially, citizenship) and exposed to imprisonment, exploitation, injury and ultimately death. The discussion in this chapter considers the extent to which detainees, short of being reduced irrevocably to bare life, might via self-injury reconfigure their incarcerated bodies, putting them to 'anti-work' or 'anti-use' in such a way as to show a consanguineous relationship between their wasted lives and the political lives of citizens. The case studies selected for analysis in this chapter sought to represent asylum seekers' incarceration and self-injury, the latter having mainly taken the form of lip-sewing, cutting and hunger striking. I argue that when extrajudicial immigration detention constructs a state of exception, separating noncitizens from what I term 'embodied citizenship' (this refers to the social and juridical functions of bodily wellness and liberty: nutrition, healthcare, freedom of movement and the right to habeas corpus), the instrumentalization of its modalities of pain in performance and activism frames noncitizenship as an infection borne by performers' bodies.

The four case studies that provide the basis of chapter four employ distinct but related techniques of performative representation. Australian artist-activist Mike Parr's performance installation, *Close the Concentration Camps* (2002), was a gruesome piece that saw Parr stitch his face and brand his body in support of asylum seekers undergoing these self-injuries in detention. Parr's work confronted the complex dynamics of watching others in pain. Lebanese Australian artist-activist Mireille Astore's performance installation, *Tampa* (2003), consisted of Astore occupying daily a cage-like structure at Tamarama beach, Sydney, over an eighteen-day period, reinscribing the leisured, moneyed space in terms of capture and containment. A series of solidarity fasts that took place across Australia in 2004 saw celebrities and activists place their fasting bodies on display in metropolitan spaces, sensitizing their own response to and responsibility for detained asylum seekers and translating this into affective public provocations. Iranian theatre practitioner and former detainee Shahin Shafaei's solo touring play, *Refugitive* (2002–04), centred on an unnamed man undergoing a hunger strike in an isolated detention cell. Shafaei's performances of this work constructed intimate spaces of connection with his audiences, intensified by his prolonged question-and-answer sessions with audiences that called up responses to the artist as an individual and as an embodied signifier of national asylum policy.

The fifth and final chapter interrogates competing ontologies of Australian sovereignty. It takes as its provocation the Aboriginal Australian performative ceremony of the 'Welcome to Country' and non-indigenous verbal acknowledgements of Aboriginal land (both of which take place frequently at events and gatherings across the country), to consider what might derive from a structurally marginalized but affectively accepted Aboriginal territorial claim (inhering in the right to welcome, or presumably reject, the newcomer) in the context of determinations of citizen and noncitizen, audacious boat-person and deserving refugee. I discuss indigenous scholar Aileen Moreton-Robinson's concept of patriarchal white sovereignty and consider the meanings and possibilities of Aboriginal sovereignty vis-à-vis the irregular arrival of asylum seekers. I trace recent points of engagement between refugees and Aboriginal activists, elders and scholars, and consider the imagining of such engagement in public activism (performatives, statements and critical discourse) and intimate activism (interpersonal contact, encompassing support as well as, more rarely, antagonism). The public and intimate activist practices examined in this chapter employ indigeneity as a tool for reconfiguring territorial relationships and hierarchies of power—effectively, for radically questioning the state's legitimacy. While noncitizenship emerges in preceding chapters as a discourse and political configuration marking unsuccessful arrival, this chapter shows how noncitizenship might also become a strategic position claimed by those who were 'there first', in defiance of prevailing frameworks for Australian belonging.

Neoliberal Consensus and the Illegality of Noncitizenship

The Howard government's refusal to admit the *Tampa* asylum seekers in August 2001 represented a crucial moment in the instigation of Australian policies of deterrence relating to unauthorized asylum seekers and a concomitant upwelling of arts and activist practice responding to these policies. While Australia is not unique in the West in its general antagonism toward asylum seekers who arrive without a visa, or specifically, its use of extrajudicial detention (similar carceral systems operate in the United States, the United Kingdom and several other European Union states)[7] it has put in place a punitive and uniquely totalizing apparatus for dealing with all unauthorized arrivals to its oceans and shores. David Farrier, who characterizes Australia's contemporary asylum policies as 'the most parsimonious […] in the western world', perceives in the enforcement of Australian territorial law a spectral twin, whereby '[t]ough dealing with new migrants operate[s] dually, both as a means of exorcizing the ghosts of contemporary Australia's difficult past and of excising "undesirables" from its future' ('Beyond Biopolitics' 263). For

Farrier, spectrality operates both in terms of the ghosted colonial past and in terms of an alternative future-to-come where violence might not be first and foremost read as 'attendant upon the law' (265).

If the upheavals of 2001 mark the starting point of this book, the last few years have, as I have indicated, seen a renewed intensification of the rhetoric on and challenges faced by displaced people. This goes beyond Australian politics. Recent waves of global economic crises have heightened the vulnerability of people living in economically and politically unstable parts of the world, prompting an increase in refugee numbers; the United Nations High Commissioner for Refugees, António Guterres, pointed out in a 24 February 2009 press conference with the then Australian Minister for Immigration and Citizenship Chris Evans that economic deterioration is an 'accelerating factor' in the existing pressures that force people to move, and moreover, a 'generator of xenophobia' directed at refugees in many parts of the world (Evans 'New Directions'). The forces that produce a twinning of global interconnection and global inequality are clearly manifest in the coercion of asylum seekers and refugees in Australia and elsewhere.

While it is important to observe the formal distinction between economic migrants and refugees—the latter are, according to article 1 of the 1951 United Nations Convention Relating to the Status of Refugees,[8] deemed to have a 'well-founded fear of being persecuted for reasons of race, religion, nationality, membership of a particular social group or political opinion'— the persecution that precipitates refugee movements cannot be disentangled from economic pressures. Certainly, the explosion of the people-smuggling boat that I cited at the beginning of the book (by no means the only maritime tragedy to befall asylum seekers in the Australasian region recently[9]) is part of an interconnected series of events that are linked, at least in part, to global economics as they are orchestrated by multinational interests in the Middle East, and yet an asylum seeker's successful activation of a claim for refugee status involves the disavowal of economic volition, as well as most other impulses or imperatives that might be read as 'ambition'.

Indeed, asylum seekers are required to carefully calibrate the appearance of agency in light of the fact that the overwhelming majority of the world's asylum seekers, refugees and internally displaced people live in border camps or at town fringes within or proximate to their unstable homelands. The work I focus upon in this book has emerged as a response to what is, in world terms, a trickle of human traffic to a place of wealth and stability, that is, to a nation unified by its ostensible neoliberal consensus and partialist politics. That performance, filmmaking and activism in Australia are overwhelmingly preoccupied with unauthorized asylum seekers, those who attempt to enter without a visa, as opposed to individuals who enter with visas granted under 'offshore' Refugee or Special Humanitarian Programme provisions, is a sign of the weight of discursive interest that is attendant on the notion of illegal arrival. In Australia the term 'illegal' has been used interchangeably with the even more morally pejorative 'queue-jumper', which seeks ideologically to disqualify asylum seekers from hospitality as a consequence of their adjudged self-interest and transgression of basic civility.[10] Under the terms of article 31(1) of the United Nations Convention, punitive treatment on the basis of unauthorized arrival is not justified:

> The Contracting States shall not impose penalties, on account of their illegal entry or presence, on refugees who, coming directly from a territory where their life or freedom was threatened in the sense of article 1, enter or are present in their territory without authorization, provided they present themselves without delay to the authorities and show good cause for their illegal entry or presence. (Convention Relating to the Status of Refugees)

Similarly, Article 5 of the UN Protocol Against the Smuggling of Migrants by Land, Sea, and Air states that '[m]igrants shall not become liable to criminal prosecution' for having been the object of the offence of people smuggling (Protocol Against 3). Applied as a descriptor of undesirable noncitizen bodies per se, and not just means of arrival, the term illegal immigrant implicitly defends the use of exceptional biopower vis-à-vis asylum seekers, chiefly the use of prolonged or indefinite extrajudicial detention. Even though the term is fundamentally problematized when a person requests protection from a Refugee Convention signatory nation, it is nevertheless a cornerstone of discourse on contemporary Australian noncitizenship.

As scholars of ethics, the body and society such as Judith Butler (see *Precarious Life*), Joanna Zylinska (see *The Ethics of Cultural Studies*) and Joseph Pugliese (see 'Penal Asylum') have illustrated, a philosophical intervention in contemporary discourse on state sovereignty and 'illegal' noncitizenship can be identified in French philosopher Emmanuel Levinas's emphasis upon a first principle of responsibility in the face of the other. For Levinas, an inheritor of Kantian moral philosophy, a relation of recognition and response epitomized in the human(e), naked encounter 'face-to-face with the Other' ('Time' 45), is a condition of being in the world that precedes politico-legal concepts. This ethical philosophy, situated in terms of what I would argue is an inevitably affective body-to-body relationality, is distinct from the partialist political position whereby, as Matthew J. Gibney explains, it is assumed 'that states, in their role as representatives of communities of citizens, are morally justified in enacting entrance policies that privilege the interests of their members' (23). In contrast with—indeed, oftentimes in direct opposition to—the idea of a relation of responsibility to noncitizens, the partialist view is concerned primarily with 'the reciprocal duties of citizens, those, in other words, already sharing a state [...] [and it] implicitly assume[s] that the question of who is and should be a member of the political community is basically unproblematical' (Gibney 24). The partialist position—which in Australia underpins the use of a citizenship test as well as the prerogative of immigration detention—differentiates the citizen from the noncitizen in apprehending responsibility, and as such stands in direct contrast with Levinas's philosophical insistence: '[m]y *self* [...] is never absolved from responsibility towards the Other' (qtd in Malka 291, italics in original). For Levinas, there can be no self in the absence of the other.

In its material and ideological forms, globalization represents a challenge to the role and value of partialist politics, and indeed, to the some of the underlying precepts of noncitizenship. The neoliberal market encompasses the transnational production and movement of goods, capital, ideas and people, and as recent and current financial crises have underlined, is highly interdependent. The concept of the nation, which, as critics such as Homi Bhabha, Ghassan Hage and Benedict Anderson have argued, depends for its cohesion upon the narration and perception of unified identity, exists in a complex dialectic with postnationalizing forces that exceed economics and the law; most obviously, the Internet revolution has precipitated a significant reconfiguration of ideas about social, cultural and political locatedness—as Graham Barwell and Kate Bowles observe, disembodied transnational movement on the Internet 'complicates our understanding of the everyday performance of nationality' (141). My purpose here is not to try to disentangle interconnected postnationalizing phenomena that are, variously, economic, technological, social, spatial and legislative, but to note that these give rise to cosmopolitan subjectivity, or the entry into relations with others from diverse backgrounds and cultures, for a variety of reasons. It may be argued that the administrative logic that tags human beings as 'illegal' ends up producing postnational intersubjectivity by virtue of the fact that illegal bodies only become illegal by their movement or attempts to move in ways that push back against a nation's laws as activated by its human agents; but to reappropriate 'illegality' as a tactic or some kind of embodied resistance seems to minimize a key point about the irregular noncitizen, which is that they access none of the intersubjective or inter-territorial privileges enjoyed by comparatively elite mobile cosmopolitans. As such, illegal bodies may activate or manifest politics, but they are not truly political actors.

'For Those Who've Come Across the Seas'[11]

Technologies of detention that operate outside of the contexts of criminality and habeas corpus are not new; as Foucault notes in *Discipline and Punish* with reference to the incarceration of the mentally ill throughout Europe, the 'principle of extra-penal incarceration was in fact never abandoned' (297). However sophisticated immigration detention may have become (not to mention monetized, with operational aspects of Australian detention centres contracted to the British multinational security corporation G4S, formerly Group 4 Securicor, and to its rival, the outsourcing company Serco), it occupies a place in a long genealogy of surveillant power. Similarly, aggressive territoriality did not emerge fully formed in Australian culture out of the *Tampa*'s wake, or after the United States was galvanized by attacks on its homeland. Rather, these and other events consolidated established currents in Australian history, culture and governance to cast unauthorized asylum seekers as the most polarizing figures in contemporary debates on Australian identity, security and (non)citizenship. Like other settler colonial nations, Australia has long nurtured foundational narratives of white[12] achievement in a vast, inhospitable land, harnessing the establishment of European forms of land use and settlement to a myth of white autochthony (see Cox, *Theatre* 36–38). But while the Immigration Restriction Act 1901, better known metonymically as the White Australia Policy, functioned to restrict non-European immigration to Australia until 1973, the territory claimed by the emergent Commonwealth of Australia contained more diverse and heterogeneous histories and populations than its narratives of nationhood and white autochthony were prepared to acknowledge. As historian Henry Reynolds observes:

> At the time of Federation [1901] the European population was small and either stationary or declining everywhere except along the Queensland coast. There were thriving Asian communities in most northern towns— Broome, Darwin, Thursday Island, Cooktown, Cairns, Townsville and Mackay. Large areas of the north—the Kimberleys, Arnhem Land, Cape York and much of the dry inland—were home to Aborigines who had little or no experience of Europeans and who could not in any practical sense be considered to be part of the new nation. (*North* xiv)

The occlusion of non-white histories is part of what William E. Connolly terms 'the politics of forgetting' (138) necessary for 'purified' imaginative processes of nation building as well as the practical consolidation of sovereignty. After the official abandonment of the White Australia Policy in 1973, federal discourse on both the left (under Prime Minister Gough Whitlam) and right (under Prime Minister Malcolm Fraser) began to advocate the idea of multiculturalism; this shifting discursive landscape was given legislative architecture in the form of the Racial Discrimination Act 1975, and in the context of indigenous grievances, the Aboriginal Land Rights (Northern Territory) Act 1976. In the two decades following the 1975 communist takeover of South Vietnam, Australia accepted approximately 137,000 Indochinese refugees, including some 2000 unauthorized boat arrivals (Jupp 69). However, as Bruce Grant notes, a 1979 poll indicated that 'Australians had, at best, mixed feelings about the new arrivals' ('After'). Ien Ang identifies the persistent fear of invasion from the Asian north as an affective key to the 'psycho-geography' of white Australia (129–30). Gibney argues that the intake of Indochinese refugees intensified invasion narratives, being 'a first visible sign to many Australians of the implications of ending racial discrimination in entrance' (179).

Slippages between the idea of *intake* and that of *influx* are familiar to immigration debates, and in 1988 the latter gained purchase in Australia via a report by an advisory committee on immigration, entitled *Immigration: A Commitment to Australia*, which warned that '[w]ithout immediate reform, current selection mechanisms will deliver many tens of thousands of immigrants more than the planned immigration program' (FitzGerald 1), and claimed furthermore that '[c]onfusion and mistrust of multiculturalism' was prevalent in Australian society, as was 'the suspicion that it drove immigration policy' (FitzGerald 2). In the same year, the then leader of the opposition, John Howard, rejected the term multiculturalism in favour of a concept of 'One Australia'. Not long after this schism in the community and political landscape was articulated, Australia's federal mandatory detention system was instituted by the Keating Labor government under the Migration Amendment Act 1992. A 273-day limit on detention was removed in 1994, making way for the incarceration of some detainees for several years. In October 1999, the Howard conservative government instituted the Temporary Protection Visa (TPV) for unauthorized asylum seekers found to be refugees. This three-year visa denied family reunion and the right of return to Australia after overseas travel, as well as access to a number of social, settlement and educational services (Mansouri and Bagdas 23). Abolished in 2008, the TPV was subject to successive reinstatement attempts in 2013 and 2014, spearheaded by Minister for Immigration and Border Protection Scott Morrison.[13] As a visa category, the TPV has no direct international precedent, although there are targeted provisions for temporary protection in United States and United Kingdom law.[14]

In 2001, in the wake of three controversies concerning unauthorized noncitizens that occurred in close succession in the latter half of the year,

Australia's steady erosion of asylum seekers' rights was accelerated. First, the *Tampa* incident sparked international condemnation, but according to various polls the government's action was supported by up to ninety per cent of Australians (Henderson 12). Second, on 6 October a sinking 'Suspected Illegal Entry Vessel' (SIEV 4) carrying 223 asylum seekers was intercepted by the Navy vessel HMAS *Adelaide* 100 nautical miles north of Christmas Island. The sea rescue obtained its misnomer, the 'children overboard' affair, after senior government ministers and the Prime Minister repeated the false claim that asylum seekers had thrown children into the ocean in order to manipulate the Navy and secure passage to Australia. Third, on 19 October 353 asylum seekers drowned when the unidentified vessel SIEV X sank in international waters between Indonesia and Australia. This most tragic of the three events of 2001 is also the least well remembered.[15]

The Howard government responded rapidly to the 'exceptional' situation of *Tampa* by passing a total of seven pieces of legislation (most of them amendments to the Migration Act 1958) through the federal parliament in the month of September 2001.[16] The main purpose of the legislation was, as noted at the very start of this book, to excise certain territories—including Ashmore and Cartier Islands, Christmas Island and Cocos (Keeling) Islands—from Australia's migration zone, ensuring that very few boats would reach Australian migration territory and thereby enabling the government to avoid processing intercepted asylum seekers under Australian law. In accordance with its economic priorities, the government's excision legislation did not diminish Australia's large Exclusive Economic Zone, in which it holds special rights regarding exploration and use of marine resources, or the rights of Australian citizens or visa holders to travel freely within and across excised places. Excision legislation worked alongside what was termed the Pacific Solution: the (costly) establishment of offshore detention and processing on the excised Australian territory of Christmas Island, as well as on the island nation of Nauru and on Manus Island in Papua New Guinea. Both states continue to be given much-needed financial aid for holding asylum seekers (see Siegal 'Crisis', and Hoffstaedter 'Rudd's'), but a 2014 riot on Manus Island, in which a young Iranian asylum seeker was killed by a local man employed by the Salvation Army, tragically highlighted the cracks in Australia's monetized transnational arrangements (see Bourke).

The Australian government's flexing of exceptional executive muscle in 2001 formed the ideological bedrock of federal asylum legislation as it exists to this day. The latest iteration of territorial excision brought the policy innovation to an (il)logical limit-point: in May 2013 a legislative amendment, the Migration Amendment (Unauthorised Maritime Arrivals and Other Measures) Act 2013, excised the entire continent of Australia from the migration zone for the purposes of 'unauthorised maritime arrival', meaning that no person arriving by such means will be able to apply directly for an Australian protection visa. This exemplifies what Agamben identifies as the 'continuing tendency in all of the Western democracies' for an explicit declaration of a state of exception to 'gradually [be] replaced by an unprecedented generalization of the paradigm of security as the normal technique of government' (*State* 14). The geopolitical technologies inaugurated by the Pacific Solution, which bear out Ien Ang's assertion that racial and territorial anxieties are intimately linked in the imaginary of white Australia (130), are precisely the kind of zealously coercive tools that define a nation's limits for its own members vis-à-vis its unwelcome noncitizens. These tools can enforce the most ludicrous of administrative contortions: at the time of writing, a bill presented to the Australian parliament, the Migration and Maritime Powers Legislation Amendment (Resolving the Asylum Legacy Caseload) Bill 2014, proposes, amongst other provisions, including the reinstatement of Temporary Protection Visas, that newborn children born in Australian territory or offshore detention centres to unauthorized maritime arrivals will also be designated as unauthorized maritime arrivals (101–102).

Artists and Advocates: Mapping Impetus

The central motive force for artists, activists, asylum seeker supporters and advocacy communities in Australia has been the emergence of the policies and cultural conditions described above. Their work is part of what is to a certain extent a national movement. However, I employ the word 'movement' with caution, as asylum seeker supporters in Australia have tended to form as essentially heterogeneous and decentralized clusters of individuals and organizations. While cultural and creative responses to asylum seekers and refugees are almost by definition supportive, the way in which that support is articulated, particularly the degree to which it opposes government policy and power, is varied, framed in terms of affects ranging from humanist compassion and hospitality to resistance that seeks to radically re-make the nation.

James Goodman argues that asylum seeker support movements that intensified in Australia in the early years of the twenty-first century were bifurcated in terms of national and global preoccupations; the former, he argues, 'is broadly instrumental, geared to national policy change, effectively to remaking "the nation", and reclaiming national pride against the shame of refugee detention' while the latter 'is more expressive, in demonstrating anger and outrage in the name of human empathy and dignity' (270–71). Both, he maintains, are underpinned by deep emotional responses to the noncitizen other, which provide the necessary impetus for cross-cultural solidarity and representation:

> Affective embedding, one may say, is a precondition for sustained mobilization. The aim here is to evoke an emotional response to an issue, one that elicits cognitive reflection and action. This involves the mobilization of moral emotions, arising from, or in reference to an experience or situation, an affective value appeal or normative judgment, and which then generates moral evaluations and social expectations, and thus actions. (272)

While I would agree that lines of connection (both embodied and ideological) between asylum seekers and supporters, Australian citizens and Australian noncitizens, are typically initiated in terms of what Goodman recognizes as 'moral emotions', they are constituted over a multifarious emotional terrain that exceeds this; certainly, the work that I examine mobilizes a range of affective engagements between artists and audiences, and a number of ways of thinking about the cultural, linguistic, political and ethical challenges of these engagements.

While a good deal of the work examined here involves collaboration and self-representation by asylum seekers and refugees, on balance, more of it involves work initiated or led *by Australians*, and indeed seeks to untangle the cultural conversations Australians are having *with one another*. This makes sense: ultimately, asylum legislation reveals more about Australia and Australians than it does about asylum seekers, and the fate of asylum seekers is umbilically tied with the question of what it means to be (and behave as) a citizen in a liberal democratic nation that is a signatory to the UN Refugee Convention and Protocol. Inasmuch as they fill some certain silences and animate certain obstructed cultural conversations, artistic and activist work on asylum may be socially or politically efficacious—a term I employ in Baz Kershaw's sense of how theatre can influence 'wider social and political realities' (1). Kershaw's theorization specifically concerns the 'ideological transaction' of live performance, where the 'community of the audience' plays a vital, constitutive role (23). However, it is important to acknowledge that the work examined in *Performing Noncitizenship* complicates, if not precludes, a uniform application of concepts like efficacy. The capacity for artistic and activist work to disrupt the potent affective pull of the nation—theorized comprehensively by scholars of nationalism—

will rarely be decisive, much less inevitable. Points of engagement and moments of mobilization may be prompted in and through arts and activism, not in a directly causal fashion, but slowly, partially, and as Helen Gilbert and Jacqueline Lo suggest, 'cumulatively' (204). More immediately, imaginative cross-cultural engagement has the potential to generate spaces of complicity among those citizens who might, in the end, become hosts to equals.

Chapter 1

THE POLITICS OF INNOCENCE
IN THEATRES OF REALITY

> I have spent all my life between yes and no.
>
> —Towfiq Al-Qady, *Nothing But Nothing*

> Innocence, in the sense of complete lack of responsibility, was the mark of
> their rightlessness as it was the seal of their loss of political status.
>
> —Hannah Arendt, *The Origins of Totalitarianism*

At the start of the book I referred to one of the many tragedies at sea that
have befallen asylum seekers transported on people-smuggling vessels across
the heavily-patrolled waters between Indonesia and Australia. As I noted, the five
deaths in this particular instance, following a large explosion of fuel on board the
asylum seeker vessel SIEV 36, were found at a coronial inquest to be the result of
deliberate sabotage by 'a passenger or passengers' (Cavanagh 5), that is, one or
more of the asylum seekers aboard the boat, in an attempt to ensure that they
would not be returned by Australian Navy personnel to Indonesia. Reports
in the wake of the 2009 event speculated that the cause of the boat explosion
had been deliberate, but before the findings of the 2010 coronial inquest were
published, it was all too easy for asylum seeker advocates, including academics,
to doubt the veracity of this claim, perhaps assuming it to be part of a general
strategy of character assassination akin to that which underpinned the 'children
overboard' scandal of 2001.[1] But the speculation turned out to be warranted,
as well as inconvenient for a politics that implicitly depends upon asylum seeker
innocence as a key reason for compassion to be extended to them. Of course,
the trouble with pegging asylum seekers' deservingness of humanitarian
protection in Australia to innocence is that it promotes a morality instead of
an ethics and that it struggles—indeed, is often unable—to absorb complex
motivations, duplicity or recklessness: in the case of the boat explosion, a plea

for asylum that turns into a deadly demand. That asylum seeking is, in Australia and other Western host nations, twinned with morality to the extent that it is sheds some light on the limited contexts in which discourses of hospitality find purchase in a globalized world increasingly dominated by partialist politics and authoritarian immigration regimes.

Media reporting on the 2010 coronial enquiry into SIEV 36 focused, appropriately enough, on the key finding of a deliberate ignition of petrol causing death, as well as on the actions of Australian Navy personnel. What didn't need to be emphasized was the way in which coroner Greg Cavanagh's report methodically registered the known particulars of the five deceased men, all Afghan nationals. Its cumulative effect is of unintentional poignancy. The following, pertaining to the first of the named deceased, is indicative:

> Particulars required to register the death are:
>
> a. The deceased was a male.
> b. The deceased was Mohammed Hassan Ayubi.
> c. The deceased was born in Afghanistan.
> d. The death was reported to the Coroner.
> e. The cause of death was drowning.
> f. The forensic pathologist was Dr Terence John Sinton and he viewed the body after death.
> g. The name of the deceased's mother is not known.
> h. The name of the deceased's father is not known.
> i. The deceased was temporarily within the Territory of Ashmore and Cartier Islands.
> j. The employment of the deceased is unknown.
> k. The deceased was 45 years of age. (7)

The other four deaths are registered in much the same way. The details (which in many cases are *non*-details) read as harrowing absences, though of course they aren't meant to carry such inflection. These are the kinds of haunting characterizations that a documentary theatre account of the event and its aftermath is likely to home in on. But theatres of reality that engage with asylum too often skip over pieces of evidence that intervene in frames of loss and victimhood. Cavanagh also concluded the following in his report:

> It is quite apparent when one compares the evidence of the Afghani witnesses to that which is depicted on the video, none of them are telling the truth. All of them are denying knowledge of events about which they must have some knowledge. Because they have all told similar lies I can only conclude that they have all to some extent colluded with each other and decided as a group to lie to this Inquest. (34)

If this statement is one that is difficult to imagine finding its way into a theatrical representation of asylum seekers' experiences under Australia's brutal immigration system, this signals, I argue, that Australian noncitizenship as it has emerged in theatrical guises has been corralled into a moral category, as innocent. Innocence here implies both constructions of non-culpability as well as meanings that are conventionally applied to minors, that is, subjects who are particularly susceptible or vulnerable to abusive power.

The presumption of innocence is a well-known cornerstone of many legal systems worldwide, including Australia's. But it is activated only in the context of criminal law, leaving in the contemporary world great swathes of civic life and political power structures in which it does not apply. Where the presumption of innocence does not negotiate the space between power and its implementation, something else emerges to fill the space. This can often be a pre-emptive presumption of non-innocence; for instance, a civic safeguard such as locking one's doors and windows or insuring one's property from theft. Antonella Galetta notes that 'the presumption of innocence does not benefit persons who are not charged with a criminal offence, as well as persons who are presumed of having committed a crime but not formally charged before a court' (Galetta). She argues that when the application of surveillance practices extends beyond the legal contexts in which the presumption of innocence is activated, significant social consequences ensue: '[t]he pre-emptive approach in policing exacerbated by the use of surveillance technologies spreads a great sense of suspicion within democratic societies. In turn, the use of technologies of suspicion threatens the typical relationship of trust that links citizens to the state, as well as the presumption of the individual's innocence' (Galetta). Galetta's discussion concerns civic surveillance technologies such as CCTV cameras (she doesn't mention surveillance of the Internet by the state, but this is a pervasive and urgent example), which may be understood as tools for a pre-emptive presumption of non-innocence.

It might at first glance appear that Australia's border surveillance technologies of maritime deterrence and forcible return, and of course its *uber*-technology of imprisonment for all unauthorized arrivals, are evidence of a pre-emptive presumption of non-innocence writ large. But they are, in fact, quite another thing entirely. I argued in the introduction to this book that Australia's asylum policies represent a comprehensive and long-standing state of exception, which Giorgio Agamben has variously characterized as a biopolitical condition where normal law and process are suspended, in exceptional circumstances, vis-à-vis exceptional bodies. Australia's border surveillance technologies and Australia's state of exception operate outside the contexts both of civic society *and* criminal law (at least in relation to asylum seekers: numerous prosecutions of captains and crew members of people-smuggling vessels have occurred in recent years[2]). For noncitizens that it has '*captured outside*' (Agamben, *Means* 40, italics in original), the exception or the ban does not activate a legal presumption of innocence *nor* a pre-emptive civic presumption of non-innocence. Andreas Schloenhardt and Hadley Hickson evaluate the principle of non-criminalization of smuggled migrants (guaranteed, as I noted in the introduction, under Article 5 of the UN Protocol Against the Smuggling of Migrants by Land, Sea, and Air) in the context of Australia's treatment of asylum seekers and identify a 'disturbing level of congruity' (61) between immigration detention and criminal imprisonment. What is just as disturbing here is how a UN principle designed to protect smuggled human beings can license its very opposite. Asylum seekers detained under Australia's asylum regime, Schloenhardt and Hickson observe, 'enjoy substantially fewer rights than persons convicted and imprisoned for committing criminal offences. They are denied the benefits and transparency of a judicial trial, face the possibility of indefinite detention if they cannot obtain a visa and if their removal cannot be arranged, and are deprived of the statutory guarantees of minimum detention conditions for convicted prisoners' (62–63). Australian immigration detention is not a measure that formally presumes innocence or guilt, even though it has the structural and symbolic effects of a guilt consensus, being enacted punitively and constructed in dominant discourse as the result of 'illegal' actions by 'illegal' noncitizens. Even worse, it is precisely through their non-criminalization that asylum seekers are cast into the most abject of biopolitical conditions.

Scholars have examined in some detail the theatricality or performativity of the law (for example, Peters; Brion), as well as theatre's capacity as social tribunal (for example, Botham; Monks) but the presumption of innocence, specifically, and the word itself have not been put under any real pressure in theatre and performance studies. Discussion in the humanities of how asylum is constructed in advocacy discourse and the arts has had more to say about the delimiting trope of victimhood than about constructions of innocence; in this sense such work has been indebted more to trauma theory than to political theory. Hannah Arendt, however, did recognize the important intersections between innocence, agency and en masse persecution; in *The Origins of Totalitarianism*, she writes that as the number of stateless people increased in Europe in the 1930s and 40s, 'the greater became the temptation to pay less attention to the deeds of the persecuting governments than to the status of the persecuted' (294), with the result that the persecuted became undifferentiated, unremarkable: 'they were and appeared to be nothing but human beings whose very innocence—from every point of view, and especially that of the persecuting government—was their greatest misfortune. Innocence, in the sense of complete lack of responsibility, was the mark of their rightlessness as it was the seal of their loss of political status' (295). The way in which Arendt uses the word 'innocence' here differs from its application in a legalistic sense; she is describing not the presumption of innocence that is activated when a person enters a power relation under criminal law, but the innocence that exists as a default when a person stands outside that law. This distinction helps to explain how it is that exceptional Australian noncitizens activate *neither* a legal presumption of innocence nor a pre-emptive civic presumption of non-innocence.

Theatre that represents or responds in some way to these irregular noncitizens enters this aporia. It seems entirely reasonable to suppose that a *moral* presumption of innocence manifests in Australian theatre that engages counter-discursively with asylum issues precisely because asylum seekers have not been able to insert themselves formally within the terms of the legal presumption or even a civic pre-emptive presumption. (In terms of creative and political motivation, this is a basic premise of representation as recuperation.) I argue, therefore, that a politics of asylum seeker innocence in theatres of reality can be indexed to the consolidation of Australian biopolitical technologies that 'criminalize' irregular noncitizens in the absence of criminal proceedings under a state of exception. Moreover, I contend that, contrary to its well-placed application in criminal law, the more thoroughgoing the application of a presumption of moral innocence in the theatre, the less scope a play has to challenge, surprise, diversify and most importantly tell fuller stories about asylum seekers' lives in the contemporary world. This extends beyond characterization: my discussion scrutinizes ways in which the theatrical endeavour can posit or problematize itself terms of representational innocence via different dramaturgical strategies or techniques.

The four plays that provide case studies for this chapter operated as various kinds of theatres of reality, and they offer contrasting examples of how innocence is implicated both at the representational level of character (particularly moral persuasiveness) and in terms of the theatrical endeavour as a total practice. The first two are verbatim pieces and the second two are expressionistic works of autobiographical theatre. The plays are *Through the Wire* (2004–05), devised and directed by Australian Ros Horin; *CMI (A Certain Maritime Incident)* (2004), devised by members of the Sydney performance company version 1.0; *Nothing But Nothing: One Refugee's Story* (2005), written and performed by Iraqi refugee Towfiq Al-Qady and supported by Actors for Refugees, Queensland; and *Journey of Asylum—Waiting* (2010), devised by Catherine Simmonds and members of the Asylum Seeker Resource Centre (ASRC) in Melbourne. The first two plays may be categorized as verbatim plays, though *Through the Wire* was much closer in ethos to the tribunal verbatim theatre that has been quite prominent in the UK and the United States over the last ten to fifteen years, while *CMI (A Certain Maritime Incident)* problematized its own status and capacity as a verbatim work. *Through the Wire* presented the testimonies of four asylum seekers and the Australian women that befriended and/or supported them whilst they were in immigration detention. In *Through the Wire*, Iranian actor, playwright and refugee Shahin Shafaei—the one person in the play to perform as himself—was instructed by his Australian director how to perform his own testimony; the other performers in *Through the Wire* are not refugees, but enacted refugees' testimonies in a mimetic fashion. In contrast, *CMI (A Certain Maritime Incident)* was devised from testimonies about asylum seekers: specifically, the 2002 Australian Senate Select Committee on the notorious 'children overboard' affair, summarized in the introduction to this book. *CMI (A Certain Maritime Incident)* was far more circumspect about the transparency of the historical record, the innocence of testimony and its own innocence as a theatrical form. The other two works discussed in this chapter were devised from true stories and were performed by refugees, but they did not employ the classic documentary theatre technique of utilizing existing 'raw materials' from interviews, statements, tribunals and so on. In his emotional, impressionistic solo work, *Nothing But Nothing*, Al-Qady performed his own story (enacting his adult and child selves) and also took on the perspectives of his mother, daughter and fellow asylum seekers. The work was suffused with the desire of its protagonist to be recognized by audiences as an innocent subject. *Journey of Asylum—Waiting* employed a discontinuous narrative of vignettes derived from stories shared in group and one-to-one environments and organized by Simmonds into a performance text. While also preoccupied with making a case for the innocence of its refugee characters, this piece blurred distinctions between dramatized truth and fiction and questioned moreover the broader use of performance as a medium for asylum narratives.

All but one of the plays (*CMI (A Certain Maritime Incident)*) involved performances by refugees, either as themselves or as non-autobiographical asylum seeker or refugee characters. And all but one of them (*Nothing But Nothing*) involved performances by Australians. These different representational modes had ethical, political, personal and aesthetic implications, as I will outline, but it is important to emphasize at the outset that representation in every case had a common starting point in the way asylum seeker noncitizenship has been made recognizable in contemporary Australia and indeed globally. As I noted in the introduction to this book, Alison Jeffers offers a compelling framework for thinking about expectations that are applied to refugee self-representation, inside and outside the theatre. She argues that asylum seekers who cross international borders become enmeshed in bureaucratic performances of 'refugeeness', being 'forced to play the role of "Convention refugees"' (*Refugees* 17) (a reference to the UN Refugee Convention), and in the process become *conventional* refugees, conforming to common expectations of suffering, powerlessness and victimhood. Conventional formulations of identity condition theatre made by and about refugees, constructing the spaces in which narratives can typically occur and the meanings that can be communicated between refugees and hosts. However, Jeffers also contends that '[w]hen bureaucratic performance reaches the limits of its usefulness, other narratives from theatrical and cultural performance take over, telling stories about some of the positive and complex experiences of refugeeness' (*Refugees* 40). But complexity doesn't always equate to moral ambiguity; indeed, I argue that the expectation that when a refugee speaks he or she is 'giving evidence' is so pervasive that it becomes exceedingly difficult to ethically circumvent constructions of refugees as innocent individuals. This goes for the kinds of stories that are told as well as the way in which they are heard. Innocence may function in this sense as a kind of narrative 'safeguard', gifted by those citizens who listen to the stories of asylum seekers and refugees, in the knowledge that the very act of narrativizing one's life is fraught with risk, and that the presumed 'guilt' of the noncitizen has already been instantiated by their exclusion under Australia's state of exception.

If a theatrical politics of innocence concerns narrative structure, tone, the performing body and how it is read, then it follows that moral presumptions of innocence function in terms of the performance of refugeeness *and* the performance of Australianness (something that may be glossed for my purposes as the performance of ethical citizenship). The latter is oriented in this context around *belief*. In a rationalist sense, belief is justified by evidence, but in theatres of reality, belief has an affective quality. In terms of asylum in Australia, belief or disbelief cannot take shape outside a frame of reference informed by an ideological disposition or opposition to asylum policies, such is the extraordinarily high profile of these policies. Just as it is impossible, as I contended in the introduction, to imagine what Australia *means* in the absence of the category 'Australian noncitizenship', so too is it impossible to orient structures of belief in or doubt of asylum seeker narratives emerging from Australia outside the nation's recent treatment of these people. Theatres of reality in this context frequently construct noncitizen subjects in two ways: first, as figures who are to be believed, that is, whose accounts of persecution are fundamentally credible, and also figures who are to be believed in, that is, emotionally and ideologically aligned with. Horin's *Through the Wire* was oriented mostly toward belief that is a recognizable cognate of the belief that orders uses of testimony in the judicial apparatus, that is, belief justified on the grounds of reasonable likelihood and corroborating accounts; version 1.0's *CMI (A Certain Maritime Incident)* was even more interested in the language of reason and evidence, but only because it found cause to cast serious doubt on such language's innocence when its aim is to discredit asylum seekers; Al-Qady's *Nothing But Nothing* and Simmonds's *Journey of Asylum—Waiting* were oriented mostly in terms of what I describe as pre-emptive belief, that is, belief of and in asylum seekers that is more akin to faith. Each of these, I will argue, has a politics and generates consequences for the terms on which asylum seekers come to be *recognizable* in representation.

Verbatim Theatres and the Evidentiary Paradigm

The two theatrical productions discussed in the following section, *Through the Wire* and *CMI (A Certain Maritime Incident)*, can be categorized under the rubric of verbatim theatre, but they represent important contrasting case studies for testing out the scope of testimony's use in Australian asylum discourse. Both works were oriented around the evidentiary paradigm inherent to verbatim theatre, in the sense that both positioned words as a primary means by which we come to know history and the other, but the second offered a more troubling perspective on the implication of all these words structuring habits of thought. Testimony's prominence in the performance of the law informs the terms upon which this form of language is commonly framed and received in theatre: as a first-person account of individual experience, a 'true' account that constitutes evidence of events in the past. Agnes Woolley articulates precisely the problem with the preoccupation with language as evidence in the context of refugee narratives, observing, '[i]f, as is usually the case, "well-founded" is interpreted as a demand for proof or evidence of the persecution from which the refugee is fleeing, then the current and prevailing concept of the refugee is rooted in the idea of a validating narrative' (124).

Of course, imperatives of truth and evidence contend with the inevitable processes of construction and mediation (connected to the fallibility of memory and the translative nature of representation) involved in testimony, problematizing the determination of 'what actually happened in the past' (Kennedy, 'Stolen' 116). Much has been written on the testimony's peculiar structure as a mode of representation that cannot constitute a transparent reflection of historical events, but is nevertheless bound to appear transparent, reflective and unmediated. In the following discussion I am particularly interested in the imperatives of those who elect to hear the testimony of a person, outside the context of the law, in terms of willingness and truthfulness. In respect of the latter, I take as a point of departure the epigraph of French resistance member Charlotte Delbo's poetic, fragmentary Holocaust memoir *Auschwitz and After* (first published in English in 1985): '[t]oday, I am not sure that what I wrote is true. I am certain it is truthful' (1). This statement may be interpreted in two ways: first, it may be an admission that one may not have got every historical detail 'right', and second, that the reality of traumatic personal experience is still so far beyond the limits of assimilable memory that it barely *feels* real. Delbo's observation in her last book, *Days and Memory* (first published in English in 2001), 'I feel that the one who was in the camp is not me, is not the person who is here, facing you' (3), implies that the latter may be more pertinent than the former, though they are not mutually exclusive.

Either way, the key word in Delbo's epigraph is *truthful*. This emphasizes intention and asks for an interlocutor's trust. It acknowledges that words do not have an unproblematic relationship to existence but that they fundamentally negotiate relationality. In the context of theatrical representations of refugees' stories, truthfulness has a politics. It structures an Australian civic opposition to an oppressive, exclusionary governmental structure. The truth/truthfulness tension lies at the heart of verbatim theatres (I use the plural here because of the divergent ways in which such theatre can manifest). Much has been written on verbatim theatre's peculiar predicament as a mode of representation that is bound to (often indeed meant to) appear transparent and unmediated, even as testimony's theatrical enactment complicates and compounds the representational problems already at stake in the act of testifying. In performance, refugee testimony becomes entangled with aesthetic concerns: it is edited or devised for the purposes of narrative or thematic structure and comes to bear some of the characteristics of dramatic narrative, such as dialogue, emotional tone or contrast, metaphor, symbolism and multiple subjectivity. Most of all, I argue, such theatre positions belief in its subjects' innocence as a political and ideological commitment.

Through the Wire is one of the most high-profile productions to have emerged in response to the issue of asylum in Australia. Devised and directed by Australian practitioner Ros Horin, it premiered at the Sydney Opera House studio in 2004 after a workshop season at the Sydney Festival at the beginning of that year, and it subsequently toured, with the assistance of production and touring company Performing Lines, to Melbourne, Canberra and regional New South Wales in 2005.[3] It was drawn from Horin's interviews with four refugees, Farshid Kheirollahpoor (played by Wadih Dona), Shahin Shafaei (himself), Mohsen Soltany Zand (played by Ali Ammouchi) and Rami (played by Hazem Shammas), who spent between twenty-two months and four years in various Australian detention centres.[4] The four men's stories were interwoven with testimonies from three Australian women who provided emotional and practical support for three of the men during their detention: Suzanne (played by Rhondda Findleton on tour and Linda Cropper in the workshop season), who supported Soltany Zand; Doreen (played by Katrina Foster on tour and Jacki Weaver in the workshop season), who supported Rami; and detention centre officer Gaby (played by Eloise Oxer on tour and Lucy Bell in the workshop season), who supported and subsequently began a relationship with Shafaei.[5] All real names remained unchanged in the play.

As I have noted elsewhere (Cox, 'Victimhood' 120–21), contemporary asylum narratives readily coalesce, as *Through the Wire* did, around certain identifiable tropes: the loss of home or homeland, the necessity to flee and a coercive relational structure whereby any real agency dissolves in the face of persecution. With its primary recourse to words, verbatim theatre tends toward explanatory detail, and as such, a certain amount of narrative rationality that can subject asylum to a taxonomy designed to elicit an audience's pity, outrage, shame and solidarity. This tends to solemnize refugees-as-victims—or more precisely, solemnize *responses* to refugees-as-victims. In Australia, verbatim theatre has been employed in several productions about asylum seekers and refugees, including *Citizen X* (2002), *Something to Declare* (2003) and *In Our Name* (2004). In the UK, it has become a mainstream form of political theatre, and in terms of asylum and refugee narratives, variations on its use have been seen in, for example, a piece set in Manchester about a failed asylum seeker, *I've Got Something to Show You*[6] (2005); performance works by the London outreach network, Actors for Human Rights;[7] the Testimonies Project South Africa, which was a 2011 collaboration at the Live Theatre in Newcastle; and *The Arrival* (2013), a touring work scripted by Sita Brahmachari and Kristine Landon-Smith, based on Shaun Tan's graphic novel. Similar narrative and thematic tendencies to those described above were evident in Rustaveli Theatre's *Do We Look like Refugees?!* (2010–2011), devised by UK practitioner Alecky Blythe with Georgian refugees, and *Aftermath* (2009) by American practitioners Jessica Blank and Erik Jensen, based upon interviews with Iraqi refugees living in Jordan.

In her role as writer/deviser and director of *Through the Wire*, Horin seems to have approached the project with a mindset that placed a certain burden of proof on her refugee interlocutors; that is, her process did not simply activate a moral presumption of innocence—or at least, Horin did not want it to appear that way. In a newspaper interview she explains, 'I went through the process of how do I know these people are telling the truth. I wasn't like some bleeding heart automatically believing everything' (qtd in Morgan 14) and elsewhere describes her approach to the project in language evocative of criminal law: 'quite forensic' (qtd in Simmonds 124). Horin distances herself here from the unreliability that is often associated with emotive accounts of traumatic experience, but even more importantly, she effectively positions herself as a gatekeeper and arbiter of veracity, thereby communicating to potential audiences that the content of *Through the Wire* can be believed. In other words, she uses her leadership role as a way of making *morally permissible* the spectator's presumption of innocence.

Certainly, *Through the Wire* was marketed with an emphasis on the truth of its content; the Performing Lines information pack for the touring production stated, '[e]ach of the characters speak[s] authentically—*in their own words*' (2, italics in original). But the play's claim to unmediated truth was emboldened most of all by the presence of one performer: Iranian playwright and actor Shahin Shafaei. As the only person to perform as himself, Shafaei was the play's 'authenticating' body. Promotional material and the programme note featured his image, usually photographed in medium close up or close up, and at the end of each performance, when photographs were projected of the people on whom each character was based, Shafaei's performance as himself became apparent in what Caroline Wake calls the 'traumatic reveal' ('To Witness Mimesis' 111). *Through the Wire*'s musical accompaniment was composed and performed live by Iranian Kurdish refugee and former detainee Jamal Alrekabi, further augmenting its credentials as an authentic enactment of and by refugees. And it was uniformly received in these terms; reviews and media promotions referred to the work's 'true stories' or 'human stories' (see, for example, Clark; Gill; Rose; 'Brutal Look'). The combination of directed self-representation with directed re-presentation of testimony makes *Through the Wire* a particularly complicated and problematic example of verbatim theatre.

The production design was sparse, consisting of a wire cage that foregrounded the play's emphasis on communication across carceral lines. The audience's attention was directed to oscillate between the performers as they 'testified' into microphones, and live-feed video projections of their faces in close-up. The confessional and often fraught nature of the text, with its implicit purpose of convincing audience members of what really happened, meant that if cinematic mediation constructed a kind of intimacy, it was the intimacy of zoom surveillance technology and voyeurism. As a symbolic device, it communicated to the audience that they were being told the truth and empowered spectators to scrutinize the unnaturally enlarged faces in a hypervisible relation. The production's evidentiary visual paradigm was underpinned by its deployment of 'believable' performances. The issue of believability is one that any actor performing testimony naturalistically (as dramatic reenactment) or as documentary realism (as a reenacted interview) has to grapple with. It is rare for refugees to perform, as Shafaei did, as themselves in professionally produced verbatim plays, for obvious ethical reasons to do with psychological wellbeing as well as practicalities to do with acting experience. Practitioners of verbatim theatre have in recent years devised various ways of conveying not only a sense of innocence in relation to the truthfulness of characters but also 'innocence' in terms of form. Perhaps most prominent in this regard is UK playwright Alecky Blythe's technique of 'recorded delivery', which is indebted to the acting techniques of Anna Deavere Smith and was deployed in the abovementioned *Do We Look Like Refugees?!*, among other works. It involves actors listening to recorded interviews and replicating not just the words, but the voice, including '[e]very cough, stutter and hesitation' (Blythe 125). As I will discuss below in relation to *CMI (A Certain Maritime Incident)*, a different way of approaching testimony is obliquely, that is, by frankly acknowledging the gap between witness and actor via metatheatrical dramaturgy. The performance of testimony in *Through the Wire* was undoubtedly an attempt to mask the gap between testifying individuals and performers not, it should be noted, by way of mimicry, but through the aesthetic of documentary realism. This included casting in a presupposed ballpark of ethnic specificity: the four female roles were performed by white Australian actors, while Dona (playing Farshid) is a Lebanese immigrant, Ammouchi (playing Soltany Zand) is the son of Lebanese immigrants and Shammas (playing Rami) is an Israel-born Palestinian Australian. I'll return to the problematics of this mimetic casting of ethnicity in a moment.

Horin's text was a discontinuous narrative that emphasized the connections that formed between the men and (with the exception of Kheirollahpoor) the Australian women who supported them. The play switched between these seven perspectives to construct a cohesive narrative trajectory, setting out the men's reasons for fleeing their homelands, their journey to seek asylum, their prolonged detention in Australia, the development of supportive friendships and finally their visa approval and release. The testimonies were interspersed with connecting dialogues and linked with thematic overlaps, the repetition or elaboration of comments and recollections, the sharing of jokes and making of comparisons. In this way, recognizable asylum seeker tropes become generalized affectively in terms of a broader plea for recognition and humanitarian response by Australians. Moral innocence in terms of character manifested as the personal integrity of each of the asylum seekers. The reasons each gave for fleeing their homeland bore this out. Soltany Zand had been a clerk of Iran's Military Courts and became a whistle-blower on judicial corruption. Rami had been a hotel concierge and was tortured in Iraq after providing foreigners with directions to a restaurant. Kheirollahpoor was a medical technician in Iran and fled after attempting to covertly investigate the suspected poisoning of Ahmad Khomeini, the son of the late Ayatollah Khomeini. Shafaei had been forced to flee Iran after a raid on a theatre that covertly staged his work, which had already been banned for challenging oppressive state ideology. The four men offered details about their personal and family lives: Kheirollahpoor's mother's murder during the 1979 Iranian revolution and the disappearance of fellow clinicians following the suspected poisoning plot; the wish of Shafaei's family that he would pursue a safer career as a doctor, then the arrest and disappearance of a director of one of his plays;

Soltany Zand being given his mother's jewellery to pay people smugglers; and Rami's desire to excel in the field of hospitality tourism, which prompted his ill-fated communication with foreigners in Iraq. *Through the Wire*'s integrity–persecution–salvation arc operated as the kind of narrative safeguard to which I referred above; audiences recognized pretty quickly the underlying pattern and so the stories became genres or types. This structured our belief of the men, and justified an ideological belief in them, as well as the collective that they represented: Australian noncitizens. These opening sections of *Through the Wire* established the moral structure of the men's persecution and constructed them as being innocent of ambition to come to Australia.

The link to the collective was not merely implicit. Shafaei described his boat journey to Australia using the first-person plural pronoun 'we', citing the nationalities of the 112 people on board, describing their fear and violent sickness. This grammatical construction reflects a poetics of speaking for others, and it is one that Primo Levi invoked self-consciously in *The Drowned and the Saved* to indicate community subjectivity with respect to Holocaust survivors: 'I can use the first person plural: I am not one of the taciturn' (150). Each of the asylum seekers was portrayed as advocating for the freedom of other oppressed people. Kheirollahpoor spoke of how at the Port Hedland detention centre he was a 'detainees' representative' and an activist, speaking on community radio about the poor conditions in which hundreds of people were being held and of the violent coercion of several individuals by guards. Kheirollahpoor and Soltany Zand became involved in a co-ordinated protest and mass break-out at Woomera detention centre, and Kheirollahpoor recounted the planning and execution of the action (of which he was an instigator), involving almost 100 people, in terms of 'we'. Soltany Zand proudly recalled an incident in which he defended a small child who was being treated with contempt by guards. Similarly, Shafaei explained his role as translator of official correspondence for fellow detainees. Even though these characterizations aligned the four asylum seekers entirely with moral (even heroic) rightness, it was in this section of the play that they overcame most decisively a frame of political innocence, being attributed volition via resistance to the very power structure Arendt saw being occluded as refugees become apprehended as blocs, that is, 'the persecuting governments' (*Origins* 294). In this regard, even though *Through the Wire*'s narrative structure rendered the four asylum narratives in terms of a moral type, it did open up space for differentiation in which we could glimpse Farshid, Shahin, Mohsen and Rami as political actors, culpable human beings.

It is important to be clear at this juncture that where moral or political innocence manifests in *Through the Wire* we should not simply attribute this to the testimony and other public representations offered by the individuals upon whom the play's characters were based; that is, the issue here is not necessarily with how noncitizens make themselves known but with how cross-cultural theatres of reality situate them. Shafaei has, as I will explain further in chapter four and in this book's conclusion, been a robust presence in community and participatory theatre in Australia. Mohsen Zoltany Zand has published and produced spoken word poetry, with the support of high-profile refugee advocates, including writer Thomas Keneally, psychologist and former politician Carmen Lawrence and politician Andrew Bartlett. Indeed, much of Soltany Zand's writing ventures outside the frame of innocence or non-volition; take for example the following brutal, challenging lines from his poem 'Dream of Freedom', first published in the anthology *Another Country* and reproduced in his first collection *Inside Out* (2010): 'I'm looking for a sharp razor/All rent is settled in a second/I can see freedom, the red of nature's sunset/and God on the sharp razor/Red is the only colour I can see/The hand is cutting/Blood is all over the room' (*Inside Out* 20). This voice is very different to the Mohsen whom audiences came to know in *Through the Wire*. It is, therefore, in the translation from refugee self-narrative to documentary theatre that non-volitional tropes about asylum seekers can become prominent, coalescing in a mutually-intensifying relation to the stories of others.

Challenges concerning the ethics and aesthetics of this translation in the context of verbatim theatre come down, probably more than anything else, to acting technique and embodiment generally. As I have explained, three non-refugee performers played three of the refugees in *Through the Wire*, speaking the testimonies and presenting themselves *as* the refugee witnesses/ subjects. In various discussions, Canadian theatre practitioner and scholar Julie Salverson has identified the risks involved in a mimetic mode of acting-as-the-other in terms of an emotionally intense identification with trauma narratives, or what she calls an 'erotics of suffering' or an 'erotics of injury' (see, for example, 'Change on Whose Terms'). When approaching the ethics of employing actors to perform as refugees, it can be argued persuasively that practical and psychological concerns must take precedence. The UK Refugee Council's Tim Finch makes a case for pragmatic ethics with reference to Sonja Linden's *Asylum Monologues*, a UK portable verbatim work created by Actors for Refugees (now Actors for Human Rights) that employs professional actors to present (but not re-enact the mode of telling of) refugees' testimonies:

> The way to change people's minds or people's perceptions on this issue is to hear from asylum seekers and refugees themselves [...] It wouldn't be appropriate and it's certainly not possible for there to be a sort of 'touring circus' of asylum seekers and refugees going around every community [...] what Actors for Refugees does is the next best thing:

uses their real words, their real experiences, but uses other people to get that across; so it's testimony. (qtd in *Asylum Monologues* promotional DVD)

Asylum Monologues is presented by actors who sit or stand before a microphone and read from a script; as the work's director Christine Bacon explains, the simple presentational style means that performances require minimal rehearsal and are easily transportable—on 21 June 2007, for instance, the work was performed in twelve British cities simultaneously (Cox interview). Finch's reference to a 'touring circus' suggests a concern with what Helen Gilbert and Jacqueline Lo describe as 'reproducing the refugee as spectacle' (196), and Bacon invokes a similar argument to explain why refugees do not perform as themselves in testimonial works like *Asylum Monologues*: '[r]efugees, unless they're actors, are not performers, so it's [...] tokenistic to do that' (Cox interview). Downplaying the problematics of the gap between actor and refugee, Bacon emphasizes the transparency of presentation in *Asylum Monologues*, arguing that 'there's no sense that we're trying to manipulate [...] or [that we] can't be trusted', and that the actors are discouraged from emotionally realistic portrayals, being instructed: 'forget *being* the character [...] you as an actor [are] investing in this testimony [...] bearing witness to this person's experience [...] standing shoulder to shoulder with them' (Cox interview). The views expressed by Finch and Bacon speak to crucial issues of psychological wellbeing and the pragmatics of political awareness-raising, to the importance of communicating the words of others in the public sphere. Bacon maintains that the fact *Asylum Monologues* is typically, though not exclusively, performed by white British actors is a reflection of the availability of actors in Britain and the non-racially-selective basis upon which performers are recruited; moreover, she suggests that it may enable the work to speak more affectively to a similarly constituted (in other words, predominantly white) British audience community (Cox interview). While problematic, this argument accords with Bacon's aim of having actors speak for but not *as* refugees as it acknowledges the vast gap between refugee and actor.

Far more controversial than this is the fact that one of the refugees whose story was presented in *Through the Wire*, Farshid Kheirollahpoor, auditioned unsuccessfully for the role of himself. Here, aestheticized authenticity trumped ethics to an astonishing degree. The Australian actor, Dona, who portrayed him was, not surprisingly, uneasy upon discovering this, commenting in a media interview, 'you can imagine how I felt in hindsight. I didn't actually know that it was him in the [audition] room. I thought it was some exotic actor that [Horin] had selected to read as well' (qtd in Krauth 28). This misidentification of Kheirollahpoor as an 'exotic' actor is sadly ironic; for the actor in a professional theatre context, it seems, the refugee is always already designated an absence to be filled by the embodied presence of the non-refugee. (This is a paradigmatically different to treatment of refugees and their stories in participatory theatre contexts, which I discuss in the next section.) Despite his shock, as an actor Dona was comfortable with a universalized rendering of testimony: '[w]ords are words […] it does not matter to me what their origin is' (qtd in Krauth 28). For some critics of *Through the Wire*, misidentification went the other way; for instance, a previewer of the Sydney Festival rehearsed reading season wrote, 'Four refugees will join theatre industry heavyweights Jacki Weaver and Lucy Bell on stage tonight', and a reviewer commented, 'there's a dignity conferred especially by the closeness of the Iraqi and Iranian players to their material' ('Brutal Look' 9). Such comments are indicative not so much of the slippage or collapsing of distinctions between witness and actor/proxy upon which much verbatim theatre deliberately turns, but of actual *misrecognition*. The fact that misrecognition is described in terms of 'dignity' is telling. It implies a readiness to accept refugee characters within a paradigm of solemn belief. Wake deploys the term 'faceness' to account for the generalized emotional structure of the collective misrecognition that *Through the Wire* seemed to generate:

> Faceness refers to the vague and generalized humanity that an audience grants asylum seekers when they see a face that looks—to them, at least—like what an asylum seeker's face might look like. In this way, faceness is indistinct, indiscriminate, and somewhat sentimental, as evidenced by comments such as "[t]he characters are never less than endearing," as if being endearing were one of the five grounds for protection as a refugee. ('Witness' 113)

It seems that the most efficient means by which *Through the Wire* provoked Australian spectators to recognize the asylum seekers it depicted was by engaging audiences in generalized narrative structures and racialized semiotics, producing a symbolic theatrical *communitas*. That is to say, the play's work inhered in engaging spectators with the idea of the asylum seeker more or less as an innocent type who appears transparently in theatrical proximity. This engagement is, I contend, deeply ideological, setting the agenda and terms of appearance and compassionate recognition of the noncitizen other.

Through the Wire's representational ethics and aesthetics were most complex with respect to Shafaei's performance, the one which perhaps should, at least from the perspective of audience identification, have been the most straightforward. Shafaei commented in several media interviews connected with the production on his discomfort being instructed/constructed by Horin: 'I do struggle with [the performance] […] It's a very bizarre thing to be on the stage as yourself but being directed by someone else' (qtd in Humphries 38); elsewhere he observed, 'there's a director who says "Walk in this way" or "Tell this line in this way" and you know that in your real life it was done another way' (qtd in Gill 100). Eloise Oxer, playing Shafaei's then-partner Gaby Schultz in the touring production, encountered a related problem in reconciling real individuals with the play's representational framework; this meant trying to do 'justice to [Gaby and Shahin's] story' (qtd in Longworth 50), while finding herself having to prioritize Horin's aesthetics over Shafaei's. As Oxer recalled, 'Shahin tells me one thing but Ros wants something else [...] It's her vision, her creative frame' (qtd in Longworth 50). While the Australian actors had to reckon with external referents, Shafaei had to battle with himself as referent. For Shafaei, the dilemma was not just a question of authority but of emotional risk. He explained in an interview: 'I feel the pain in each dialogue [...] it was very hard for me to reveal every personal detail of my life' (qtd in Gill 100).

Reviewer Kirsten Krauth found Shafaei's performance, ostensibly that of the 'true' witness, less compelling than those of the other actors: '[t]he first time I see *Through the Wire* I am least engaged by Shafaei's performance. This unsettles me for weeks but when I go the second time I realize this man tells his story with the distance and abstraction of a writer/actor through necessity; he can be deported any time' (28). Given Shafaei's acknowledged struggle with self-enactment, the risk of psychological re-traumatizing must surely be added to immediate visa-related fears. Reflecting on his work in *Through the Wire* in 2008 (after an interval of four years), Shafaei acknowledged that the emotional stakes of his self-representation justified Horin's directorial interventions:

> There were nights that I was emotionally connected to my story; you would imagine as an actor that that would have to be the best performance, but that was the most monotonous performance because I was emotional. And straightaway it would affect six other professional actors. That performance would be completely flat [...] That is why Ros *needed* to take me somewhere else. (Cox interview)

This retrospective observation seems to bear out Bacon's argument that the iteration required for performance constitutes too great an emotional demand: 'you can't ask asylum seekers to continually get up and tell their story' (Cox interview). While Gilbert and Lo suggest that the emotional distance detected by Krauth indicated Shafaei's 'successful insertion of a critical caesura between the related subjectivities of performer and refugee' (197), Shafaei's own recollection of his work discloses that these more distant performances were actually the ones in which that caesura had collapsed. The nights when he was able to alternate between various emotional states as required by the role were, as he explains, the occasions in which he felt least emotionally engaged and was therefore able to render an affective, communicable image of himself (Cox interview). Shafaei's experience shows up a problem with instrumentalizing (and fetishizing) a performer as both signifier of trauma and the real thing: in order to be believable and to be believed in by an audience, Shafaei could not speak as himself.

In a televised interview with Shafaei, Australian broadcaster Andrew Denton made a point of the fact that Shafaei and other detainees were subject to a numerical identification system: '[y]ou got to Curtin and you [...] ceased really being Shahin Shafaei, you became refugee number 1319' (*Enough Rope*). A curious equivalence to this administrative transformation from individuality to anonymity via name substitution appears in Krauth's discussion of *Through the Wire*; she dedicates her article to 'S*', a man in Baxter detention centre with whom she had corresponded. It is clear that the use of a number or letter in place of a name can serve to dehumanize or to protect identity. It can also be appropriated as a radical political strategy of resistance, a locus around which a community of witnesses can coalesce and be spoken for. An example of this may be seen in Holocaust survivor Yehiel De-Nur (born Yehiel Feiner), who wrote of his experiences under the title Ka-Tzetnik 135633 (Concentration Camp Inmate 135633). Of De-Nur, Jeremy D. Popkin argues, 'the complete emptying out of his identity symbolized by the adoption of a number in place of a name also marks the fusion of the identities of all those who bore numbers' (348). While he does not use a number in place of a name in his creative practice, Shafaei/1319 did use his numerical identification in tactical resistance to the dehumanization that such categorization performs; in *Through the Wire*, the characters of Shafaei and Gaby wryly explained that Shafaei belonged to a group of detainees whose numbers started with the 'unlucky' 13 and who became known as a vocal, politicized collection of young men. In resistances such as this the assigning of numbers is subversively reinscribed according to the terms of those who are forced to bear them.

A markedly different approach to verbatim material, one underpinned by self-conscious awareness of the problems of testimonial representation, was evident in *CMI (A Certain Maritime Incident)*, which was first produced at the Performance Space, Sydney, in 2004, touring later that year to a Canberra venue The Street Theatre. A theatre company based in Sydney, version 1.0 devised the work as an alternative (and challenging) account of the structures of recognition applied by Australians to noncitizens that attempt to enter Australian territory and political community. Crucially, it did this by working with testimony that is almost overwhelmingly *about* rather than *from* asylum seekers and refugees. The project was led by Australian theatre practitioner David Williams and devised collectively by the performers and dramaturge Paul Dwyer. The text used Hansard transcripts of the Senate Select Committee on A Certain Maritime Incident, tabled in October 2002; this Committee investigated the information flows surrounding the events of 6–8 October 2001, when the HMAS *Adelaide* intercepted the distressed smuggling vessel SIEV 4 (Suspected Illegal Entry Vessel 4) and rescued its passengers. As I outlined in the introduction to this book, the incident has come to be known as the 'children overboard affair' because of a widely repeated report, later found to be incorrect, that a child (or children) had been thrown into the water by a person (or persons) on board the SIEV 4. With additional text written by the performers and dramaturge, the extracted Select Committee transcripts elucidate some of the ways in which accounts of the incident were reported and interpreted by various individuals, including Navy personnel who were present at the event, senior Navy personnel and politicians to whom these eye-witnesses reported and a selection of senators from various political parties. The final section of the play utilized refugee testimonies, but in a way that was entirely outside the frame of mimetic representation.

Fig. 1. Production still from *CMI (A Certain Maritime Incident)* by version 1.0. Performance Space, Sydney, 2004. (Photo: Heidrun Löhr.)

Obviously, version 1.0's production represented a departure from verbatim theatre projects about asylum seekers and refugees, of which *Through the Wire* is the most prominent example, produced in Australia around the same period—indeed, in his introduction to the play in *Australasian Drama Studies*, John McCallum goes so far as to define *CMI (A Certain Maritime Incident)* as a 'mock-verbatim' work (136). Formally, the piece was linguistically convoluted, complex, indeed, enamoured of its words, but it refused to allow its audiences to perceive words as conduits to truth. Instead, it employed various dramaturgical devices to call directly into question the use of verbatim testimony not only in theatre but in politics. With regard to the latter, the Select Committee was characterized as achieving little in terms of the verification and analysis of events, much less in apprehending asylum seekers as human witnesses rather than abstract players. Williams observes, in a comment whose present tense implies analysis of the theatrical text but which is also an assessment of real people, '[t]he Liberal senators behave shockingly, they stonewall and deny and waste time, but the Labor Party doesn't care about the asylum seekers, it just wants to embarrass the government' (qtd in Norrie 15). This characterization of Australian politicians reflects, of course, version 1.0's political agenda, but as I'll explain, the company did not position this agenda as innocent, much less profess its counter-narrative as a moral corrective. And yet, it was much more than just an exercise in postmodern ambivalence, but a production that was at once ethical, chilling and satirical.

The most important point to be made about *CMI (A Certain Maritime Incident)* in the context of this discussion concerns its deliberate absences. I argued at the start of the chapter that Australian noncitizens activate *neither* a legal presumption of innocence *nor* a pre-emptive civic presumption of non-innocence; they are held outside jurisdictions that would recognize them in these terms and as such they embody a radical innocence, in the sense that Arendt understands it: '[i]nnocence, in the sense of complete lack of responsibility, was the mark of their rightlessness as it was the seal of their loss of political status' (*Origins* 295). Rather than bringing asylum seekers into a representational frame, transforming their radical innocence as exceptional noncitizens as a moral innocence structured around belief in the way of *Through the Wire, CMI (A Certain Maritime Incident)* (until its final scene, at least) reproduced the silencing that the Select Committee enacted. This Committee heard no testimony from any of the 223 asylum seekers that were aboard SIEV 4. The reasons for this map the agenda of a state of exception, in which radical innocence resides; the Chair's foreword by Labor Senator Peter Cook states that because the Committee's jurisdiction only extended to Australia, asylum seeker witnesses had been effectively excluded from having their accounts appear on the public record:

the Committee received correspondence from many of the asylum seekers who were on 'the overboard boat' SIEV 4. The Committee's jurisdiction is limited to Australia and its territories. These asylum seekers were in detention on Manus Island at all the relevant times of this inquiry. This meant that their evidence could not be heard under privilege, nor could the usual protections be extended to them should they be adversely treated as a consequence of what they may have said. (Senate Select Committee xv)

By choosing to use as its key source material Hansard from the Committee, itself such an exemplary case study of the effect of noncitizens' capture outside political community, *CMI (A Certain Maritime Incident)* confronted the ways in which noncitizenship as identity politics and biopolitics is constructed in dominant Australian discourse. In other words, the play turned a mirror on Australian narratives of nationhood and belonging vis-à-vis its exceptional others. As such, asylum seeker innocence was rendered by this production in the radically silenced guise identified by Arendt, and crucially, it was rendered *knowingly*. It is worth acknowledging that this knowingness served to theatrically underscore some of the perspectives voiced in the enquiry itself, which was by no means a consensualizing process; for instance, following the observation quoted above, Cook registered his disapproval of the way asylum seekers were effectively silenced by the enquiry's jurisdiction and the scope of its protection: '[i]t has always seemed to me to be one-sided that the asylum seekers as key players in the event could not have their evidence heard and tested by the inquiry. Given the limitations it is not surprising that the asylum seekers themselves declined to participate in a telephone link-up with the Committee' (Senate Select Committee xvi).

As far as acting was concerned, and again, in contrast to *Through the Wire*'s mimetic veracity, version 1.0's company of actors did not seek to mask the inherent problem of enacting testimony. The nine performers (Danielle Antaki, Nikki Heywood, Stephen Klinder, Deborah Pollard, Christopher Ryan, David Williams, Frank Dwyer, Ren Khava and Minna McClure) essentially appeared as themselves, 'playing' the thirteen people involved in the Select Committee with self-reflexive metatheatricality. A reviewer of the Canberra production noted of the work's studied non-mimesis, 'the actors play in character, but drop out at times as if it is almost too difficult to play the role' ('Awash' 23). The gap between the Committee itself and version 1.0's performance of it was underlined with comic self-consciousness in the opening scene, which consisted of an interview with Defence Minister Peter Reith, played by a small child (Frank Dwyer, Khava and McClure, alternating) who read the testimony aloud while their words were processed and evaluated on a lie detector machine. From the outset, then, *CMI (A Certain Maritime Incident)* reflected upon its own non-innocence in terms of representation, accentuating spaces of mediation; a reviewer of the Sydney production discerned that the child's reading at the opening 'establishes a performance code in which voices and gestures sifted from the Senate transcript are assumed, dropped and wrestled with as a way of imagining the kind of dubious political operations that can make national headlines alternately happen or disappear' (Trezise 6). Several minutes into the production, an overhead projection announced to the audience: 'WE KNOW THAT YOU KNOW WE ARE NOT REALLY THE SENATORS WHO TOOK PART IN THE CMI SENATE INQUIRY. STEPHEN IS A LOT SHORTER THAN SENATOR COOK AND DEBORAH WHO PLAYS SENATOR FAULKNER IS ACTUALLY A WOMAN. WE FOUND THAT OUT AFTER THE AUDITION' (13). As well as parodying the misinformation that was at the heart of the 'children overboard' affair, this statement inserted a satirical alienation effect, reminding the audience of what they already knew about the gaps between historical event, testimony and theatrical representation.

The statement was one of several interventions and subversions that generated a sense of disorientation amid the taut verbatim text. When the Committee descended into chaos and confusion and a wheel-mounted enquiry table, dominating the stage, began to spin, another overhead projection read: 'NO TABLES WERE SPUN DURING THE CMI ENQUIRY. EXCEPT PERHAPS THE TEA TROLLEY. BUT THIS IS SPECULATION, NOT FACT' (20). This and similar explanations of theatrical manipulation mimicked the concern with linguistic precision that is apparent throughout the Select Committee testimonies. While witnesses at the Committee employed exacting, careful language, they drew on ambiguous evidence and interpretive assumptions. Particularly striking was the slippery concept of the 'fog of war' upon which Vice Admiral Shackleton based his account of the events of October 2001. *CMI (A Certain Maritime Incident)* seized on this, quoting him at length:

It is related to the reality that everything is real but it is not real. You are trying to pull threads and strands from many miscellaneous and sometimes disconnected information flows. You are trying to build a puzzle from many disconnected pieces [...] You are dealing with millions of shades of grey [...] This is constantly moving and going up and down all the time. (12)

In the performance, as in the Committee hearing from which it was devised, this evasive articulation of the difficulties of perception was met with approval from Senator Brandis, who remarked that Shackleton's statement is '[m]ost eloquent' (148); the theatre audience was left to ponder the nature of the fog in which Shackleton found himself, or as Williams incisively asks in an essay on the production, '[d]oes such a "fog or war" actually exist, or is there simply a fog machine?' (116). If there was a fog machine, part of its magic was to infer with confidence the motivations of asylum seekers: in act two of *CMI (A Certain Maritime Incident)*, Senator Mason read from a Navy officer's report which stated, 'self-harm and threats to children became commonplace and were not seen to be out of the ordinary—almost a "modus operandi"' (24). In a strategic paradox, these moral characterizations were combined with the distancing device of a language of bureaucratic acronyms, in which most of the Committee was fluent: asylum seekers were referred to variously as SUNCs (Suspected Unauthorised Non-Citizens), UAs (Unauthorised Arrivals), PIIs (Potential Illegal Immigrants) and UBAs (Unauthorised Boat Arrivals). As one reviewer of the production discerned, the subjects of the enquiry 'exist only as acronyms' (Norrie 15).

Peggy Phelan's contention, '[t]he condition of witnessing what one did not (and perhaps cannot) see is the condition of whatever age we are now entering' (577), was glaringly exemplified in the context of the Senate enquiry's statements from politicians who were not present as witnesses of the (non)event of 'children overboard'. This was comically underscored at the beginning of *CMI (A Certain Maritime Incident)* when the child-as-Reith asserted that children were thrown into the water on the basis of photographs and a low-quality film that he has not seen:

> these photos show absolutely without question whatsoever that there were children in the water. Now we have a number of people, obviously RAN [Royal Australian Navy] people who were there who reported the children were thrown into the water [...] I have subsequently been told that they have also got film. That film is apparently on HMAS *Adelaide*. I have not seen it myself and apparently the quality of it is not very good, and it's infra-red or something but I am told that someone has looked at it and it is an absolute fact, children were thrown into the water. (9–10)

The child's account is evaluated on a lie detector, which delivers a 'truth' reading, or at least, this is implied when the interviewer praises 'Reith' for having spoken the words 'much better than you did last time' (10). Truthful communication and structures of belief are stripped here of all pretence of innocence, but at the same time, the audience is invited to witness something 'true' on the level of embodied presence, in the face of the child (who is not 'performing' so much as reading off a laminated text) who indexes the seen/ unseen refugee children about whom Reith obfuscates.

In its fourth and final act, 'Sunk without a trace', *CMI (A Certain Maritime Incident)* changed gear. This section dealt with the secondary focus of the Senate Select Committee, the SIEV X disaster of 19 October 2001, in which 353 asylum seekers drowned en route to Australia. As I outlined in the introduction, and will expand in chapter three, this tragedy occupies the fringes of the nation's commemoration narratives. The production by version 1.0 concluded with a computerized voice 'speaking' testimonies from the few survivors of the disaster, while a corresponding written transcript was projected onto the back wall of the theatre. The testimonies, indistinguishable from one another in this mode of presentation, were drawn from translations of interviews filmed in Indonesia in the wake of the tragedy (McCallum 140). The computerized voice dehumanized the witnesses, and therefore, even as it sought in the final act to represent the testimony of asylum seekers, *CMI (A Certain Maritime Incident)* insisted on the distance that separates Australian society from the survivors and from the numerous drowned for whom the survivors speak. It also seemed to imply that the testimonies occupied a fractured, radically contingent representational space between survival and death, chiming with Agamben's characterization of 'the intimate dual structure of testimony as an act of an *auctor*, as the difference and completion of an impossibility and possibility of speaking, of the inhuman and the human, a living being and a speaking being' (*Remnants* 151). As the human/inhuman 'voice' was heard in the final moments of *CMI (A Certain Maritime Incident)*, the performers (the 'Committee') began to clear away props until all but one performer, who had been laid out, naked and washed, as if in a mortuary, remained. Here, in leaving audience members literally to make their own ends, the production offered an account of a tragic history, but did not give spectators moral cues by which to judge the innocence or otherwise of the inhuman voice: the record was not for evaluating, but simply there to be heard, and to be put on the theatrical record.

Autobiographical Performance and Pre-emptive Belief

The categories of innocence that do not permit the inclusion of irregular asylum seekers—the legal presumption of innocence and a pre-emptive presumption of non-innocence—have little to do with belief; they are categories from which criminal proceedings may be built. This section looks more closely at the function of belief in recuperating the moral innocence of asylum seekers, where other forms of innocence are absent. Iraqi refugee

Towfiq Al-Qady's solo, self-penned play, *Nothing But Nothing: One Refugee's Story*, was an emotional, lyrical and impressionistic work that was marketed in terms of truth, but not in a testimonial mould. It was presented in 2005 at Brisbane's Metro Arts Theatre, an important professional space in the city for the staging of new and emerging work, which during his production run also hosted an exhibition of Al-Qady's paintings. *Nothing But Nothing* was supported by the advocacy collective Actors for Refugees and was created with directorial assistance by Australian theatre practitioner Leah Mercer. With live accompaniment by Iraqi musician Taj Mahmoud (playing the oud), Al-Qady's performance testified to a lifetime's accumulation of trauma: a fearful and deprived childhood, the deaths of family members and friends, political persecution and imprisonment as a young adult and the arduous boat journey to Australia. Belying its claim to tell 'one refugee's story', the work continually had recourse to the trauma of a community—a family, a nation, a group of asylum seekers, and civilians during war. While audiences for performances of *Nothing But Nothing* were mostly comprised of Australians, members of Brisbane's Iraqi community attended in significant numbers (Hunter 30); the work was positioned, therefore, to speak not only for, but also *to* members of a minority community and as effectively a representative, Al-Qady's need to make the moral case for Iraqi refugees was acute.

Al-Qady worked autonomously on the piece from inception to realization. Mercer insists that her involvement 'was not a collaboration' and that she along with other key individuals 'was really just helping to facilitate [Al-Qady's] vision and his vision was very clear and very specific. It was as if he already had it all clearly performed in his head. For the most part we were just assisting him with the logistics of that vision' in terms of English pronunciation and phrasing (personal correspondence). Because it was not mediated by conventional direction, Al-Qady's enactment of his intersubjective testimonial narrative differed significantly in terms of agency and authority from Shafaei's representation of the self in Horin's *Through the Wire*. Al-Qady's narrative was fluid, unstable and often dreamlike, privileging expressionistic and heightened emotion over linearity or structural coherence. Any solo, autobiographical project that recounts traumatic experience will reflect the witness's desire not only to communicate and construct his or her life in narrative, but also fundamentally to be believed. For Al-Qady, being believed seems to have been indexed to emotional exposure and heightened theatricality. His occasional bombast likely masked deeper anxieties associated with the burden of the witness to compel the listener or interlocutor. Al-Qady's mode reflected a different approach to the weight of history and dominant discourse from a rationalist, evidentiary one. Consider by way of contrast how the imperative of being believed, and being believable, informs Primo Levi's positioning of his subjectivity in the Afterword to *If This is a Man* and *The Truce*: 'I have deliberately assumed the calm, sober language of the witness, neither the lamenting tones of the victim nor the irate voice of someone who seeks revenge. I thought that my account would be all the more credible and useful the more it appeared objective and the less it sounded overly emotional' (382). His self-narrative rendered as event rather than as literary record, Al-Qady's subjectivity in *Nothing But Nothing*—which was no more or less aestheticized than Levi's—did not equate emotional excess with unreliability.

At the beginning of his performances, Al-Qady would enact himself as a child: 'I am a child, I like to play./I am a child, I like to play,/with everything,/I like to play soccer, and play the guitar./I would like to be an artist' (192). The use of the first-person 'I' activated the singular specificity of testimonial speech, while the use of present tense in the voice of an adult-as-child created a poetic disjunction that disarticulated the words from time and a fixed perspective. Slipping in and out of re-experience or reenactment and testimony, Al-Qady switched from present to past tense as he described events in Iraq: 'What is this?/Is this love?/Her name was Leila./With Leila, I saw my dreams./I liked her; I loved her, Leila' (195). An expressionistic presentness was also evident in a one-sided, repetitious conversation with his deceased father, in which Al-Qady enacted his grief as the imperative of the child-self: 'DAD!/Please come back, I dearly miss you./Please come back./You've taken too long./Please Dad, come back' (193). Far removed from an evidential mode, these words, performed by Al-Qady in a defeated, crouching position with his back to the audience, testified incisively to the traumatic loss of the father. A stream-of-consciousness technique gives the impression of flow, or direct transmission of a subject's emotional state, but it is of course always a deliberate and crafted mediation of subjectivity, and in Al-Qady's case it was an explicitly reconstructed first-person disclosure, being in English rather than his native Arabic. This linguistic translation was one that he found intellectually and emotionally challenging; as he explains, 'I hadn't studied English before and it was hard to express my feelings with little English. The language problem was another suffering for me' (personal correspondence). If telling his story served certain therapeutic ends for Al-Qady, it clearly posed difficulties as well. The highly emotive present tense sections of the monologue, most of which were performed under dim, red lighting, created the impression of a man haunted by traumatic memory, bringing to mind psychoanalytical concepts of the unwilling repetition and re-experience of trauma in dreams or hallucinations. The obvious and crucial difference is that Al-Qady's use of repetition via first-person narration was not unwilling, but situated and purposeful. Or at least, it was purposeful for the most part: Al-Qady's lack of fluency in English lends credence to the notion that he was only partly in command of his slippages between tenses, and if this is the case, we may see emerging in his performance an 'innocent' picture of how trauma is structured in memory, and specifically, of its relationship to time.

While in one sense Al-Qady was conspicuously alone both onstage and as a persecuted figure in *Nothing But Nothing*, the importance of interlocutors, whether friendly, hostile or indifferent, was reinforced throughout the performance; every point of the physical and emotional journey was contingent upon the outcomes of human relationships and encounters. Al-Qady engaged in various conversations: between his child-self and his mother, with Leila, with his young daughter, with an Iraqi official and with an Australian immigration official. He also sang an Arabic song taught to him by his mother, a recollection of childhood that invited spectators to glimpse an intimate, early lifeworld. The narrative was anguished and expressive of Al-Qady's individual grief and loss, but it also testified to the casualties of successive wars in Iraq—in other words, to the community of civilian witnesses to which he belongs. Even during the worst of the boat journey to Australia, with all avenues for intervention seemingly exhausted, Al-Qady's narrative enacted one-sided dialogue, an attempt to engage the ocean, sky and boat as benevolent interlocutors: '[g]ood morning, sea./I like you and I am scared of you at the same time./You are very big, very deep./Please be quiet and soft with us, we are weak people' (199). Here, again, Al-Qady's present tense narration of history conjured the past as imminent.

The lines of causality identified by Arendt from rightlessness, to lack of responsibility, to political innocence were traced in *Nothing But Nothing* via its pervasive trope of disempowerment, articulated to a rigid yes or no binary that the audience was told has instrumentalized Al-Qady's life. At the very start of the performance, Al-Qady stated, 'I have spent all my life between yes and no' (191). (This echoes a brutal line about contingency from the poem with which Levi begins *If This is a Man*: '[w]ho dies because of a yes or a no' (17)). In *Nothing But Nothing*, a very large wooden cut-out of the word 'NO', painted in grey, stood at the back of the stage, exemplifying Al-Qady's position outside of political agency. Throughout the performance, he repeated the words 'please', 'sorry' and 'thank you', often when such courtesies were patently unwarranted: '[p]lease, can I sleep here?/I just want to sleep./Please, can I sleep in this alley?/Can I sleep in this corner?/Can I sleep on this footpath?/Thank you, thank you' (198). Enacting an interview with Australian immigration officials, he repeated the word 'sorry' several times. Frequently, he would use the 'NO' as a grim or threatening symbol—his father's grave, a prison cell, the boat to Australia. Al-Qady's narrative was in many ways a lamentation on loss and powerlessness: 'at night I would miss my friends./I would ask, where are my friends? Why did they leave? Are they ever going to come back?/The darkness seemed to always say, "no"' (191). Jenny Edkins observes that '[t]he concept of trauma oscillates between victimhood and protest and can be linked with or articulated to either' and maintains, further, that 'victimhood offers sympathy and pity in return for the surrender of any political voice' (9). Certainly, in terms of much of the content of his story, Al-Qady's work constituted just such a surrender.

But he asked more of his audience than might have been expected. Baz Kershaw describes the constitutive role of audience members in political performance: 'the spectator is engaged fundamentally in the active construction of meaning as a performance event proceeds. In this sense performance is "about" the transaction of meaning, a continuous negotiation between stage and auditorium to establish the significance of the signs and conventions through which they interact' (16–17). Al-Qady constructed a relation with his audience that was overtly transactional. At the beginning of his performances, he would implore his audiences/interlocutors to answer his candid questions; he would walk up the theatre's central aisle and gesture directly to individuals, asking ad-lib variations of the question, '[w]ould you like to be my friend?', followed by, 'could you help me?' The exclusivity of solo performance and the otherness of Al-Qady as an Iraqi refugee intensified this interrogative technique. Jo Bonney observes of solo work, '[m]ore than any other form of live performance, the solo show expects and demands the active involvement of the people in the audience. They are watched as they watch, they are directly addressed, their energy resonates with that of the lone artist' (xiii). If interrogative theatre has a reputation for making audiences uncomfortable, Al-Qady was also somewhat ill at ease as interrogator, working across cultural and linguistic barriers; as he recalls, 'I feel nervous because I think that the people don't know what I said. I also had a problem with the pronunciation of some words. For this reason I feel that I can't make contact with the people' (personal correspondence).

Eliciting, as he inevitably did, affirmative responses to his questioning, Al-Qady sought to pre-empt spectators' belief and more fundamentally their moral alignment with him. Upon initiating the call and response, Al-Qady began his story. In this way, *Nothing But Nothing* unashamedly emphasized what is often implied in autobiographical representation: the need to establish terms of belief as pre-emptive moral alignment, that is, to establish a readiness to believe that is akin to faith. In performances of *Nothing But Nothing*, the construction of consent as contingency was invoked continually via Al-Qady's dynamic use of space in his liminal character/refugee position. He would walk up the theatre's central aisle, move behind the audience to a side mezzanine, insisting that he could not fight in war, and directing frantic pleas for asylum from numerous vantage points around the space. Al-Qady activated in such ways a series of Levinasian face-to-face summons: '[t]he Other becomes my neighbour precisely through the way the face summons me, calls for me, begs for me, and in so doing recalls my responsibility, and calls me into question ('Ethics' 83). His repeated questioning sought to cohere the audience as an ethical community, something Kershaw (following Raymond Williams) argues is necessary for performance to work as cultural intervention, since community is 'the concrete medium of face-to-face interactions through which we transact ideological business' (29). Here, the tension between initiating contact and waiting for permission meant that the question of Al-Qady's volition was complicated. Obviously, the transactional role of the audience in 'befriending' and 'helping' him modelled the role of the Australian immigration authorities that are the elected representatives of the Australian people, but the transaction was made using aesthetic and affective rather than bureaucratic currencies. Given that audience members had, in attending the performance, indicated a degree of sympathy with the plight of asylum seekers and had already consented to hear Al-Qady's story, the contingency implied by his request for affirmation has low stakes in a literal sense; what his gesture invoked, though, is the cross-cultural framework, the relation of alterity, within which asylum seekers must strive to be heard. Moreover, the appeal to the audience highlighted the relationship between actor and spectator in terms of power and moral permission. The addition of post-show question and answer sessions with Al-Qady intensified the capacities for engagement with his perspective on history and asylum.

As intimate as his appearance on stage was, much of the time Al-Qady's perspective was subsumed very explicitly into the collective, rendering him a type. This occurred with varying degrees of self-consciousness. As he enacted the boat journey to Australia, he told of how he would represent the global community of refugees: 'I would like to make a huge sculpture of the refugees of the world from this water, to say to the world, look, look what the war has made for the people' (199–200). Instead of a strategy of making known through individualization, Al-Qady imagined the amalgamation and de-individualization of the world's refugees as a way in which to communicate their plight; obviously, the precarity of his fantastical image of a water sculpture is loaded with all the risks that Arendt saw for the refugee whose innocence is 'the seal of their loss of political status' (*Origins* 295). On occasion, Al-Qady seemed to acquiesce to this loss in a way that implicated the aggressor; at one point he wryly subordinated his identity to an orientalist stereotype of the Middle Eastern voyager, telling an immigration officer: '[a]ll right... yes... yes... my name./I forget, I can't remember./Please write down my name is Sinbad./My number? Five million./Five million refugees, they escaped from my country./My address? Okay, please write airports, checkpoints, ocean, boat./My problem?/I hate the war' (202). The use of the name 'Sinbad' here is double-edged, concurring with Western stereotypes of the foreign, exotic seafarer, as well as with Middle Eastern narrative traditions. Al-Qady's semi-strategic slippages are evident elsewhere in his public representation; in a newspaper interview connected with *Nothing But Nothing*, he referred to the personal and the communal interchangeably: 'I like the art. I like museum. We like to paint. We like to write. Iraqi people are very nice' (qtd in Dalton 1). In her analysis of Aboriginal women's life narratives, Debbie Rodan observes that the decentring of the 'I' can function to strengthen community connections and identities within the context of a minority collectivity or shared 'lifeworld' (60). By designating himself as belonging to a collective lifeworld, Al-Qady's essentialism served a purpose of countering pejorative identifications (militant Islamist, terrorist, illegal immigrant) that after 9/11 were attached to Iraqi people. Characterizing Iraqis instead as 'very nice', that is, invoking moral innocence, Al-Qady sought to defend his and others' deservingness of asylum.

As I have outlined, Salverson is critical of the victim trope in performative representations of trauma, arguing that a 'preoccupation with the experience of loss and a privileging of trauma [...] provides an essential yet limiting framework that fixes testimony within a discourse of loss and the tragic' ('Change' 122); this, she contends, ultimately 'sustains the psychic residues of violent histories, codifying the very powerlessness they seek to address' ('Transgressive' 35). It is certainly arguable that in *Nothing But Nothing*, Al-Qady's victimhood served to elicit uncomplicated pity from an audience comprised mostly, though not entirely, of Australian citizens, who in their belonging occupied positions of power relative to himself, and in whose name the federal asylum mechanisms by which victimhood is codified and sustained operate. On the other hand, by creating a work as unashamedly earnest as *Nothing But Nothing*, one that appealed via raw emotional exposure directly to an audience's pity and sorrow—indeed, precisely the type of representation of refugee identity that writers and critics such as Salverson and Edkins warn against—Al-Qady may have served to remind us that the judicious irony of a work like *CMI (A Certain Maritime Incident)* represents a luxury when it comes to the exigencies of traumatic histories. Moreover, for all his victimization, Al-Qady is not politically naïve. His imprisonment under Saddam Hussein's regime—itself the result of resisting authoritarian power by refusing to paint the leader's portrait or join the military—was recalled in his performance, crucially, in order to claim 'the best thing [he] did' (195), which was to paint a dove of peace on the prison wall. Although he obeyed an order to wipe it away, Al-Qady resolved 'that art was more powerful than prison./More powerful than the government' (195).

His interpretation of this experience enabled him to perceive purpose and agency, opening up a space to insert himself into a political struggle. His scrawled inscription, immediately following the closing night's performance of *Nothing But Nothing*, of the words 'thank you' and 'freedom' across the large wooden 'NO' appropriated the pleas of subservience that punctuated the work and transformed them into a political mark or tag (akin in some ways to his painting in the Iraqi prison—albeit met with an entirely different response). In this moment, the spectator was able to glimpse a man in the process of wresting himself from a position of non-volitional innocence and into a sphere of political, social and artistic agency.

The final production discussed in this chapter was a group-devised and performed work, *Journey of Asylum—Waiting* (2010), created by refugees, volunteer community support workers and students, under the leadership of community theatre practitioner Catherine Simmonds. The work was initiated and funded by the Asylum Seeker Resource Centre (ASRC), one of Australia's leading non-governmental refugee advocacy, aid and health organizations. The ASRC was founded in 2001 by Konstandinos Karapanagiotidis and has a primary base in Melbourne's inner-west. Like *CMI (A Certain Maritime Incident)*, *Journey of Asylum* was collaboratively devised, but it was not a documentary work, even though many of its narrative threads had origins in the testimonies of participants. The play was poetic and symbolic, presenting parallel and discontinuous narratives in such a way that time, place, history and imagination were unmoored and interwoven. As director-facilitator, Simmonds was responsible for shaping the piece by working closely with refugees and Australian participants, most of whom did not have theatre backgrounds. While the core objective of the project was the theatre production that was staged at Bella Union in Melbourne in 2010, *Journey of Asylum* was of at least as much significance as a process engendering creativity, skills development, confidence and friendship. Uniquely among the works discussed in this chapter, *Journey of Asylum* was not produced against the backdrop of John Howard's conservative government, which became so divisive in Australia in terms of asylum seeker debates, but the increasingly bipartisan nature of punitive asylum legislation means that this is actually of little consequence as far as the broader political and social context for the theatrical project is concerned.

Of more consequence for this discussion, as I have indicated, is that *Journey of Asylum* is distinct from the other productions I have examined so far because of its participatory form. Certainly, Al-Qady's piece had certain participatory characteristics and was supported by an advocacy collective, but it was not a community project and took place in a more prominent, professional theatre space. *Journey of Asylum* was a community development project whose primary orientation was toward ethical process, but which was also ultimately to serve as public representation and political communication. While Al-Qady actively solicited his audience's pre-emptive belief via interrogative performance techniques (pre-emptive in that the spectators' affirmations preceded the validating narrative), we can say that inasmuch as it is possible to characterize dispositions among an audience made up mostly of refugees and refugee supporters, *Journey of Asylum* proceeded with structures of pre-emptive community belief more or less in place. Simmonds's project began in 2009 as a series of dramatic storytelling workshops. In a detailed reflection published in the extensive programme note, academic Anne McNevin, who documented the process, describes how Simmonds 'worked with individual asylum seekers to digitally record their stories and to explore their boundaries and desires around telling those stories in public. Weekly workshops and weekends away brought asylum seekers together with volunteer actor collaborators to work on content and dramatic skills development' (*Journey*, programme note). This describes an ethical process whereby boundaries are set by the individuals who tell their stories, not by a director who processes them; it is qualitatively different to Horin's 'forensic' approach and mimetic rendering of verbatim accounts in *Through the Wire*. Horin's work played to a much larger audience and therefore had greater scope to intervene in habits of thought and action outside the rehearsal room, and what is more, professional and participatory theatre imperatives are never going to align perfectly, but the import of *Journey of Asylum* as political and aesthetic work should not be underestimated; as McNevin insists, the ASRC's project was at once 'therapeutic, artistic, and political' (*Journey*, programme note). I shall examine the aesthetics and politics of its narrative techniques shortly. The facilitators of *Journey of Asylum* sought to offer a safe space for self-representation and for the portrayal of fictional characters by the refugee participants, and it appears to have been efficacious. As McNevin explains in her reflection:

> A number of participants talked about a sense of being "unlocked" and finding a voice to express not only the trauma of their journeys but also the humour and energy that was part of their everyday lives. Here they were more than the sum total of grief, loss and victimhood. In this space they were also friends, musicians, comedians, and a group with a shared social and political purpose. (*Journey*, programme note)

Certainly, none of the refugees' enthusiastic first-person accounts of the project, published in the programme, hint at the traumatic effects and loss of agency that undermined Shafaei's faux-mimetic self-representation in the professional context of *Through the Wire*.

In the remainder of this discussion, I consider, first of all, the ways in which *Journey of Asylum* exceeded tropes of moral innocence via its non-mimetic, deliberately inconsistent and at times confrontational aesthetics, and second, I evaluate the production's politics of innocence in terms of the affective work of pre-emptive belief amongst Australian participants and spectators. The work's large cast of characters was divided into asylum seeker and refugee 'protagonists' and non-refugee 'collaborators'. *Journey of Asylum* exhibited clearly its genesis in inclusive devising processes responsive to the backgrounds and characteristics of its participants. All of the Australian characters' names and most of the asylum seekers' were the performers' real names. This created constant slippages, where a named individual behaved in various ways, taking on a number of characters whilst still remaining in some essential way *themselves*. These slippages between actors and roles had the effect of highlighting the lenses though which interactions between asylum seekers and those from whom they seek assistance or protection are filtered: commercial (for those who smuggle people), bureaucratic (for government and legal representatives), disinterestedly polite (for cabin crew), pedagogic (for teachers) and so on. The question for the audience then became, who exactly is interacting with whom—are we seeing individuals or their socially constituted roles? Is there much of a difference? *Journey of Asylum* did not strive to construct internally or externally consistent characters, but was more interested in how asylum seekers and refugees adopt particular *characteristics*. As project leader, Simmonds explained in the programme note how she understood the work's relationship to dominant evidentiary paradigms:

> Our protagonists are people who have sought asylum in Australia. For most, their stories have been represented and judged within legal frameworks where they've had to prove their "truth" time and time again. It has been my privilege, challenge and honour to steer another kind of journey in which the "truth" of human experience can be expressed with all its vulnerabilities and contradictions. (*Journey*, programme note)

In this way, the production emerged as one in which asylum seekers and refugees (as characters as well as performers) were invested with volition, self-awareness and indeed self-interest—all traits that permitted them to emerge, insofar as the theatrical frame was concerned, as complex, contradictory and transparent only when they chose to be. To put it simply, these characters were neither innocent in the way Arendt uses the term (non-volitional, without responsibility), nor were they morally innocent. For this reason, the work challenged audiences to recognize the protagonists not as people owed protection in Australia because of their virtues nor refused it because of their vices. More than this, *Journey of Asylum* refused to entertain the idea, discernible in a lot of asylum theatre, particularly verbatim theatre, that the audience should in any way be in a position to determine or decide whether characters and the real people they portray are worthy of asylum.

Bureaucratic performances of refugee identity of the kind Jeffers theorizes inflected the ASRC's production in several metatheatrical scenes. *Journey of Asylum* was especially preoccupied with the ways individuals play roles in circumstances informed by vast power differentials. It presented legalistic interactions that frame conventional refugeeness, but it also staged resistance. In doing so, it sought to implicate the audience and to provoke critical evaluations of the desire to hear traumatic asylum stories in the first place. For example, in the play's second vignette, asylum seeker Haydar expresses a deep weariness: 'I'm sick of telling my story; talk talk talk talk talk. I already told my story. It doesn't work. I don't want to. Don't make me do this. Sorry, I don't want to play' (145). Here Haydar is saying something Jeffers recognizes clearly: that adhering to bureaucratic performance codes often brings little hope of formalized refugee status. At the start of the next vignette, asylum seeker Yomal, lying seductively in a Perspex box, teases the audience: '[g]ive me a banana and I will tell you a story. Give me two bananas and I'll tell you my story, but maybe you won't sleep for the rest of your life' (138). The words ask us to think about what an individual might be reduced to in the face of demands to tell and retell their 'story'. They also, subversively, present the prospect that stories might be tailored to satisfy spectatorial appetites. Subversiveness could also be discerned in *Journey of Asylum*'s portrayal of diverse experiences—humorous, agonizing and prosaic—of resettlement in and around Melbourne. In one scene, the process of reorienting oneself to a new home drew upon African refugees' memories of culture shock upon first encountering Melbourne's busy Flinders Street Station; in this scene, as elsewhere in the play, the shock was distilled in physical theatre techniques that showed just how intimately culture is written on the body. In another scene, Yomal ran out on a date at a restaurant with an Australian woman because he could not afford to pay for the meal; the scene represented Yomal's awkwardness and shame, but as he exited, at a jog, he smiled at the audience, metatheatrically hinting at his own sense of agency in the midst of powerlessness.

Cumulatively, the vignettes that made up *Journey of Asylum* built a picture of how countless interactions, big and small, personal and impersonal, crucially determine the course of asylum seekers' lives. If noncitizens are to be 'protagonists' in these interactions, citizens must, as *Journey of Asylum* signaled, be 'collaborators', with all of the moral ambiguity that word implies. To a greater extent than the other three productions examined in this chapter, *Journey of Asylum* demonstrated that it is possible to hold in productive balance the moral complexities of refugees and a community's moral alignment with them. On this latter point, then, I want to argue that the collaborator function of the citizen-supporters in the project was one that pre-emptively presumed the moral innocence of asylum seeking noncitizens. The ASRC's founder and CEO, Karapanagiotidis, set out the terms of engagement with asylum seekers in the production's programme note:

Fig. 2. Production still from *Journey of Asylum—Waiting* by Catherine Simmonds and the Asylum Seeker Resource Centre. Bella Union Theatre, 2010. (Photo: Riza Manalo.)

Our people share these stories with you to place a human face on what it is to be a refugee; to remind us all that injustice anywhere is a threat to justice everywhere; that our federal government's inhumane policies such as mandatory detention and denying people their most basic human rights has a terrible and untenable human cost.

What you are witnessing is a universal story that we all share in—the dream of freedom, of sanctuary from oppression and the belief in a better world. We all have a responsibility to act to ensure the human rights we enjoy are shared by all. The flame of freedom will only burn as brightly as we allow it to in our hearts and in our actions. The time to act is now. (*Journey*, programme note)

This comment situates *Journey of Asylum* as an affective trigger to political mobilization. It articulates to both of the strands of refugee support that James Goodman identifies as the most prominent modes of post-2001 Australian political activism. As I explained in the introduction to this book, these strands are the instrumental 'national' strand, which concerns the nation-state, its organization of national community and its structural power, and the expressive 'global' strand, which is concerned with emphasizing humanity-in-common (270–71). It is evident from Karapanagiotidis's comment that a pre-emptive moral belief as applied to asylum seekers and refugees pertains both to believing what they say (and by extension, how they have been subject to governmental power) as well as a more fundamental ideological belief in their right to social and political participation. When Karapanagiotidis explicitly identifies Australia's federal asylum policies as the status quo that informs his and the ASRC's presumption of moral innocence and situates this status quo in terms of its violation of human community, he signals that his position is a strategically universalist, recuperative one. I want to suggest that we may recognize this as a position espoused because of the intolerable aporia whereby Australian noncitizens activate neither a legal presumption of innocence nor a civic pre-emptive presumption of non-innocence.

Impossible Politics of Innocence

As far as theatre is concerned, a key problem with this aporia of innocence in Australian biopolitics is that if moral innocence emerges to break the impasse, if characters in a play appear as morally innocent (on top of being susceptible or vulnerable to power), they run the risk of appearing as unformed subjects or types. They are unlikely to be permitted complex, objectionable, discrepant or self-interested motivations or behaviours. And as I have argued, a politics of innocence concerns more than just characterization and narrative, but manifests in the way theatre negotiates its agenda through its technique. Of course, the stakes of complicating the politicized figure of the asylum seeker or refugee in theatre are high: in Australian work, characters based upon real people and (even more urgently) refugees performing as themselves have tended to serve the instrumental function of clarifying or exemplifying practitioners' and audiences' responses to tough legislation and its hegemonic rationale. The works discussed in this chapter effectively insisted that if certain rights (most pertinently, in this context, to habeas corpus, legislative appeal and non-refoulement) accrue to personhood, not citizenship, then their removal or deprivation must be a violation acted upon an innocent subject. The ever-present risk, which this chapter has sought to trace, is that when the right to humanitarian protection in Australia is posited as having a moral dimension, asylum seekers are too often excluded from being political actors and in their rightless innocence are seen, and indeed may end up presenting themselves, as always and fundamentally *acted upon*.

The space for a politics of innocence emerges in the collectivizing of the oppressed; Arendt is clear that it is through the numerical increase of an undifferentiated mass of persecuted peoples under totalitarianism that the refugee is evacuated of political agency and rendered a rightless innocent. In this sense it can be argued that the refugee has as its spectral twin the high value terrorist, in contemporary parlance, who by extreme volition has become a named, known, distinctive political actor. It is deeply ironic, then, that when a politics of innocence in theatrical representation works to distance the asylum seekers or refugees as far as possible from their spectral twin, attempts to characterize the asylum seeker's own 'high value' can end up dispossessing them of political volition. Arendt observed that as refugee populations grow, focus is diverted to them as a group and away from persecuting governments or states; as such, a structure like Australia's immigration detention regime defines asylum seekers first and foremost by their undocumented, 'illegal' entry, even as it withholds the privilege of prosecution under a criminal jurisdiction that would presume individual innocence. As such, asylum seekers' capacity as political actors is already curtailed.

Theatres of reality of the kind discussed here enter the impossible space opened up by Australia's dystopian biopolitical reality, whereby the unauthorized appearance and extrajudicial imprisonment of undocumented noncitizens does not activate a legal presumption of innocence, nor a pre-emptive presumption of non-innocence (in the way that civic surveillance technologies do). Australian noncitizens are the exception even to criminal justice. By understanding this we can reconcile the way Arendt deploys the term 'innocence' in *The Origins of Totalitarianism* with the way innocence operates in criminal law, and furthermore, with the moral pre-emptive belief that is so readily activated in theatres of reality. The purpose of this discussion has not been to conclude cynically that structures of pre-emptive moral belief resemble a hegemonic order, but rather to recognize the extent to which they set the terms of representation and response. In this sense, theatre that engages with contemporary Australian asylum histories posits belief *of* and *in* their 'innocent' subjects as a political, ideological and affective commitment.

Chapter 2

DOMESTIC COMEDY AND THEATRICAL HETEROTOPIAS

...a comic character is generally comic in proportion to his ignorance of himself.

—Henri Bergson, *Laughter: An Essay on the Meaning of the Comic*

On the face of it, the categories of refugee and comedy appear to be segregated into an incompatibility that has ethical or moral basis. Certainly, there is little to be found in prevailing conditions and definitions of a 'well-founded fear of persecution' that would warrant the characterization of comic. But even that sentence seems wry. Theories of comedy and humour have identified incongruity as an important ingredient in the juxtaposition of meaning and outcome that makes something funny.[1] The other most commonly identified mode of comedy, that of laughing at the victim or victims of a joke, is explicated by so-called superiority theories[2]—which perhaps underscores why refugee comedy might be at once out of order and entirely, subversively, in order. While the plays examined in the previous chapter were confined by their relationship to true stories to a certain spectrum of tone, characterized by greater or lesser degrees of solemnity, the plays under discussion in this chapter, Victoria Carless's *The Rainbow Dark* (2006) and Ben Eltham's *The Pacific Solution* (2006), open up a different range of possibilities for representing and responding to the topic of asylum. These one-act plays had their premiere productions within weeks of each other in 2006 at Brisbane's Metro Arts Theatre, an inner-city space that, as noted in the previous chapter, has become prominent in the development and staging of works by new and emerging performance makers.[3] Both Carless and Eltham were first-time playwrights in their twenties when the plays were produced.

It is certainly the case that comic theatrical approaches to refugee narratives are uncommon, but a handful of other Australian productions have engaged with humour in this context. Certainly, *CMI (A Certain Maritime Incident)* (2004), discussed in the previous chapter, integrated very many comic elements. One of the first plays to emerge from the bitter post-*Tampa* landscape, Ben Ellis's *These People* (2003), utilized various documents—interview materials, fact sheets, reports—relating to refugees in order to construct a scathing satire on Australian family and social life and its relationship to the (anti)sociality of immigration detention. Outside the dominant framework of documentary theatre, Linda Jaivin's play *Seeking Djira* (2003), also an early foray into post-*Tampa*, pro-asylum seeker cutural engagement, offered up an unabashedly farcical premise not unlike the infiltration narrative employed, as I shall outline, by Eltham in *The Pacific Solution*. But in Jaivin's play, it is a group of variously self-absorbed writers at a retreat in the Blue Mountains, west of Sydney, rather than a group of surly housemates, who find themselves interrupted by the unexpected arrival of an asylum seeker. When comedy has been employed in the context of asylum narratives, its targets have tended to be unwitting Australian characters who find themselves attempting effectively to respond, or else determinedly unwilling to do so, in the face of a stranger appearing quite literally in their midst. To this extent, refugee-themed comedy in Australian theatre may broadly be recognized as an inheritor of the social realist theatres of suburban ennui that date back to Ray Lawler's landmark *Summer of the Seventeenth Doll* (first performed in 1955), only politically recast in order to test out and come to understand what the demonization of the noncitizen other means for the citizen and, ultimately, for their capacity to practice hospitality.

The *Rainbow Dark* and *The Pacific Solution* are comedies set in domestic living spaces—the homes of ordinary Australians. Setting their sights on Australian suburbia, Carless and Eltham identify in its daily banality tactics of and justifications for xenophobic exclusion that are recognizable as allied to federal machinations. While neither playwright intervenes in the delimiting formula of refugee noncitizenship as an innocent subject position, the illumination of refugee identity is not their purpose, unlike most of the plays discussed in the last chapter. Even though both plays imagine encounters between Australians and asylum seekers, both are careful *not* to construct the latter as fleshed-out characters (indeed, in Carless's play, asylum seekers are only spoken of; they do not appear on stage at all). Instead, asylum seekers exist in the same way they do in the lives and imaginations of most Australians, that is, as objects for defining or challenging what it means to belong. And in this, the two plays offer darkly comic reflections on how important the idea of noncitizenship has become in the minutiae of life as a citizen. Both works generate comedy out of incongruity, which I consider here in the context of Michel Foucault's theorization of heterotopias, and to a certain extent from superiority, making material, social and intellectual spaces for their mostly-Australian audiences to align themselves against a conservative Australian identity defined by the coercive exclusion of the asylum-seeking stranger.

In each play we find a contradictory organization of spaces, material and imaginary. In a striking parallelism, the works both posited cupboards as sites in which asylum seekers are forcibly placed, thereby situating carceral zones as bizarrely and disturbingly contiguous with homely zones, and locating both in one domestic territory. That both plays devised versions of this scenario seems symptomatic of the kinds of social and ethical questions asylum policy was provoking among Australians at the time: who should be permitted to make a home in Australia? What is the responsibility of the citizen-at-home to the irregular noncitizen who seeks protection? Might the advent of the irregular noncitizen have a detrimental impact on the perceived 'homeliness' of the nation? The origin of dark humour in each play came from the creation of theatrical heterotopias that were continuous with political heterotopias. Of course, for Foucault heterotopia, which is the opposite of utopia, doesn't have comic implications, but neither is it always hegemonic. Foucault's theorization of heterotopia is contained in his 1967 lecture, 'Des espaces autres', published in 1986 as 'Of Other Spaces'.[4] As an idea which describes spaces that contain contradictory elements, meanings or practices, heterotopia offers a means by which to integrate not just physical but also symbolic or ideological inscriptions within a particular space in time. Foucault characterizes heterotopias in the following terms: '[t]he heterotopia is capable of juxtaposing in a single real place several spaces, several sites that are in themselves incompatible' (25). Foucault's theorization of heterotopias corresponds with his well-known philosophical concerns with space, biopower and the organizational technologies that connect the two. Positing a rough genealogy of space and society, he contends in 'Of Other Spaces' that in the Middle Ages, space was structured in a 'hierarchic ensemble of places: sacred places and profane places; protected places and open, exposed places; urban places and rural places (all these concern the real life of men). In cosmological theory, there were the supercelestial places, as opposed to the celestial, and the celestial place was in turn opposed to the terrestrial place (22). Foucault claims that the 'heterotopias of crisis' that marked time or life stages in pre-industrial society by emplacing individuals who were in a sacred or liminal state, are diminishing.[5] He suggests that social organization of space (and bodies in space) is now typified by simultaneity and relations of contiguity rather than opposition or dichotomy.

Heterotopia has been a useful notion in social and urban geography for some decades and has more recently emerged in the work of theatre and performance scholars. In this they are following Foucault's lead: in 'Of Other Spaces', he refers in passing to the theatre as a heterotopia, noting, 'the theater brings onto the rectangle of the stage, one after the other, a whole series of places that are foreign to one another' (25). Joanne Tompkins observes, '[h]eterotopias are particularly productive in theatre, which is predicated on the structuring of imagined worlds. Not only does this concept help reconfigure non-places, it also provides further anchoring in stage space for the multiple worlds that may coexist with, interact with, and resist the "real", mimetic one' (95). The concept of heterotopia is also productive in the context of theatre's function as a social practice; in this context it pertains to considerations of gender, race, ability and socio-economics or access in relation to performing and spectating bodies convened in time, in a theatre space. *The Rainbow Dark* and *The Pacific Solution* derive layered meaning from uneasy relationships between seen and unseen spaces as understood in terms of their fictional frames, their performance spaces and the real-world cognates of their satire in contemporary Australia as it is organized vis-à-vis its proximate noncitizens. The works' preoccupations with the organization of legitimate and illegitimate bodies, and their respective capacities as theatrical heterotopias in which these preoccupations are tested out, articulate a key dilemma identified by Foucault:

> the problem of siting or placement arises for mankind in terms of demography. This problem of the human site or living space is not simply that of knowing whether there will be enough space for men in the world—a problem that is certainly quite important—but also that of knowing what relations of propinquity, what type of storage, circulation, marking, and classification of human elements should be adopted in a given situation in order to achieve a given end (23).

Foucault also notes that heterotopias must 'have a function in relation to all the space that remains' (27). As a heterotopia, theatre is peculiar in its *deliberate* correspondence to proximate real-world heterotopias—in the present context, we have carceral domestic spaces devised to respond and correspond to a carceral state. This gives it, I would argue, a radical potential: theatre can simultaneously reflect socio-political conditions, refract, distort or pervert them, all in the context of a collocation of artists and audiences who move between and across representational and socio-political grids.

The paradigmatic heterotopias in modern society, according to Foucault, are 'heterotopias of deviation [...] in which individuals whose behavior is deviant in relation to the required mean or norm are placed' (25). Heterotopias of deviation do the work of disciplining bodies, and in the context of asylum, they obviously manifest as sites of exception via the incarceration by a surveillant state of its noncitizens. Heterotopias of deviation reify refugee noncitizenship as a contradictory corporeal condition of surveillance outside the eyes of the law, as well as that of life outside the frame of contemporary citizenship. In making this observation I am, of course, indebted to Giorgio Agamben, whose theorization of the extrajudicial detention camp helps to explain why zones of incarceration can be understood as heterotopias; particularly key here is his observation that, in an apparent paradox, 'what is being excluded in the camp is *captured outside*, that is, it is included by virtue of its very exclusion' (*Means* 40, italics in original). Underscoring this point, Agamben notes that the etymological meaning of the Latin root for exception is *ex-capere*, which translates as 'captured outside' or 'taken outside'. The domestic-carceral zones set out in Carless's and Eltham's plays offer striking imaginative frameworks for grasping Agamben's theorization of paradoxical capture inside; it is arguably, in this sense, in and through the spatial organization of the home that we might most acutely perceive the ban. On the level of social practice, heterotopias of deviation can appear in theatrical productions like *The Rainbow Dark* and *The Pacific Solution* to the extent that they set out to critique and reimagine coercive zones; in the context of such practice, the deviation inheres not in the bodies of oppressed individuals, but in the resistant bodies of those in attendance (performers and audience) who oppose the premise of state-coerced territorialization of human lives. Foucault notes, '[h]eterotopias always presuppose a system of opening and closing that both isolates them and makes them penetrable. In general, the heterotopic site is not freely accessible like a public place' ('Other' 26). Crucially, entry into the heterotopia of theatre differs from entry into a classic heterotopia of deviation: put simply, the latter is rarely a choice.

Practices of Comic Theatre and Heterotopia

In *The Rainbow Dark* and *The Pacific Solution*, elements of farce, satire and the absurd generate potent imaginative and embodied environments for the contradictory proximity or nearness of citizens and noncitizens. What might be the value in thinking about theatre, and specifically comic theatre that stages the antagonistic 'capturing outside' of the noncitizen, as a heterotopia, or indeed as a heterotopia of deviation? In the context of this discussion, there are several ways of approaching the question: one is in terms of, to repeat Foucault's phrase, 'the storage, circulation, marking, and classification' ('Other' 23) of theatre makers and audiences who come together in time and place to present or watch a performance; a second is in terms of 'the storage, circulation, marking, and classification' of characters in a play; a third is in terms of the real-world bodies to whom all of these people, real and fictional, are indexed.

In its capacity as artistic and social practice, comic theatre permits of the performing body ridiculous behaviours, incongruous interactions and linguistic dexterity. The praxis of comedy is heterotopic at the level of embodiment inasmuch as the 'undisciplined' body in a comedy must actually mask its diametric opposite. A skilled farceur or clown, for instance, has to develop bodily discipline, expert physical timing and spatial awareness; a satirist will typically have a highly disciplined linguistic facility; in absurdist theatre, illogical ideas or sentiments must be carefully timed and inflected. From the audience's perspective, comic theatre permits the kind of laughter-in-common that would generally be out of place in public spheres of work, education, sport and the law. Indeed, aspects of comedy and the staged sociality it codifies—bombast, subversiveness, accidents, tricks, cruelty—would also be out of place in the private sphere of the family (or certain configurations of it). The last of these aspects, cruelty, is worth pausing over in the context of the 'superiority' theories of comedy to which I referred at the start of this chapter. Joan F. Dean notes that laughter elicited by the inadequacies or excesses or accidents of bodies in theatrical farce can betray an element of ego-maintenance on the part of the spectator, pointing out that 'descriptions of comedy have always stressed the superiority that the audience enjoys over the play's characters' (483–84). In the context of Carless's and Eltham's plays, the objects of comedy are Australians and to the extent that the laughter of audiences for both was in response to representations of xenophobia as ludicrous and unenlightened, it is perhaps the case that the works risked consolidating the opposite impulse— that of welcoming strangers—in terms of their mostly Australian audiences' feelings of superiority. Put simply, the laughter of those in the theatre, 'in on the joke', might more than anything have been a way of recuperating ethical Australian citizenship.

In their capacity as fictions, characters in farce, as well as satire and the absurd, are frequently 'deviant in relation to the required mean or norm' ('Other' 25); characters in farce tend to be deviant in respect of their unpredictability and their transgression of physical and interpersonal boundaries, while the latter two genres trade more in ideological and conceptual subversion. While neither of the plays I discuss in this chaper can or should be categorized precisely, Carless's tends mostly toward the satirically absurd, while Eltham's is more readily identifiable as a satirical farce. Tracing impure lines of theatrical descendence from ancient Greek satyr and phlyax plays, from Atellan farces and of course from more recent European comedy and clowning traditions, farce, satire and the absurd are performance modes that purport to present the antithesis of the disciplined individual. Characters in farce, in particular, are comically unpredictable, extravagant, accident-prone, lustful, and frequently grotesque. Interactions between characters in farce and absurdist theatre are often violent or cruel—the latter facet is important in the plays I discuss over the following pages. On the level of the imaginative frame, it may be said that characters in farcical, satirical and absurdist theatre are comic to the extent that they exist in heterotopic space; or to put it another way, to the extent that they are oblivious to their predicament, its implications and their ridiculousness, whilst their audience is aware of all of these. As Henri Bergson observes in *Laughter: An Essay on the Meaning of the Comic*, 'a comic character is generally comic in proportion to his ignorance of himself' (16).

The third way in which we might think through heterotopias in theatre is, as I noted above, in terms of the real-world corollaries of the figures that occupy the theatrical frame. In this capacity, the broader socio-political one, we can understand Carless's and Eltham's works in terms of placement and power in ways that link them to the politicized representation of asylum seekers in Australia. The plays' most obvious corollaries are immigration detention centres; these are clear examples of heterotopias of deviation, border zones in which noncitizens are situated and which citizens must, by definition, patrol. In *The Rainbow Dark* and *The Pacific Solution*, the placement of asylum seekers is transposed into direct equivalents (within the plays' imaginative universes) of the territorial logic of the camp as Agamben identifies it: 'it is not simply an external space' (*Means* 40). In this sense, the plays also politicize another real-world corollary: the domestic sphere. Both rehearse what goes on in comic collision of unwelcome stranger with(in) the Australian suburban home. The sphere of noncitizenship, as Carless and Eltham present it, is subject to the desires of citizens for an uncontaminated sphere of citizenship. Both zones constitute, however, one carceral-domestic space, a heterotopia, and it is in this that the plays emerge as critiques of the binary that scaffolds their comedy.

The Rainbow Dark

Victoria Carless was awarded the 2006 Queensland Theatre Company George Landen Dann award for *The Rainbow Dark*, which was first performed during the Backbone Youth Arts 2006 Fragments season of short plays at Metro Arts Theatre (which staged Al-Qady's *Nothing But Nothing*, discussed in the previous chapter). The play has since been performed at the Jute Theatre in Cairns (2008). *The Rainbow Dark* pivots on an imaginative and spatial heterotopia. The stage design consists of two homely spaces, a living room and kitchen in the home of sixty-something sisters Gloria and Babs (played by Jan Nary and Kaye Stevenson in the 2006 production), while the narrative also incorporates an unseen, unhomely space, a cupboard under the stairs in which a group of strangers are imprisoned (the terms 'asylum seeker' and 'refugee' do not appear anywhere in the script). The suburban home, then, both nourishes the lives of citizens and produces the bare lives of noncitizens. Carless's narrative tests out the idea, articulated by Foucault, that power, including biopolitical coercion, is not the exclusive domain of sovereign authorities, but a series of decentralized, dispersed structures and engagements. *The Rainbow Dark* orients itself toward questions of consent and action (or inaction) among citizens and insists on ethical proximity, the idea that asylum seekers are imbricated in the nation, even as they are marked by their noncitizenship.

In its premier season in Brisbane, directed by Kat Henry, *The Rainbow Dark* was prefaced with an opening sound bite of John Howard's vilifying narration of the 'children overboard' affair, including the statement, 'I don't want people like that in Australia. Genuine refugees don't do that [...] They hang onto their children' (qtd in Marr and Wilkinson 251). This dramaturgical choice (which is not indicated in the script) served the purpose of situating the play by recalling the events of 2001, which saw unauthorized asylum seekers transformed into a major national problem, and maritime borders concretized in the consciousness of many citizens as a vast zone that might be breached in the absence of vigilance. In scaling political discourses and manoeuvres down to a domestic sphere via farce and absurdism, as well as the topical satire signalled most clearly in the Howard sound bite, Carless crystallizes the structures, attitudes and impulses that underpin the biopolitics of contemporary Australian noncitizenship.

Henry's production utilized the intimate space of the Metro Arts Theatre, with its close proximity between stage and audience spaces, to create a sense of insularity; the set design heightened the feeling of unchanging domestic order, with floral couches still covered in their protective plastic creating contaminant-free zones. A satirically distorted version of Australia, the world of the play is one in which carefully screened Australian families take on the responsibility of incarcerating 'Peoples from Elsewhere Who Don't Recognise Perfectly Good Borders [...] in an appropriate vestibule' within their homes (9). This simple premise situates 'legitimate' and 'illegitimate' Australia under the same roof, metaphorically and literally. Gloria and Babs espouse a similar attitude towards defending the nation's integrity to that expressed by Howard in his infamous statement on 'people like that', and while they may, in the scheme of things, be blameless in comparison to the former Prime Minister, the moral high ground that they claim is, for Carless, just as unstable. According to the logic of *The Rainbow Dark*'s theatrical heterotopia, we can recognize a portrayal of a nation that in seeking to immure itself from what it deems non-belonging, is forced to enact systems that keep this illegitimacy close; the condition of being 'captured outside', in Agamben's phraseology, becomes, in the sphere of comedy, a condition of capture in an outside that is also an *inside*.

The space of imprisonment might be invisible to the audience, but it's all the sisters can think about; its non-presence permeates the house. For this reason, and prompted by the play's absurdism, we may apply a reading of the unseen carceral space as a zone of haunting and its noncitizen inhabitants as spectral figures generated out of the citizens' unease with the state's organization of living space. Foucault identifies Gaston Bachelard as one of the key theorists that 'taught us that we do not live in a homogeneous and empty space, but on the contrary in a space thoroughly imbued with quantities and perhaps thoroughly fantasmatic as well' ('Other' 23). In *The Poetics of Space* (1994, first published in French in 1958), Bachelard's lyrical reading of how we inhabit intimate domestic spaces, the philosopher considers the way cellars can represent the intensified emotional life of a house's inhabitants, becoming spaces associated with 'buried madness, walled in tragedy' (20). While Gloria and Babs's cupboard isn't subterranean, it is beneath stairs and may be read as the repository of their exaggerated fears and creeping guilt. If the home as an image is appreciated in Bachelard's terms as 'the topography of our intimate being' (xxxvi), the spectral detainees in Carless's narrative can be conceived of as penetrating the unconscious of her two protagonists. Certainly, it isn't easy for the sisters to uphold the state-initiated sublimation of noncitizens; whenever Gloria and Babs feed the detainees, they seek to avoid the face-to-face encounter that would compel them to attend to the other *as other*. As Gloria whispers, haunted, 'I don't look. Can't bear their eyes' (9).

The phrase, 'Peoples from Elsewhere Who Don't Recognise Perfectly Good Borders', is repeated seven times throughout the one-act play, each time with a sense of pious insistence, as if the sisters are seeking to reinforce the idea it contains as a natural law. The repetition of the phrase is one of the most prominent ways in which Carless derives comedy from the incongruous. and in this case it's an incongruity between the human and mechanical, the very intersection that Henri Bergson regards as the site or source of laughter. In relation to verbal mechanization and the eliciting of laughter, Bergson employs the analogy of a Jack-in-the-Box, identifying repetition as key to the comic element: 'a stream of words that bursts forth, is checked, and keeps on starting afresh' (71). Gloria and Bab's language, which we might expect to be human precisely in its unpredictability (according to Bergson, 'thought [...] is a living thing. And language, the translation of thought, should be just as living' (119)), is shown via repetition of phrases of identical word order—here, the ventriloquizing of bureaucratic formulae—to be mechanistic or involuntary; certainly, it's far removed from *creative* speech. And perhaps more importantly, the mechanistic features of the sisters' dialogue represent moments in which the manifest content of their words and their feelings about what they're saying aren't entirely congruent; Bergson contends that the repetition of words is a sign of repression and diversion of an idea: '*In a comic repetition of words we generally find two terms: a repressed feeling which goes off like a spring, and an idea that delights in repressing the feeling anew*' (73, italics in original).

Alongside their verbatim repetition, Babs and Gloria's duologue circles compulsively around similar ideas and is full of fussy mutual assurances, especially about being 'very civil-minded' and 'not made of money' and acting 'for the greater good', and assertions about life being '[r]eally quite good'/ 'Wonderful. No problems at all. None whatsoever'/'peachy'/'just super'. By not saying what they seem to want to say, but nevertheless maintaining a stream of words, Babs and Gloria display the 'automatism' that Bergson describes as 'closely akin to mere absentmindedness' (16). By presenting us with characters whose verbatim knowledge of federal law on noncitizens and acceptance of its effects on them is a sign of absence of mind rather than precision of mind or force of will, Carless sets up a critique of unthinking acceptance of a 'perfectly good' laws. Bergson shows how the body's relationship to mechanization, and the laughter that is thereby generated, can become more and more sophisticated until 'in the end we find a mere administrative enactment occupying the same relation to a natural or moral law that a ready-made garment, for instance, does to the living body' (48–49). That, for much of the play, Gloria and Babs wear their ready-made, state-sanctioned linguistic codes with apparent ease is both chilling and comical.

Surrendering, in Bergsonian terms, entirely to mechanization by allowing themselves to act as obedient administrators of the state's organization of social life, Carless's protagonists also sublimate their knowledge of humanness and vitality of the noncitizens under their roof as anxieties and self-congratulatory comments about what other neighbours are or aren't doing. The play's audience is confronted with what this sublimation means and what emotional shadows it casts because we never see any asylum seekers, or to put it another way, no actor is required by the script to embody an asylum seeker on stage. The incarcerated 'Peoples from Elsewhere', held by Babs and Gloria in cramped, dark conditions for approximately one year ('[g]ive or take a week' (9)), function only as imagined figures, ciphers within the narrative, apprehended in snatches and traces—through the discussions of Gloria and Babs, muffled cries and moans, the appearance of a baby's slipper. The noncitizens are 'secret', sublimated subjects, unseen but continually imagined.

The human sphere of morality merges with the mechanistic sphere of economics in the context of one of the sisters' most cherished notions, 'civic responsibility'. Like Australia's poor island neighbours, Nauru and Papua New Guinea, Gloria and Babs are given financial assistance from the government to detain their quota of strangers. Anxious to downplay an economic motivation, the women assure themselves and each other of the modest nature of the assistance, and bemoan their poverty. To justify their task, they employ the language of civic citizenship, congratulating themselves on their 'civil-minded' willingness to take on such a challenging responsibility—as Babs declares, '[w]e don't shirk our duty' (6). When Babs gives voice to her gnawing concern about muffled voices in the dark and cries in the night, Gloria is quick to remind her not to dwell on what is a 'minor inconvenience. Compared to the good we're doing' (7). However much it might present the compromising of a fundamental humanitarian instinct, the government's delineation of human legality is watertight for Gloria and Babs, and moreover, a concept to which obedience is a deeply felt moral responsibility.

The women are cases in point of Nick Dyrenfurth's observation that in Australia, the discourse of citizenship, under the domination of mainstream politics, 'has often been infused with varying degrees of morality, with civic citizenship positioned as a 'desirable activity'' (184). Prem Kumar Rajaram argues that moral invocations against unauthorized arrivals (encapsulated in the terms 'illegal' and 'queue jumper') make 'the 'problem' of asylum seekers a common one: the goal of ensuring sovereignty thus becomes not the sole obligation of a border-fixated state, but the responsibility of all Australians' (''Making Place''' 297). This construction of individual responsibility is a feature of the democratic nation-state; William E. Connolly observes, '[t]he democratic, territorial state sets itself up to be the sovereign protector of its people, the highest site of their allegiance, and the organizational basis of their nationhood' (135). It positions itself in this way, Connolly argues, through a convergence of the '[n]ostalgic realism and nostalgic idealism' (135) underlying democratic theory. The democratic political imaginary, he contends,

> fosters the experience of connection between the life of the members and the common meanings that draw them together, between the desire to shape the common fate through democratic politics and the construction of territorial structures of public accountability, and between the territorialization of democratic politics and the production of the national security state. (136)

The notion of a common obligation to serve the sovereign security interest underpins the satirical world of *The Rainbow Dark* and is a crucial moral touchstone for Gloria and Babs.

One of the central tropes around which the sisters' acts of exclusion are played out concerns food. The women control the degree of nourishment that they will ration to the detainees, conscious that generosity with food would indicate that the people under the stairs deserve hospitality as houseguests and that this would blur the distinction between Peoples from Elsewhere and guests. Indeed, Joseph Pugliese distinguishes the provision of food to detainees from nourishment, observing, '[w]hat must be relentlessly evaded is hospitality: don't expect refuge, only shelter; don't expect nourishment, only food;

don't expect comfort, only harassment. All these practices position refugees as interlopers parasiting the body of the nation' ('Penal Asylum', para 21). Inevitably though, in Carless's theatrical heterotopia even a modest allocation of food instantiates the detainees' occupancy of Australian territory: the sisters complain about the extra mouths to feed in terms of an iconic Australian food product—'the extra Vegemite on the bill' (18). Midway though the play, the two women are visited by the local butcher Donald (played by Hugh Taylor in the 2006 production) who as well as pursuing a romantic interest in Gloria is prompted to call in order to offer surplus meat stocks for the detainees; as he points out, 'Gloria, I'm a butcher not a bureaucrat. The fact of the matter is, you have starving people living under your stairs and I have leftover food!' (19). The symbolism of the offer of meat is potent; in the context of Carless's absurdism, it evokes associations with animal impulses and greed, as well as the idea that certain lives are literally sustained by the sacrifice of the bodies of others.

The sisters refuse the offer because it contravenes government policy; as Gloria insists, her and her sister's sacrifice is also a moral necessity: 'I refuse to allow Peoples From Elsewhere Who Do Not Recognise Perfectly Good Borders to benefit *illegally* from my Land of Plenty! [*pause*] There are limits Donald!' (19). Here Gloria is effectively invoking a partialist philosophy (Gibney 23–4), whereby allegiance and assistance are due first and foremost to legitimate members of a national community. She is, moreover, assuming that the rules of membership of that community are orderly and self-evidently moral. One of the central narratives of Australian nationhood concerns the land's bounty as a food source, consequent to hard work—as the national anthem affirms, '[w]e've golden soil and wealth for toil'. The impulse to peg national community to a productive relationship with the land speaks, Matthew J. Gibney argues, to anxieties about the manner in which sovereignty originated in Australia: 'white settlers needed to make good use of the land if they were to be justified in excluding others. The ease with which the previous inhabitants had lost control of the territory testified starkly to the importance of populating Australia if the British were to possess the moral right as well as the practical ability to exclude' (169). Gloria's and Babs's assertion of entitlement can, then, be linked to the anxiety that sharing too much with strangers might erode their (the women's) sovereignty.

In the end, the source of intervention in the sisters' insistence on respect for 'Perfectly Good Borders' comes from their dog, Sylvia. Dirk Hoult's portrayal of Sylvia in Henry's production deployed comic incongruity: embodying traits of autonomic and somatic canine embodiment (vomiting, farting, scratching) and, increasingly as the play progressed, human intellectual concentration (methodology applied toward a conceived objective). Sylvia's subject position and her relationship with the humans in the play may best be described as liminal, as opposed to a classic human–canine comic inversion; her trajectory

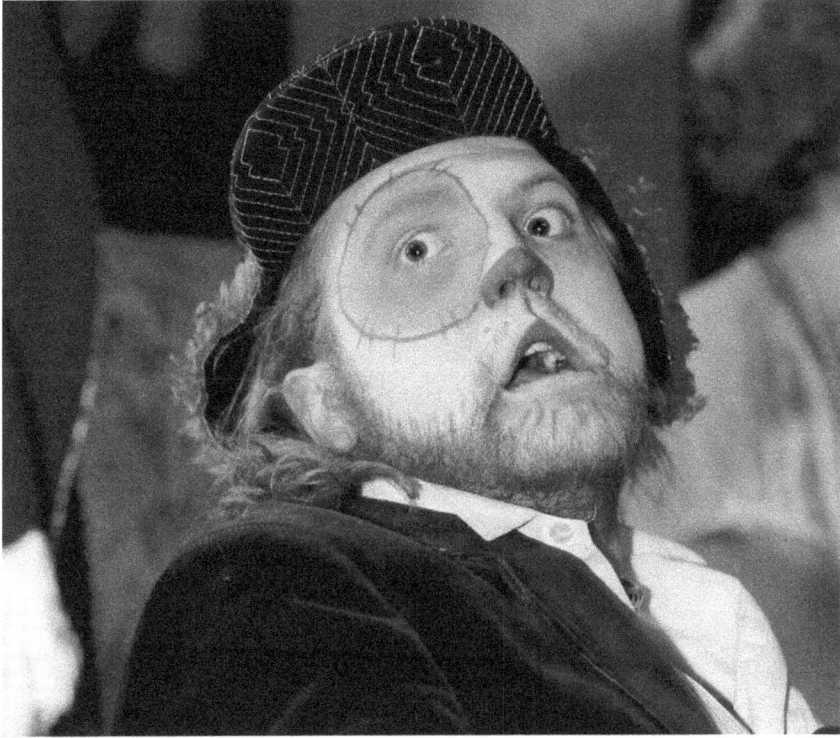

Fig. 3. Production still from *The Rainbow Dark*, by Victoria Carless. Metro Arts Theatre, 2006. (Photo: Nick Martin.)

is of continual 'becoming', but instead of becoming a character we would recognize as human she very deliberately borrows the communication tools of unsubtle humans. Sylvia alone grasps the plight of the Peoples from Elsewhere in terms of the ethical imperative of liberty rather than the civic imperative of organization. She unsettles normative stratification of living creatures by speaking for those who are subjected to treatment both sub-human and sub-animal.

Over the course of the narrative, Sylvia seeks by various means to communicate on the asylum seekers' behalf. Her attempts become more and more complex and less and less what Bergson might recognize as mechanistic, but of course, because she is a dog, whose behaviour should, we might suppose, be pure mechanism or reaction, her increasing deliberation and creativity elicit laughter. One of Sylvia's first efforts to draw the attention of Gloria and Babs to the detainees' cries for release takes an autonomic form: the dog begins a conspicuous display of retching and eventually vomits up a baby's slipper. Gloria enacts an immediate denial ('[n]othing to speak of. She's been through the bins again' (10)) while Babs inspects and quietly pockets the slipper. Sylvia's mechanistic act of ingesting and disgorging an object found in the cupboard under the stairs signals the bodily proximity of the house's free and detained inhabitants. In her next attempt to communicate with her mistresses, Sylvia trots on stage, scratches herself and sits expectantly, a cardboard sign around her neck with a rudimentary drawing of a window on it. Here, the dog's simultaneous insight or inventiveness and absent-minded scratching upends Bergson's image of '*[s]omething mechanical encrusted on the living*' (37, italics in original). Sylvia's mechanistic movements begin to be imparted with what Bergson refers to as a 'soul' (28), and at this 'mental crossways' (37) she becomes even funnier than at the play's outset when she was just a canine character embodied by a male human actor.

Finally, in an apotheosis of the human-acting-dog-acting-human, Sylvia makes her case in spoken language, addressing Babs, the sister most outwardly troubled by moral misgivings. In a cross fade to the kitchen, Babs and Sylvia exchange a few words about Donald's offer to donate surplus meat to the detainees, when Babs suddenly becomes aware of her interlocutor:

SYLVIA: Well it's very contentious issue Babs, but like the man said, he does have leftovers.

BABS: It's certainly very *humane* of him. [*pause*] Sylvia—goodness, gracious—you're talking!

SYLVIA: Yes.

BABS: But—I—you—you've never spoken before!

SYLVIA: As they say, desperate times call for desperate measures. Maybe you just weren't listening hard enough. [*pause*] I mean, come on, Babs, what do I have to do? All the barking, the begging, the passing of wind—do you think that was all for my own amusement? Do you consider that normal behaviour?

BABS: Yes, well I do, rather. For a *dog*. (60–61)

Hoult's vocal work in this section of the play betrayed no trace of the canine grunting and growling that marked his appearances in earlier scenes. Sylvia succeeds in prompting Babs to rethink the premise upon which her actions are founded, coaching her in a quintessentially human technique of creative visualization:

SYLVIA: Press your hand to your eyes. Close out the light. Now what do you see?

BABS: Nothing dear. Only black.

SYLVIA: Press harder. Concentrate.

BABS: I am concentrating.

SYLVIA: Forget about everything else. Forget about trying to see something. Forget about remembering what was there before the darkness. What do you see?

BABS: I told you. Nothing dear. Blackness.

SYLVIA: Listen closely. Look past the black. Forget what you have been told, or what you know to be true. Look beyond your hands. Look beyond the colour of the dark. What do you see? (62)

When Babs sees colours emerge, when her mechanistic body becomes an imagining body, Sylvia explains, '[t]hat's why these people have come here, Babs. This is why they wait in the dark. Even under your stairs. This is why they have not Recognised Perfectly Good Borders. It is because they see colour beyond the darkness. They can see a rainbow in the dark' (63). It takes a figure of radical in-between-ness, a dog with human(e) instincts, a mechanized animal, to understand the necessity for imagination to fill the space of ethical response to the other.

After she is coached into visualizing the lifeworlds of the imprisoned strangers, Babs defies the law and releases the Peoples from Elsewhere—some twenty-five people, including several children and a baby—via a window in the cupboard. Along with alleged escapes and releases across the country, one of which, Donald notes in one of the play's quotidian details, occurred recently 'from a sewing room in Marraborne' (56), the liberation of detainees signifies the seepages that compromise the imagined impermeability of the nation-as-home. In the final scene of *The Rainbow Dark*, it emerges that even the outwardly staunch Gloria has secretly acted more benevolently towards the Peoples From Elsewhere than the government-issue handbook will officially permit by knitting slippers for a baby that had been born in the cupboard. As hard as the women try to effect their own domestic-scale 'politics of forgetting' (Connolly 138), or more precisely, to substitute one set of intersubjective responsibilities for another set of civic ones, it becomes impossible for them to contain their knowledge of the asylum seekers' fundamental humanness.

Nevertheless, the most enduring image with which Carless leaves the audience is of Gloria and Babs's home as an outwardly serene but internally horrendous heterotopia of deviation. The abuse inherent in rendering a category of human beings mute and denying them access to social life is a dark undercurrent that runs through the play's absurdist humour. This dark vein, I argue, shouldn't be mistaken for a variant of schadenfreude or encompassed by superiority theories of comedy (laughing at comic victims). Audiences of Carless's play are more likely to feel something closer to horror upon imagining the predicament of people locked in a cupboard for a year. John Mullarkey suggests that the '*origin* of the comical' in the Bergsonian sense of life becoming machine-like is 'the flip side of the origin of horror', observing that 'where the comical concerns what is alive and of value *making itself* inert and worthless, horror relates to a subject *being made* worthless and inert *by another*' (248, italics in original). Mullarkey emphasizes the relation of abuse, whereby subjects are not held 'as vital beings at all, but indifferently as quasithings' (248). Partly because she does not represent the subjects of abuse, and partly because of the hopeful trajectory of her absurdism, Carless does not take the relation of abuse to its limit point. For this reason, even though its premise is horrific, the world Carless constructs in *The Rainbow Dark* stops short of the horror that Mullarkey identifies as being twinned in complex ways with laughter. Gloria and Babs, in this way, exist as comic figures of incongruity, not agents of cruelty. And this is what distinguishes them most clearly from the comic characters in *The Pacific Solution*.

The Pacific Solution

It is tantalizing to speculate about what Ben Eltham's protagonist in *The Pacific Solution*, diehard 'cricket tragic' and unabashed racist, Johnny, would make of Pakistan-born Usman Khawaja, the first Muslim to play for Australia. Or of Fawad Ahmed, a first-class cricketer who fled north-west Pakistan in 2010 and whose application for Australian citizenship was fast-tracked via legislative amendment in order that he could play in the 2013 Ashes test series. Playing representative sport at the national level is an activity exclusive to citizens of that country and Ahmed's treatment in Australia illustrates perfectly how easily—indeed, how sportingly—'Australian noncitizenship' can be transformed into its opposite number.

Johnny, played by Jonathan Brand in the 2006 production directed by Marcel Dorney, has committed himself to seeing every ball of the 2005 Ashes series. He represents a form of bullish Australian masculinity that has not traditionally made much space for difference. In their book chapter on 'hegemonic masculinity' and Australian sport, Jim McKay, Geoffrey Lawrence, Toby Miller and David Rowe observe that 'sport in Australia (as in most other countries) has a profoundly masculine inflection, operating as a major means through which ascendant forms of masculinity are asserted, promoted, tested and defended against "rival" articulations of masculinity and femininity' (233). Johnny's love of the game is something his housemates, pothead Mandy (Louise Brehmer) and studious Phil (Lucas Stibbard), half-heartedly go along with, and while neither is scared of Johnny, his dominant, demanding personality nevertheless sucks them into his orbit. The names of Eltham's characters were immediately resonant for Brisbane audiences at Metro Arts Theatre's production: two successive Ministers for Immigration, Philip Ruddock and Amanda Vanstone, spearheaded indefinite and offshore detention and deterrence in Australia under Prime Minister John Howard's leadership.

But Eltham's Australian protagonists aren't constructed in such a way as to alienate the metropolitan Australians who made up the majority of the play's audiences. At the start of the play, Johnny proffers a stream of cricket commentary, which housemate Mandy half listens to as she tends their 'Orchy-bottle bong'.[6] Johnny's armchair expertise is funny; it's also impassioned and erudite in the same way ABC TV's weekly sports discussion show *Offsiders* is and familiar to *The Pacific Solution*'s cricket-literate spectators. The specificity of the debates of which Johnny is self-appointed chair is such that audiences are induced into mentally agreeing, countering, qualifying or detracting. To convey a sense of the tone Eltham establishes, it is necessary to quote a section at length:

JOHNNY: It's the First Test in living memory that might actually be bloody interesting. Harmison mate. Freddy Flintoff. Simon Jones with the reverse swing later in the innings. Even Hoggard's a bit under-rated actually, actually if I can say that, I think Hoggard's really quite a penetrating bowler early on. It's one of the finest fast bowling quartets assembled against Australia since the great West Indian pace attacks of the 80s and early 90s. [*pause*] I'm sure you remember Ambrose and Walsh at their peak, they were really something pretty special and I have to say this Australian team is not traveling that well, they really aren't, they're looking vulnerable and it's going to make for some wonderful cricket, surely one of the closest series in years. [*pause*] I think the Poms could do it. [*pause*] Flintoff's good, hey.

MANDY: Yeah, but we've got Warney.

JOHNNY: Warney's a trooper, don't worry about that. He'll tie one end down. And then with McGrath at the other end—

MANDY: Warney's a fat, balding womaniser. He's doing most of his damage with his mobile phone.

JOHNNY: [*getting agitated*] Now don't you start on about Warney, Amanda. Warney's a great. He is a great. He is a true Australian legend.

When you are talking about leg-spin bowling in test history, there is no one who can claim to come close to Warnie's achievements, although of course it's risky to compare eras and Bradman did maintain that Tiger O'Reilly was the bowler he least liked to face—

MANDY: I'd say plenty of English nurses would say Warney's the bowler they'd least like to face—

JOHNNY: Close to 600 wickets Amanda. The man has taken close to 600 wickets. He's an Australian legend and he'd be the second picked in my team of the century, I can tell you that right now, along with Keith Miller, McGrath, Steve Waugh, Victor Trumper, Greg Chappell, Sid Barnes to open, obviously a 1972-era Lillee would be a walk-up start to take the new ball—

MANDY: Funnily enough Johnny, you've actually told me before who's in your Australian Cricket Team of the Century— (75–76)

The conversation's drift following this early dialogue to Johnny's, and to a slightly lesser degree, Mandy's, rage over 'dole bludgers', 'lefties', 'Abos', 'Goths', 'Pakis' and taxation, prompts audiences to adjust their responses to these entertaining and generally chilled-out characters. When law student Phil enters, we get a taste of a more cerebral set of prejudices that contrast with Johnny and Mandy's knee-jerk ones. Phil's particular brand of self-interest is calm and confidently rational.

These three Australian characters are the main focus of the play's interest. It isn't until half way through that the character of an asylum seeker appears. His appearance represents a rupture: the housemates are caught off guard by the arrival at their front door of Asif (Amin Deering), an Iraqi man who requests their protection. While in Carless's surreal narrative Australian characters are contiguous with the federal government, servants in a network of governmental surveillance, Eltham's Australians disavow power and responsibility, Johnny explaining to Asif, '[r]ight: see, the thing is mate, I'm not the stinking government. I only run a servo down the road' (96). When Asif persists, entering Johnny's personal space and holding on to him to underscore his desperation, Johnny reacts violently, knocking Asif against a wall, from which he falls unconscious:

ASIF: [*still holding on*] No, not over the road. I have come so far, you do not understand—no-one will help me. Please help me sir!

JOHNNY: [*struggling with* ASIF, *batting him down*] Now just—steady—on mate.

ASIF: I want only your help for a short time–

MANDY: Go on Johnny—tell him to get out!

ASIF *takes the opportunity to try and hug* JOHNNY *tightly around his waist.*

JOHNNY: Steady on mate!

JOHNNY, *startled, heaves* ASIF *off him, throwing him against the wall, where he hits his head and falls motionless on the floor.*

JOHNNY: Oh for fuck's sake, now look what you made me do Mandy, I've gone and hurt the little bastard. (96–97)

Johnny's violence is portrayed here as being partly accidental, a consequence of him not being aware of his own strength relative to Asif. Johnny's next act is much more deliberate:

JOHNNY *gets up from the couch and walks over to* ASIF, *who lies where he fell. Cautiously,* JOHNNY *gives him a nudge with his shoe. No response.* JOHNNY *nudges harder. No response.* JOHNNY *gives him a short kick, then a harder one.* ASIF *recoils sharply, and moans.*

JOHNNY: Yeah, he's alright.

JOHNNY *picks* ASIF *up and drags him to the cupboard door. He moans but doesn't move much or resist.* JOHNNY *laboriously holds the cupboard door open with one foot while dragging* ASIF *inside. He drops him inside the cupboard with a loud thud.*

MANDY: What are you doing?

JOHNNY: Putting him into detention. While we figure out what the fuck we're supposed to do. (97)

At this moment, citizen engagement with the unauthorized noncitizen is distilled as a relation of brute force. For the rest of the play, Asif is a present but invisible body in relation to the other characters and to the audience. And it is in this point that Eltham's narrative takes on some of the surrealism that runs through Carless's *The Rainbow Dark*, but here it is of a darker hue. Indeed, while neither play deploys representational techniques that belong to the horror genre, Mullarkey's observations on how the horrific, particularly the abuse of 'quasithings' (248), can elicit laughter as well as shock, does seem to be borne out in Eltham's play.

In performance, Asif's ill treatment and imprisonment, while shocking, was not devoid of comedy. Its comic antecedents include the staged, slapstick violence of situational comedy and farce. Bergson's reflections on laughter are once again instructive; citing examples of literary and theatrical comedy, he contends, '*[w]e laugh every time a person gives us the impression of being a thing*' (58, italics in original). Much of his discussion concerns repetitive stage violence, bodies colliding and blows exchanged, of the kind seen in clowning double-acts: '[g]radually, one lost sight of the fact that they were men of flesh and blood like ourselves; one began to think of bundles of all sorts, falling and knocking against each other' (59). While the violent encounter between Johnny and Asif is not reciprocal—here, the victim is clear—it is constructed around a comic accident or pratfall: Asif won't let go of Johnny, so Johnny throws him off and Asif smashes into the wall. The violence takes place in a classic scenario of the comic protagonist escalating his or her own predicament, and as such the engagement, in performance, had a sense of choreographed inevitability. But the scene's dénouement, in which Asif's body is wedged into a cupboard, complicates Bergson's reading of a human being transformed into a thing through comedy because while the unconscious Asif is stripped any autonomy or vitality as a living human, the fact that Johnny is made to feel the weight of his body, to confront the distinct awkwardness of lifting an adult human as opposed to a 'thing', reinforces Asif/Deering's materiality and in turn the corporeality of asylum seekers in Australian detention centres to whom both character and actor are indexed.

The ambiguous effect of the stage violence in *The Pacific Solution* pertains to its meaning and characterization as well as its physical structure. In her discussion of theatrical farce, Joan F. Dean, cited earlier in this chapter in the context of laughter and theories of superiority, refers to Thomas Hobbes's definition of laughter in order to underscore her identification of the ambivalence of audience response to comic cruelty: '[t]he passion of laughter is nothing else but sudden glory arising from some sudden conception of some eminency in ourselves, by comparison with the infirmity of others' (qtd in Dean 484). The violence in *The Pacific Solution* is disconcerting yet compelling. Eltham's protagonists have up to this point in the play been constructed as the objects of a mostly-Australian audience's affectionate identification; in the 2006 production, the comic incongruity between Johnny's and Mandy's ignorance and their conviction, between their verbal dexterity and recourse to crude contemporary vernacular, made Brand's and Brehmer's performances enjoyable in the way that satire typically is. What was the audience to make, then, of Johnny's clumsily brutal assertion of citizen territoriality? The manifest moral content of the play is clear and the obvious response is to feel disturbed and indignant at the cruelty that has been inflicted on asylum seeker Asif. But comedy is more complicated than this.

Asif's brief appearance represents the problem or crisis in the dramatic narrative, and he is as such an object to be fixed rather than a subject with which to engage. In other words, Johnny's treatment of Asif is appalling, outrageous, *and* entirely appropriate as a climax in his characterization and in terms of the construction of contradictory territorial ordering within the domestic heterotopia.

The imprisonment of Asif in the cupboard is followed immediately with a solution that takes the form of pure political satire. Level-headed housemate Phil—who, Eltham notes with irony, is 'President of the local University's chapter of Amnesty International'—devises a means of dealing with Asif and of absolving the housemates of responsibility for him. Phil's eureka moment, gleaned from his study of the Residential Tenancies Act, is a piece of bureaucratic sophistry:

> PHIL: The Act states that we have no responsibility to look after him if he's not on our property. Therefore I propose that we excise the cupboard from the lease, for the purposes of being able to refuse responsibility for [to JOHNNY] not only for the thrashing he appears already to have received, but for his physical well-being *prior, during* and *following* his 'request', which is now, legally, rendered null and void, in that there is no legal basis for it to have happened at all. (107)

This is, of course, a reference to Australia's notorious excision legislation—a cornerstone of the solution from which the play takes its name—first implemented, as I noted in the introduction, in 2001 with the removal of certain maritime territories from Australia's migration zone and since extended.

The play's treatment of Asif's injury and incarceration and of his jailers' way of resolving these incidents situates *The Pacific Solution* as a transgressive farce, designed to provoke a series of complex responses among audiences which have little to do with agitprop-style moral agitation or mobilization on behalf of peoples detained by the Australian government, much less with a direct imagining of the personal stories of asylum seekers. Certainly, the sharp narrative seems to be underpinned by Eltham's bafflement, if not fury, over successive Australian policy innovations pertaining to asylum seekers, but its psychological mirror is very much oriented at his fellow Australians, who are, like him, represented by and to a large extent the beneficiaries of a national geopolitical status quo.

If the premise of *The Pacific Solution* bears striking similarities to that of Carless's *The Rainbow Dark*, the plays' respective uses of the domestic home as an analogy for immigration detention and the impulses underpinning it differ in crucial ways. Carless's characters ultimately decide that another form of sociality and community may be possible. Eltham's farce has a darker edge. His play leaves Asif's incarceration as its 'resolution'; the man's victimization isn't ameliorated, and his story isn't really heard, beyond a few desperate snatches. The play's final interaction coolly returns the play to the suburban realism with which it began:

> MANDY: Lighter.
>
> JOHNNY *passes it to her. Lights down.* (112)

Johnny, Phil and Mandy are a comic trio whose response to Asif seems ultimately to suggest that a drive to exclude may represent the underbelly of Australian mateship. In the end, the letter of the law, not Asif's call for help, 'human being to human being' (*Pacific* 96), is the medium through which they will engage with the noncitizen in their midst. What Eltham shows us is how close such bureaucratic magicking-up actually is to domestic anarchy. The space of the home is here figured as a heterotopia in which is contained not only the deviant, threshold-crossing body of the asylum seeker, but also deviant citizens divested of culpability by their freewheeling application of the law. It is a private space in which political arrangements are devised.

The passage of time since *The Pacific Solution* was written has overlaid Eltham's picture of suburban heterotopia in ways few would have predicted. Today, Johnny would have to deal with the double blow of figuring out how cricketers Usman Khawaja and Fawad Ahmed fit into his worldview *and* contemplating the waning of Australia's once formidable dominance of international test cricket. But Phil would be able to cheer Johnny with the prospect of even greater scope to disavow Asif. As I have noted, under a legislative amendment passed in May 2013, territorial excision now encompasses the entire continent of Australia. Transposing this to the world of *The Pacific Solution*, the 'logical' response of Johnny, Phil and Mandy to Asif's arrival would be to excise their entire sharehouse from its own lease agreement. In this way, there would be no circumstance in which Asif could arrive uninvited and unannounced at the house and expect to be let in.

The Structure of Political Critique

The images of domestic living space conjured by Carless and Eltham parody discourses that have circulated in defence of immigration detention policy in Australia. A stark example of such discourse appears in a letter of reply written by Mandy's real-world counterpart, former Minister for Immigration Amanda Vanstone, to Thomas Keneally, reproduced in the expanded edition of an anthology of refugee writing, *Another Country: Writers in Detention*, which Keneally co-edited with Rosie Scott in 2007. In her letter, Vanstone invoked the metaphor of the home as nation and the householder as sovereign in order to argue for the right of a nation's authorities to determine the terms on which noncitizens may enter its territory:

[It] is very similar to the right of any householder to decide who will enter their home and how long they will remain welcome there. None of us would turn away a stranger who is fleeing immediate danger, but how many of us would unquestioningly accept someone into our home who simply wants to move from another home that they do not like and where they are not in danger? (120)

The logic that rationalizes immigration detention within a rubric of household etiquette and interpersonal sociality is precisely what is interrogated via the comedy of *The Rainbow Dark* and *The Pacific Solution*. In both plays, the rules of the house are deeply disquieting.

At the start of this chapter I noted that *The Rainbow Dark* and *The Pacific Solution* emerge as critiques of the citizen–noncitizen binary that scaffolds their comedy. This is clearly true: both plays reflect their authors' wholehearted condemnation of Australian asylum seeker policy innovations pertaining to detention and territorial excision, and these policies are presented via comic theatrical metaphors as inhumane, prejudiced, and perhaps most of all, ridiculous. But to say that the two plays critique the violence of Australia's legislated categories of belonging should not be taken to mean that they *denaturalize* these categories. And there isn't a compelling reason why they should; after all, the biopolitical technologies to which the plays respond have formidable territorializing power that reifies unauthorized noncitizenship in terms of concentrations of bodies in carceral space.

It is important, then, to clarify the nature and terms of the political critique presented by the plays. Both works prompt audiences to think through the impetus for categorizations of human lives, to imagine how allegiance to categories might manifest and to consider what happens when the categories are forced to co-exist within a single domestic heterotopia. And they do this via the heterotopia of comic theatre. In these ways, the plays can be understood as rehearsing and structuring certain habits of thought and behaviour; in terms of the former, thought, there is the political and ideological critique, and in terms of the latter, behaviour, there is the theatre space in which audiences gather to demonstrate habits of thought within the framework of the political activity that is going to seeing a play about asylum, in 2006, in Australia. *The Rainbow Dark* and *The Pacific Solution* don't deter audiences from thinking about the world in terms of citizens and noncitizens any more than contemporary immigration and citizenship legislation does—the plays *need* these categories—what they do is recast them in such a way that we might join the dots between different forms of habitation and belonging in Australia. The plays don't ask us to imagine what Australia might look and feel like in the absence of Australian noncitizenship; rather, they ask us to imagine what it looks like and feels like *because* of it.

Chapter 3

TERRITORIES OF CONTACT IN DOCUMENTARY FILM

Ali told me he had no ancestors/His parents came from elsewhere/Just one family, nothing else.

—*Letters to Ali*

The case studies that form the basis of this chapter are documentary films, and while they share with the theatrical productions featured in chapters one and two a concern with the challenging question of how belonging and inhabiting are to be reconfigured in the face of the person who seeks asylum, they raise different sets of questions with respect to the ethics and aesthetics of representation as well as to how they engaged affective audience/viewer responses to the portrayal of relationships between citizens and noncitizens. Over the following pages, I situate two Australian feature length documentary films, *Letters to Ali* (2004), written and directed by Clara Law and co-written by Eddie L. C. Fong, and *Hope* (2007), directed by Steve Thomas, in terms of how they portray complex textures of emotional contact between filmmakers and their subjects, and between citizen and noncitizen subjects. Law's extensive body of film work dates from the early 1980s and has mostly been occupied with transnational cultural identity and Asian diasporas; *Letters to Ali* was her first documentary. Thomas, on the other hand, has made several issues-based social interest documentaries since the early 1990s. In both films, interpersonal relationships, newly forged in the conflux of trauma and sympathetic response, take on ambiguously familial qualities, raising questions about ancestry, relatedness and territoriality.

On a very basic level, the reflective capabilities of film and digital technologies facilitate the forensic intimacy of the close up or zoom and can also take in visual expanses, scoping potentially vast geographies; documentary film, in particular, can enable subjects, including asylum seekers and refugees, to appear, and to speak as and for themselves without risking the public, aestheticized repetition inherent to theatrical appearance. Documentary film has obvious elements in common with the types of verbatim work and theatres of reality discussed in chapter one, but whereas such theatre's technical scope and counter-hegemonic ideological purpose tend to attenuate or even prevent the appearance of certain individuals—children, non-actors, stakeholders from metropolitan and rural backgrounds, including those whose views and rationales oppose those of the director or writer—documentary film can encompass some or all such individuals. This is not to claim the documentary as an innocent or less consensualizing form: the voice an asylum seeker or refugee, for instance, may use and the terms on which he or she may be heard and made recognizable are dependent upon a series of representational acts, and crucially, on the spaces and historical contexts in which cross-cultural contact takes place.

Notwithstanding this, documentary film can illuminate directly and seriously the exclusivist or partialist perspectives on citizenship and belonging that the productions examined in the previous chapter approached satirically. The comedies discussed in chapter two did not set out to represent asylum seekers or to ask audiences to imagine them as individuals in any significant sense, but rather deployed asylum seekers as ciphers for critiquing the spatial and social organization of contemporary Australian life and for squaring off against the nation's structural violence and xenophobia. In contrast, relationship- and personality-driven documentaries produced in Australia in recent years have traced (and manifested) emotional conflict between citizens and refugees. An interest in conflict was prominent in two Australian documentaries made for television by the national hybrid-funded broadcaster SBS: the second episode in the series *Living With The Enemy* (2014) and the six-episode series *Go Back To Where You Came From* (2011). Both were concerned primarily with studying the social realities and perspectives of Australians, who make up the majority of viewing audiences, and both used social experiment techniques of the kind that has achieved mainstream popularity via so-called reality television in order to 'hot-house' cross-cultural contact in social or domestic microcosms. Episode two of *Living With The Enemy* placed as guests in one another's homes an Australian woman who professed feelings of hostility and suspicion toward unauthorized asylum seekers and a male Iranian refugee who had spent some four years in Woomera and Villawood detention centres. *Go Back To Where You Came From* gathered two groups of Australians, one supportive of and the other opposed to asylum seekers, and followed them as they traced in reverse asylum seekers' journeys to Australia. Tom Zubrycki's documentary, *Molly and Mobarak* (2003), while ostensibly centred around the hospitality and kindness of a rural New South Wales community where Afghan asylum seekers have been resettled, also confronts the tensions, abrasions and disappointments of resettlement from a number of perspectives. Another key mode of Australian documentary-making about asylum has been to examine the nation's maritime interception, detention and deportation policies as well as their implementation and effects, and two examples of this type of work are *Anthem: An Act of Sedition* (2005), directed by Tahir Cambis and Helen Newman, which focused in particular on detention centres and Bentley Dean's investigative documentary *A Well-Founded Fear* (2008), which set out to uncover the fates of returned asylum seekers.

Letters to Ali and *Hope* engage with policy and implementation, but relatively tangentially and mostly insofar as this serves their core dramatic focus on the lives of the films' human subjects. Both concern themselves with personal relationships between Australians and refugees, utilizing the personalities and experiences of their refugee and non-refugee subjects as the keys to viewers' emotional identification and interest. In *Letters to Ali*, affective epistolary contact is the key mode of cross-cultural engagement between an Australian family and 'Ali',[1] an unaccompanied fifteen-year-old Hazara Afghan asylum seeker who, for most of the filming process, was detained at the Port Hedland immigration detention centre in Australia's remote north-west.[2] Using a DV camcorder, Law documents the Australian family's three-week, 5,000 kilometre journey through the desert to visit the boy, to whom they have been writing and speaking over the phone for a period of eighteen months and whom they have already met on one occasion. The journey calls into question the relationship between national territory and national identity for the family members, Trish Kerbi, Rob Silberstein and their four children, and the filmmakers, themselves immigrants from Hong Kong. In *Hope*, Amal Basry's self-representation as an Iraqi woman is positioned amid politically contentious crosscurrents, her story being synonymous with the regional tragedy of SIEV X. On 19 October 2001, 353 asylum seekers drowned when the unidentified 'Suspected Illegal Entry Vessel' SIEV X, sank in international waters between Indonesia and Australia. Of forty-five survivors, seven were resettled in Australia. Basry was one of them, and prior to her death in 2006 she served determinedly as an advocate for other survivors and as the voice, by proxy, of the drowned.

Both films follow their filmmakers' trajectories from local urban and suburban living environments to the fringes of Australian nation space—in *Letters to Ali*, the vast desert interior and north-western coast, and, in *Hope*, the closely patrolled ocean extending to Indonesia. These are the films' contact zones, the literal and metaphorical margins where Australians and asylum seekers encounter one another. The films embed stories of transnational displacement in contexts of home and family, at the same time as they test the spatial and embodied limits of the local and the familial; as well as this, they cohere a certain kind of Australianness, a politicized moral humanitarianism galvanized by affective (whether saddened, ashamed or outraged) rejection of state biopolitics. The documentaries perform, then, dual cultural work: offering certain kinds of representation, of voice, to newcomers, and reformulating or remaking an Australian identity that is seen to have been hijacked by militarized, exclusionary sovereign power in the post-2001 era. Because they raise several quite similar or comparable critical questions, the two case studies will be interwoven thematically here, rather than examined in turn.

Witnessing, Appearing, Performing

I discussed in chapter one how in the representation of stories of traumatic displacement, a great deal of capital is attached to words: specifically, the 'real words' of witness-subjects, which are held to offer a direct connection to the truth of experience. The notions of authenticity that are typically bestowed on documentary film are a consequence of the convergence of the real word with the real body, something that is of critical significance in contexts of asylum and detention. But, as *Letters to Ali* and *Hope* show, documentaries are not always and simply a format for unified appearance. Trish FitzSimons, Pat Laughren and Dugald Williamson explain that as a technique for representing reality, documentary film developed along two key lines: first, the early 'classic expository mode' with 'voice-of-god' narration, and since the 1960s, the 'observational mode' (broadly synonymous with cinéma vérité), which presents the 'viewpoint of an onlooker not interfering with events, ostensibly, or imposing a master narration on them' (5). Of the latter, they identify two main strands, the 'direct cinema' approach of professed detachment and the 'intercessional' approach, characterized by the overt agency of the host-narrator or camera crew (5). The latter technique, which is employed in *Letters to Ali* and *Hope*, is one that according to FitzSimons, Laughren and Williamson, 'promotes communicative exchanges between filmmakers and participants through, for instance, techniques such as interview, talking heads and testimony' (6). I would add that the intercessional approach also reflexively acknowledges its own technique (and its practitioners), even if in doing so it reinforces a film's credentials as a portrayal of the real. In his discussion of the history of documentary film, Thomas Waugh identifies the difference between modes of appearance in this genre, which emerges uniquely out of a visual tension between recording the world and making it; in the documentary film, he argues, '[t]he difference between representation and presentation is not that one uses performance and the other doesn't, but that the former disavows and hides its performance components through such conventions as not looking at the camera, whereas the latter openly acknowledges and exploits its performance components' (79). While neither *Letters to Ali* or *Hope* use illusionistic or mimetic representational performance modes, such as dramatic re-enactment of history, they both incorporate what Waugh terms presentational performance, such as interviewing or observing people whilst they are placed in particular settings from their daily life or personal history. Rather than attempting to weigh the question of how, or indeed if, verisimilitude is produced in *Letters to Ali* and *Hope*—indeed, this question seems to miss the point about documentary as technique—I want to foreground the conditions under which appearance, sociality and intersubjectivity occur, to highlight the inseparability of witnessing and performing, seeing and making visible, in the manipulation of who appears, where, and how.

Both films engage a linear narrative logic whereby the filmmakers claim to proceed from positions of unknowing—of not having an expectation of where their subject matter might take them or what kinds of stories their interlocutors might tell. In part, this exemplifies the paradigm of radical uncertainty in which asylum seekers and refugees must routinely live, but for both directors, it also seems genuinely to reflect a degree of unwittingness in terms of purpose and indeed a lack of topical expertise; certainly, both Law and Thomas profess exploratory rather than authoritative interests in their subject matter (though neither pretends to a non-partisan viewpoint with respect to the morality of federal asylum seeker policy). In *Letters to Ali*, unknowing is linked to Law's relative newness to/in Australia—certainly, her unfamiliarity with the experiences her Australian subjects introduce her to, such as camping under the stars—as well as her unfamiliarity with asylum debates (she initiated contact with Kerbi after reading a newspaper article written by Kerbi on the issue). Law takes time at the start of the film to establish how, through letters, telephone calls and one visit, the Kerbi–Silberstein family have already set up a trusting relationship with the teenage detainee, Ali. Law and her partner Fong (who is not shown in the film) take up a position as guests on the road journey, and at times their migrant status is clothed as a kind of naivety: one of Law's intertitles, invoking well-worn mythologies of the Australian landscape, informs us, 'I had never camped in my life. They said there were snakes and dingoes in the outback. And serial killers'. By contrast, the confidence and experience of the tight-knit Kerbi–Silberstein family is something that the audience is invited to gaze at but not share. As Olivia Khoo, Belinda Smaill and Audrey Yue observe, '[t]he audience is forced to rely on Law's "outsider perspective", to engage with an ethics of *following*, of contingency and new experiences, rather than on an assumption of (prior) knowledge and control' (102, italics in original). Similarly, Thomas positions himself in *Hope* as a passionate latecomer to asylum debates; he states in voiceover that when he first met Basry, she had already become 'something of a celebrity in refugee circles'. This establishes his relationship with Basry as one of joining rather than initiating a conversation, with her having already entered into the public sphere as a vocal Australian noncitizen. Thomas positions Basry (as I will explain in more detail) as a collaborator in setting certain terms, if not the road map, of the film.

Letters to Ali and *Hope*, then, model and invite non-refugee audiences' identification with Law's and Thomas's respective experiences of becoming socially and affectively engaged in response to the predicament of the noncitizen other. The exploratory, non-expert model is a familiar device in contemporary hosted-narrator documentary filmmaking; oftentimes the host-narrator is inserted so comprehensively into a film that he or she is effectively its protagonist, the experiencing self through which spectatorial identification is mediated (as in, for example, the personality-driven exploratory documentaries of British filmmaker and journalist Louis Theroux). Thomas's role in *Hope* represents a hybrid of the hosted-narrator and the voiceover narrator; he appears on screen, but only intermittently, and never looks directly into the camera lens. Most of the time his voice is heard as a non-diegetic insert. Law plays neither the hosted nor voiceover narrator roles; her voice and body barely feature in *Letters to Ali*. In material derived from conversations and interviews with Kerbi–Silberstein family members, politicians and activists, the camera remains fixed on interviewees and Law's voice is typically excised, leaving the viewer to concentrate on the verbal responses and associated body language of her interlocutors. Almost all of Law's narrative interventions are presented non-diegetically as intertitles. While Law's and Thomas's respective subtleties and restraints distinguish their intercessional documentaries from the hosted-narrator mode, their autobiographical traces are calibrated in such a way as to ensure that each is nevertheless an integral subject of their own film, as well as its director. More specifically, Law's and Thomas's subjectivities are meant to mirror the subjectivity (and knowledge trajectory, over each film's duration) of the non-refugee spectator who comes to know the essential humanity of the noncitizen other through a process of compassionate seeing and hearing.

In *Letters to Ali*, the journey to visit Ali at Port Hedland detention centre gives Law's film its narrative architecture and chimes with the well-established genre of the Australian road movie, of which Stephan Elliott's *The Adventures of Priscilla, Queen of the Desert* (1994), Sue Brooks's *Japanese Story* (2003) and Michael James Rowland's *Lucky Miles* (2007) are three well-known examples. But one thing Law's documentary road movie cannot do, which its non-documentary counterparts can, is enlarge or refine the characterization of one of its key subjects. In Law's film, young Ali cannot appear as and for himself; his identity is protected for legal reasons and cameras are forbidden inside the detention centre, so for most of the film he is at a remove from the viewer. Ali is positioned at the outer limits of belonging and therefore at the limits of representable personhood. At the same time, we see evidence of the burgeoning parental and fraternal attachments that Ali evokes in his Australian family. Law's interviews with the four Kerbi–Silberstein children have an important function in this respect; they offer honest accounts of their trepidation and feelings of awkwardness upon first meeting Ali in the alienating environment of the detention centre but explain that their anxieties soon dissipated; as Bernadette Brennan notes, '[f]or a film designed to give a message that it is "ordinary" Australians, people "just like us", that can make a constructive difference to asylum seekers and the policies that govern them, these interviews are of central importance' (21). For Ali, an unaccompanied minor, correspondence with the Kerbi–Silberstein family precipitates a particularly intimate reorientation of kinship links, as he starts to call Kerbi 'Mum', implying a renunciation of his own mother that unsettles Kerbi. But the viewer is permitted to know that even as she is unsettled by Ali's attachment and expresses a certain amount of caution, Kerbi's motivation for bringing the boy so intimately into her life is complexly enmeshed with maternal grief; at the start of the film she contextualizes her own actions with reference to the trauma of a miscarriage that she suffered in the months before she wrote her first letter.

Law harnesses this tension between curtailed appearance and intimacy as unifying threads of the film's aesthetics, and in turn, its ethics. As I have noted, Law rarely appears on screen nor does she vocally narrate the film, which instead combines Kerbi's voice, and to a lesser extent that of her husband and children, with on-screen text (subtitles and intertitles) that creates a meditative mood and suggests the intimacy of a hand-written letter. Writing is the film's visual and thematic leitmotif. For the most part, Ali's history is inscribed in writing, which seems to crystallize the information offered in interviews with Kerbi–Silberstein family members and in one-sided snatches of phone conversations. One of the clearest examples of the interpenetration of spoken words and on-screen text comes in the film's second half, after the completion of the road journey, when Law sets Kerbi and Ali the task of responding to various word-prompts, taken from a selection that appears as scrolling on-screen text: family, war, food, music, sadness, tears, childhood, sea, ancestors, fear, suffering. Kerbi's relatively detailed oral response to the word 'ancestors' tells a grim story of her family's deracination. Her voiceover, set against images of sand dunes and Paul Grabowsky's understated piano score, is unsentimental and quite monotonous in tone, clearly read from a text. She gives nothing away about her feelings on the story she tells:

My ancestors come from England and Ireland. My mother's parents, Nana Barfield and Poppa Tom, were cold and unfriendly people, whom I met on perhaps a dozen occasions during my childhood. They died when I was a teenager. My dad's father was killed in the War. My dad died whilst I was still in medical school. Whilst my mother is still alive, I have no ongoing contact. My husband lost both his mother and father many years ago. My husband has no living relatives in Australia. My own children have no extended family, no grandparents, no great grandparents, no idea of their ancestry.

This is followed by on-screen text that conveys, in the third person, Ali's response to the same word prompt: 'Ali told me he had no ancestors/His parents came from elsewhere/Just one family, nothing else'. The similarity of the two responses, inasmuch as both speak of an absence of ancestors, seems to imply that family is a sociality rather than a biological relatedness. Next, Kerbi responds to the word 'sea', recalling vivid childhood days at the beach:

I grew up beside the sea [...] As a youngster, my siblings and I would chase the waves as they raced up and down the sand, laughing and screaming, pushing and shoving [...] As teenagers, my sister and I entered the frothy surf with a decorum that befitted our teeny weeny togs and gorgeous all-over golden tans. The monotony of the rolling surf soothed my teenage impatience.

Ali's response to the word 'sea' is very different. The following on-screen text appears against background images of dark clouds and the sound of thunder followed by creaking, straining boat rigging: '[t]he sea turned stormy, the sky dark./Ali thought he was going to die./He had been drifting in the ocean/ for 3 days with 300 people./Then he saw a light, in the horizon. It saved him./In his dark life, he said, his light is his "mum"'. The poignancy of the voice and text derives from their paradoxical illumination and veiling of both Kerbi and Ali. The viewer may wonder about what caused the severing of Kerbi's relationship with her mother and siblings; indeed, Law is perhaps inviting a comparison between the loss of family as an apparent choice and the loss that is not a choice. As for Ali, the viewer is able to imagine from the text on the screen just enough of the individuality of this boy, his history, his fears and his desires to care about him—indeed, to feel that he is missing or missed from the film—even as we are reminded again and again of the fact that he is prevented from becoming known outside of state-sanctioned relations of power and violence.

Toward the end of *Letters to Ali*, the viewer is offered a rare prolonged shot of Law, in side view, silhouetted against a window as she sits on the floor in the darkened interior of her house. She is speaking to Ali on the phone as he recalls a nightmare. Her minimal spoken words are accompanied by subtitles that paraphrase his side of the conversation. The 'Ali' that emerges is an amalgamation of message fragments. Law's lightness of touch here as a filmmaker works to communicate the care and concern that Ali elicits in her but does not overplay the transformative potential of the contact for Ali, her, or the viewer. Law spends much of the conversation listening to Ali, but we cannot hear him. Consequently, the scene does not offer a realist dialogue, much less an opportunity for a spectator's emotional voyeurism (which, in a differently configured documentary film, we can imagine it might have been). There are simply too many gaps here: we can only presume Ali is distressed—though perhaps not in an obvious way—and we might guess at how his distress is communicated to Law over the phone, but any real characterization remains speculative. Law's technique of representation, in this important scene where her own relationship with Ali is glimpsed, seems to be sensitive to the boundaries of privacy in which their quiet intimacy is contained and to reflect an understanding that these boundaries should not be breached even if it were safe to present the transaction more fully. We as spectators can merely, via subtitles and intertitles, in snatches of conversation, bear a kind of tertiary witness to Ali's emotional and biopolitical reality.

So far as the central paradox of Law's documentary is concerned—that is, its simultaneous making permissible and curtailing of an asylum seeker's self-representation—its orientation toward the written word, both on-screen text and letter writing, can be understood as an exemplary metaphor and mode. Over the last twenty years, a well-established literary and historical interest in letters has spread to cultural studies and sociology, with a body of scholarship on epistolarity tracing the social relationships or pacts letters establish between writer and addressee (see, for example, Stanley, Salter and Dampier, 'The Epistolary Pact'). In politicized contexts of forced migration, letter writing often takes place within the framework of a campaign whose purpose is to mobilize and practice responsiveness between citizens and noncitizens. Gillian Whitlock observes, with reference to an archive documenting just such a letter-writing campaign between Australians (including Kate Durham, whose series of paintings are a central feature of *Hope*) and asylum seekers held at Nauru detention centre, that the letters represent a unique kind of 'theatre for the performance of the self', holding up the promise of empathic reciprocity (in stark contrast to the cautious self-performance demanded by the official immigration interview): a 'delicate transaction' where the vast gap in status, autonomy, and opportunity that separates Australians from asylum seekers might temporarily be subsumed by mutual human recognition (211). While Whitlock is right that the Nauru *epistolarium* stands in stark contrast to the formalized, evidence-based communication demanded by the refugee determination process, in another sense the letter as a mode can have traumatic associations for asylum seekers whose refugee status applications are in process. Jonathan Darling examines the significance of UK Border Agency (UKBA) letters in the lives of asylum seekers, taking account of these items as chief among 'the materials that perform relations between [...] people, places, and institutions', and moreover, 'as governmental interventions' (485). He argues that the letter 'serves to inscribe the authority of the state onto the lives of those seeking asylum' and 'directs asylum seekers to respond in specific ways' (487), within specific time frames; with respect to the last point, the letter is linked 'to the temporality of asylum' (488), marked as it is by anxious periods of waiting. Notwithstanding the distressing affective qualities and potentialities of the UKBA letters, they are frequently also, Darling suggests, treasured items: 'asylum seekers often display a stark absence of possessions and it is perhaps in relation to this absence that letters take on greater affective significance. Not only are letters protected, held on to, and carried as markers of a process, they are held on to precisely as things, as possessions whose material form might allow for the projection of hopes and aspirations' (491). *Letters to Ali* constructs a certain degree of slippage or indistinction between on-screen text that is derived from letters written by Ali and that which is distilled from conversations with him; in her discussion of the film, Brennan detects an ambivalence in Law's use of on-screen text, noting that many of the film's 'captions are presented in two or three striped bands. Visually they suggest rigidity or containment' (20). They also, I would argue, suggest the letter as at once an affective lifeline and a token of coercive power.

Even after his release into community detention in the South Australian city of Adelaide, Ali continues to evade the scopic medium. A relation of exclusion is upheld due to Ali's status as a noncitizen captured outside (to reiterate Agamben) Australia's sovereign community, and this has consequences for him both in his capacity as a body occupying civic space and a body on film. The news that Ali has been released is revealed near the end of Law's film, but rather than functioning structurally as a conclusion, the release is tinged with a sense of unsettlement, the pseudo-familial relations between the Kerbi–Silberstein family and Ali being put under the pressure of an ambiguous pseudo-freedom. Law accompanies the family as they drive to visit Ali. Puncturing the viewer's natural anticipation, she blurs all shots of the boy, a legal caution, but one which actually brings ethics and aesthetics into striking alignment: reducing the contours of his body to a smudge of colour on screen, Law underscores Ali's precarious presence in the 'free', civic spaces of Australia. The technique both marks and masks him, rendering him phantom-like as he interacts with Australians, both adults and children, whose faces and bodies are clearly visible, clearly there. Ali's subjectivity in the film is translated and transformed—he is literally renamed, disembodied—and he can only emerge as an anonymized residue of the sovereign power that filmmakers and Ali's Australian family alike decry, even as he is invested with their hopes and desires for a reconstituted Australian community. This is not to discount the political and affective value of the traces of Ali offered in the film, much less the reciprocal benefits of the Kerbi–Silberstein family's touching relationship with him, but to recognize that *Letters to Ali* is as much a testament to the totalizing power of a sovereign authority to curtail acts of (self-)representation as it is a vehicle for a marginalized voice.

In contrast to *Letters to Ali, Hope* is dominated by the bold self-presentation of its refugee-witness. Basry devoted her life in Australia to speaking publicly about SIEV X. Despite the emotional pain involved in repeatedly recounting trauma and her initial hesitance about being interviewed by Thomas for his film, Basry's desire to speak on behalf of those who lost their lives and the other survivors propels the making of *Hope,* and as Australian film critic David Stratton observes, she 'easily dominates the film in which she's the star' (Stratton). At one point in the film, Thomas follows Basry to a SIEV X fourth anniversary memorial event in Canberra, noting, 'Amal is the only survivor here who didn't lose loved ones in the ocean, but her command of English enables her to speak for those who did'. The need to remember is made more urgent by the lack of formal resolution regarding SIEV X: references in survivor accounts (including Basry's) to a ship's lights, aeroplanes, and reports that the boat had been under surveillance when it left Indonesia have left troubling questions unanswered. The Executive Summary of the 2002 Australian Senate Select Committee on A Certain Maritime Incident—at which, as I noted in chapter one, no survivors testified—concluded of SIEV X: 'the Committee finds it extraordinary that a major human disaster could occur in the vicinity of a theatre of intensive Australian operations, and remain undetected until three days after the event, without any concern being raised within intelligence and decision making circles' (Senate Select Committee xlii). Early in Thomas's film, Basry reveals, in her halting but confident English, how the historical necessity to memorialize, to testify to the tragedy, is imbricated with a personal necessity to make meaning out of inexplicable survival:

I ask my God why I'm still alive; I said maybe I still alive because maybe I going to tell the world what happened to us; I going to tell the story about the tragedy of our boat; I going to tell what happened to Iraqi people, why we escaped from our country; I want to explain why we travel by this boat; there is no way; there is no choice; we must travel by boat.

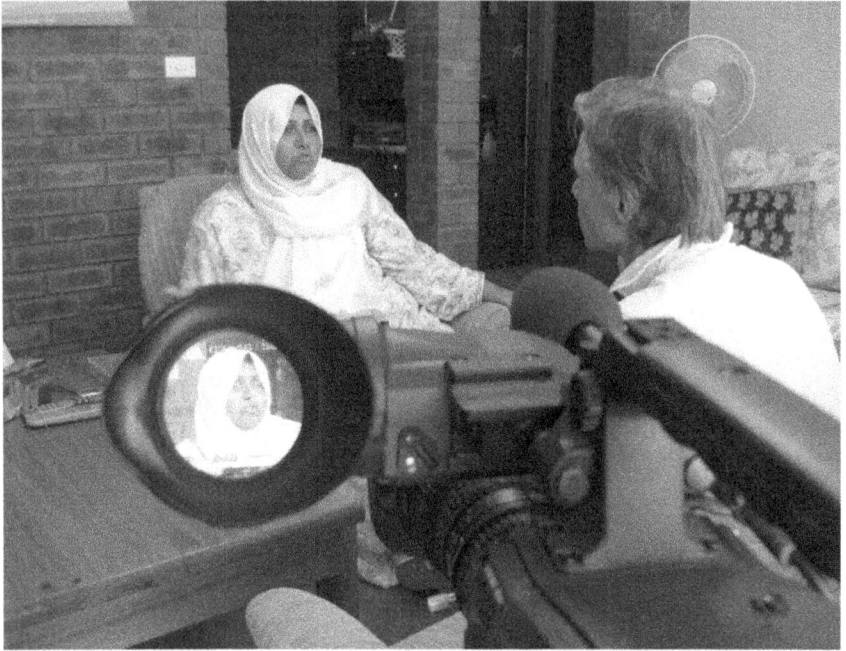

Fig. 4. Production still from *Hope*, directed by Steve Thomas. Flying Carpet Films, 2007. (Photo: Steve Thomas.)

It is worth noting here that Basry adopts the language of non-volition or non-culpability in which, as I argued in chapter one, asylum narratives are all too often made palatable to Australian listeners; Basry seems to recognize that in explaining why she got on the ill-fated boat she must not appear to be guilty of choice, much less ambition, although the overall effect of her commanding self-representation counteracts constructions of victimhood. Later, she describes a dream in which drowning children are pulling at her hair, demanding that she should tell what is happening to them, and she is reminded that she has a 'big responsibility, because I saw everything in my eyes'.

As a woman both haunted and energized by the need to testify, Basry exemplifies what Holocaust survivor Dori Laub, drawing on Cathy Caruth's work on trauma and repetition as well as his own conversations with other survivors, describes as the opposing impulses within the survivor: '[t]he survivors did not only need to survive so that they could tell their stories; they also needed to tell their stories in order to survive. There is, in each survivor, an imperative need to *tell* and thus to come to *know* one's story', even though 'the story [...] cannot be fully captured in *thought, memory,* and *speech*' (63, italics in original). Basry also occupies a position akin to that articulated so incisively by survivor Primo Levi in his account of the Holocaust survivor who can never be the true witness, if the true witnesses are, paradoxically, those who did not survive—the drowned (obviously, Levi's term takes on a terrible literalness in the context of Basry and SIEV X). For Levi, the position of survivor in the midst of so much death prompts self-berating rationalization: 'the worst survived, the selfish, the violent, the insensitive, the collaborators of the "gray zone", the spies' (*Drowned* 82). Whilst it must be acknowledged that trauma is a unique and indivisible psychic burden, Levi's profound account prompts closer consideration of whether its representation is similarly singular. The argument that true knowledge of the camps is impossible led Levi, in identifying the (lost) subjectivity of the drowned, to account for their experience and for their constitutive position within the historical collectivity of which he is part. In this sense, the very structure of his testimonial self-representation serves to witness for the drowned—as he writes, '[w]e speak in their stead, by proxy' (*Drowned* 84). While it is not at all clear, not should we assume, that Basry's questions to her 'God why I'm still alive' compel her to speak for the drowned as an act of atonement, she certainly embodies the characteristics of one who speaks for, and as, something larger than herself. Her style of speech is performative and utterly captivating: she demonstrates rhetorical instincts, using repetition, protracted pauses, and metaphor as she braids her individual story with the collective story of those who experienced SIEV X and ultimately with the people of Iraq. Her sense of historical relationality, which is essentially a compassionate intersubjective consciousness, enables Basry to recuperate and refract her experience as an international asylum story.

Although *Hope* is dominated by the increasingly close relationship between Thomas and Basry, other intimate relationships and exchanges provide crucial components of the film. One of these is Basry's friendship with Kate Durham, the painter and activist at whose exhibition of SIEV X paintings Thomas first heard of Basry. While *Letters to Ali* is marked by the visual leitmotif of on-screen text, *Hope* owes much of its aesthetic and affective intensity to Durham's series of SIEV X paintings, one 20 cm × 20 cm panel for each of the 353 drowned. Throughout the film, these images are faded in and out of close shots of the ocean's surface. This underscores a remarkable imaginative exchange between Basry and Durham. For Basry, the paintings—ghostly, staring faces and lifeless bodies being submerged by the waves—encapsulate precisely the horror of her memory of the event. She describes her response to seeing the images for the first time:

> Look to the colours, to the water. When I saw her picture the first, I'm shocked. Oh God, I feel I'm still in the ocean. I ask Kate, "you travelled with us?" She said, "no, I just imagined". I told her you are very clever.

Because your picture talk […] it look like me; it look like my eyes in the darkness; it look like my eyes when I believe that I am going to die.

Durham's concentrated creative engagement and Basry's response show just how much the story of SIEV X comprises an intersubjective weaving of memory and imagination, intimate survivor testimony and empathic supporter representation. Basry's striking response to the paintings also seems to point to the unique capacities or qualities of image-making, which may transcend some of the limits that accompany language as a communication tool. A key dimension of the problem of representability with respect to trauma in particular has to do with the limits of language; Jenny Edkins apprehends trauma testimony within this paradigm with her observation, 'the difficulty that testimony experiences—that there are no words to express what the witness needs to say—is an extreme and exemplary form of the difficulty with language more broadly' (*Trauma* 188). As an experience of extremity, trauma is, as Edkins explains, '[i]n Lacanian terms […] an encounter with the real […] that which is outside the linguistic realm, outside the symbolic or social order' (*Trauma* 213–4). In this regard, the 'gap […] at the heart of subjectivity' (*Trauma* 214) can be seen to be more than usually apparent in the context of trauma. Basry's enraptured response to Durham's paintings does not mean she subordinates her own attempts as a survivor to communicate her trauma in language—indeed, Basry is linguistically adept, as I have explained—but it does indicate that the paintings may have brought into the symbolic or social order something that had been outside language.

The other intimate relationships portrayed in *Hope* are between Basry and her family. In this respect, the film reflects Basry's strong desire to enact unextinguished familial ties in the context of her exile. Indeed, Thomas's account of his relationship with Basry is that he started making a film *about* her and ended up making one *with* her. In the first third of the film, Thomas states in voiceover, 'after tolerating my earnest filmmaking intentions for a while, Amal told me what *she* wanted to do'. The short interlude that follows is inspired by Basry's vision of a video clip that would capture her exilic longing: she is filmed walking along the banks of Melbourne's Yarra River, which she explains reminds her of the Tigris, while a love song that she heard in Iran after fleeing Baghdad plays in the background. Later, upon her request, the film incorporates an extended interlude excerpted from a family video that Amal brought back from a visit to Iran. Thomas's voice frames these moments, as it does the entire film, providing an authorized, but not overbearing, narrative. Finally, Basry's battle with breast cancer and her death, movingly portrayed towards the end of the film, transforms a dialogic process into a eulogic one.

Landscapes and Oceanscapes

Letters to Ali's wordless opening minutes offer a juxtaposition between Law's former and current living spaces. On-screen text guides the visual transition from a wide shot of the bustling Hong Kong harbour and the interior of a high-rise apartment (Law's former aerial view on the city that was her home) to suburban Melbourne, where, as we read, she lives 'close to the earth'. A series of images of Melbourne re-sensitizes viewers to a familiar—for Australian audiences—suburban environment, but as well as inducing a close looking, the re-sensitization is unsettling, in many ways constituting a simultaneous defamiliarization. The neighbourhood that Law shows us is eerily quiet; the camera surveys streets and green parklands, birdlife and seasonal changes, all in one way beautiful but markedly empty of people. Law's vision of her adopted home, rendered in on-screen text as 'a vast country/With very few people', pointedly questions the rationale for mandatory detention, but here it also evokes a feeling that the nation may lack civic engagement, that people are absent in the lives of their neighbours, much less noncitizen others. The film then proceeds to introduce us to the idyllic Kerbi–Silberstein home in the hills east of Melbourne and to the family members, who despite the isolated environment of their home represent an impulse to engage with outsiders.

The images of suburban somnolence effect a contrast with the desert landscapes that dominate most of the rest of the film. The ambitious road trip to Port Hedland takes the Kerbi–Silberstein family and the filmmakers into the red centre, a desert landscape that is iconically Australian and yet rarely encountered directly by the vast majority of the nation's inhabitants, who cluster around the coastal metropolitan regions of the east, south, and south west. Australian film critic Margaret Pomeranz describes the film's desert setting as 'that red heart that [...] is [at] the back of all of our brains' (Pomeranz). *Letters to Ali* suggests that this 'red heart' is a territory in which Australians must reckon with their own belonging, that the idea of it has a kind of haunting effect on the national psyche. Once again, the film projects a sense of unease on this issue. At one point the travellers pass through the location of an Aboriginal community. Shots of dilapidated buildings and burnt-out cars and fleeting images of townspeople watching the convoy pass are followed by text that informs us of appalling Aboriginal mortality statistics: '[t]hey die younger than the other Australians, by 20 years.' This is accompanied by a sombre section of Grabowsky's piano and string score and punctuated by the roar of Law and Fong's vehicle on the dirt road, barking dogs and the throaty, almost-human call of the Australian raven. As Brennan discerns, the scene briefly apprehends another dimension of sovereign–stranger relations: '[a]t this moment we understand that "Ali" is not the only person who has come to this land uninvited' (19). The desert tests the very meaning of settler Australianness and its practices of territorial authority, as well as an affective moral commitment to an Australian noncitizen.

In *Hope*, a different border zone is brought into view. The film's opening scene establishes the ocean as a pervasive presence: taking in the rhythmic crash of waves and squawking seabirds, the camera pans across the water at a small Melbourne beach to reveal Basry walking along the sand. The ocean is figured as an isolated space, a deathscape (a vision encapsulated in the Durham paintings), but also as inseparable from Australian civic and political life. When Thomas accompanies Basry to Australia's Parliament House in the capital city, Canberra, she looks down at the empty House of Representatives from the viewing gallery and states emphatically: 'Here. Here. In this place. They decide to forget us. Here. They didn't say the truth'. Basry's words not only instantiate the controversy that still lingers over the SIEV X tragedy but also show up in stark spatial or territorial terms the interdependency of the formal, efficient seat of Australian power and the disorderly swathe of the ocean. Basry's use of vocal emphasis and repetition in the Parliament House scene, while once again demonstrating her performative instincts, reflect her awareness of the power of speech, and speech acts, in the context of sovereign power. By entering the seat of executive power in which speech acts produce ontologies, Basry enacts and embodies a tactical defiance. The scene becomes, for her and for Thomas, a way of refusing to acquiesce to a politics of forgetting; Basry here politicizes her survivor's body as evidence of what she regards as the lies spoken by politicians about SIEV X.

A significant section of *Hope* depicts Thomas's visit to Indonesia. This pilgrimage of sorts was also supposed to be undertaken with Basry, but when Thomas arrives on his flight from Australia, two hours after Basry, he discovers to his horror that she has been refused entry at Jakarta airport because she is on a blacklist (most likely due to her previous illegal entry). He books into the hotel where Basry and her son lived for seven months after being rescued from the ocean and visits the hotel they stayed at before setting out for Australia, filming a children's playground in the hotel garden, a place with fond memories for Basry. A telephone call between the pair is dominated by Basry's frantic confirmation that Thomas had indeed retraced her footsteps as she wished. Here, Thomas takes himself and the viewer on a journey into Basry's past; these scenes are overlaid, however, with a mood of melancholy because the viewer is aware that this return to the places of the past brings Thomas a clearer understanding of what has been lost, that these places no longer contain the bodies of the people who set out in the ill-fated SIEV X.

In an act not, in the audience's view at least, reported back to Basry in Australia, Thomas travels to a wharf from which it is most likely the SIEV X departed. He walks to the end of the empty wooden platform and performs a simple ceremony, placing flowers in the water and tearfully speaking of the known and unknown victims and of the survivors. Basry had expressed her desire to place flowers in the ocean to say farewell to the drowned, but in this emotional scene the viewer is acutely reminded that the story being told is not just Basry's. Thomas maps a personal journey here, performing an act of mourning for the SIEV X asylum seekers, which is also an expression of guilt for geopolitics in which he is implicated. In doing this, Thomas solemnizes his self-identification as a compassionate Australian. This is not to say that the ritual is merely solipsistic; in enacting and also documenting his expression of sorrow, Thomas re-enfolds those who died back into history, a political as well as personal action that marks the deaths of the drowned as grievable in the context of Australian social realities.

Letters to Ali does not concern itself as overtly as *Hope* with Asian spaces, but as I have noted, Law's decision to juxtapose at the start of the film an image of Hong Kong harbour with her quiet Melbourne home is important. Not only does it remind the viewer that belonging is always contingent and represents, for many, a difficult process of continual becoming in Australia, but it reinforces the regional nexus in which Australian asylum politics are enmeshed. Several scholars have read *Letters to Ali* directly in the context of race relations and specifically Law's Asian Australian identity (see Mitchell; Johnston; Shen; Khoo, Smaill and Yue). Law's Hong Kong Chinese roots explicitly inform the film's mythopoetics as well as its cultural and political perspectives: the evocative final image reveals a cloud formation of, as the on-screen text tells us, a mother dragon bringing its child home. Law reads the cloud image, a distillation of the film's sustained concern with family and particularly parenting, as a sign of the 'miracle' Ali needs. As in Thomas's ritual act at the Indonesian wharf, Asia is seen in this moment to offer symbolic or sacred understanding. In the case of Law's film, the symbolic understanding is also part of her coming to be at home in Australia, to the point where she permits herself to read the natural environment, the meteorological signs, in a way that enfolds her ancestral cosmology.

Although the majority of those who have sought Australia's protection in the last decade have originated from Afghanistan, Iran or Iraq, their setting-off point from ports in Indonesia means that the transnational lens through which they tend to be refracted is an Asian one. The relationship that Australia and Australians have with asylum seekers, whether policy-based, embodied or, as in most cases, imagined, is inextricably tied to Asia, particularly Southeast Asia. A persistent psycho-geography of invasion from the Asian north that, as Ien Ang argues, has long underpinned the settler Australian imaginary (129–30) is complicated more recently by certain geopolitical realities in a globalized world: notwithstanding economic interdependence, the connectedness of Australia and Asia has been underscored by discourse that now explicitly works to formulate asylum as a regional issue, to be dealt with by regional 'partners'. Former Prime Minister Rudd maintained that even as Indonesia is chief among the 'friends and partners' with whom Australia has 'integrated [its] [...] border protection efforts', it is also a repository of people smugglers, 'the vilest form of human life' who should 'rot in hell' (qtd in 'PM Tells'). Subsequently, Prime Minister Gillard attempted to authorize her government's version of 'regional relations' vis-à-vis asylum seekers via a plan—which was halted by the High Court in 2011—to send asylum seekers to Malaysia for processing. Currently, Manus Island in Papua New Guinea and Nauru are key extra-territorial detention sites utilized by the Australian government, while in 2014 a financial and diplomatic memorandum of understanding between Australia and Cambodia was signed, facilitating the transfer to Cambodia of processed refugees rejected by Australia (Crothers and Doherty). The Middle Eastern origins of many of the individuals who seek asylum in Australia are frequently collapsed, both discursively and administratively, into an ongoing national project of articulating an ambivalent relationship with Southeast Asia that is at once 'across borders' and 'between neighbours'.

Remaking Australianness

Like the politically motivated documentaries that have garnered international attention in recent years, such as Michael Moore's *Fahrenheit 9/11* (2004) or *Sicko* (2007), or Davis Guggenheim's *An Inconvenient Truth* (2006), Law's *Letters to Ali* and Thomas's *Hope* have clear social agendas and liberal political orientations. The filmmakers may position themselves, as I have noted, as explorers or newcomers to the issues with which they engage, but even a cursory viewing of the documentaries confirms that filmmakers and subjects alike stand in opposition to Australian federal asylum policies and moreover that the purpose of the films is to document this opposition. Law's intertitles repeatedly describe the Kerbi–Silberstein family's three-week road journey to visit Ali as 'a long march', a significant choice of words that simultaneously situates the journey in the context of international referents, of course to China and the Long Marches that led to the instalment of the Communist Party, but also to forced marches that took place at the end of the Second World War. The concept of a 'long march' also has local resonance, having been invoked by Aboriginal Australian activists for decades in their resistance to oppression and injustice; some of the best-known actions in this context are the 1966 Wave Hill walk-off by Aboriginal cattle station workers, which mobilized the land rights movement and in 2004 Aboriginal AFL football player

Michael Long's 650 kilometre 'Long Walk' from Melbourne to Canberra, which culminated in a meeting with Prime Minister John Howard. By invoking the spectre of the 'long march', Law establishes the journey to Ali as a moral act of endurance for the purposes of mobilization and change.

Letters to Ali invokes the historical resonance of the Second World War more extensively via interview material with Kerbi and Silberstein on their decisions and perspectives, as well as the latter's family history. Kerbi speaks of her desire to learn more about Australia's detention centres in the context of a recent visit to the site of the Dachau concentration camp, while Silberstein speaks of his Polish father's and German mother's resistance against the Nazis and likens the profoundly detrimental effect of incarceration on his father with Ali's detention. Law lingers on the trauma in Silberstein's recent past, at one point setting his voiceover remembrances of his father against an image of Ali's blurred silhouette as the boy sits looking across a beach to the ocean:

> He never felt that he had a home. [Although] I think he did here because [...] our family home was on the beach, in the suburbs [of Adelaide] and my father would come from work and go down to the beach and jump into the water [...] And there was something very, very significant to that that I didn't recognise until maybe ten years ago, I think that was a real cleansing process that he was going through. [...] It was a ritual and even in cold days [...] he'd jump in the water [...] I feel that there was something there that linked him to maybe a purification process or something, I'm not entirely sure.

The film's concern with memory, the ambivalence of home, and the unspoken textures of family history are woven with its interest in documented historical and contemporary politics. The implications of abuse of outsiders in terms of political leadership are communicated in the film in an interview between Law and former conservative Prime Minister of Australia Malcolm Fraser, who has been a vocal advocate of asylum seekers' rights in recent years (and whose government oversaw Australia's resettlement of Indochinese refugees after the Vietnam War):

> One of the things that political leaders ought to do, I believe, is to fight discrimination, racism, hatred, religious bigotry with all the force and with all the power and persuasion that they can use. Because if they don't then these things grow and they spread. And we saw, certainly in the Second World War, how those feelings could engulf almost the whole world.

Fraser's role here is to offer the universal humanist reading of immediate policy measures, and in doing so he performs the discursive move—a fraught one, certainly—of holding up fascism in general and Nazism in particular as ever-malleable moral touchstones or cultural cautions (this is not an uncommon tactic in Australian refugee support discourse, and it can be used effectively as radical provocation, as illustrated by Mike Parr's durational performance, *Close the Concentration Camps*, discussed in the next chapter). Fraser's position as an Australian elder statesman lends his words gravitas and political credibility, and his interview stands as a counterpoint to Law's interview at the start of the film with a young Australian musician, Adam Myonvell, who was charged with harbouring escaped detainees after a protest in 2002 outside Woomera detention centre. Again, the spectre of the fascist state is raised when Myonvell explains how he wrestled with the question of when and how a law may be morally wrong. Through these interlocutors, as well as other interviews interspersed with the core material with the Kerbi–Silbersteins, Law establishes the idea that moral opposition amongst Australians cuts across political affiliations and generational lines; what emerges is an image of a heterogeneous Australian 'we' who are not represented or served by harsh asylum politics. For the viewer, then, one of the overriding affective invitations established by the film is to align oneself with this Australian 'we'.

At the very beginning of his film, Thomas situates *Hope* in relation to a single administration: the opening intertitle explains that '[a] feature of the Howard Federal Government from 1996 to 2007 was its determination to turn back or detain asylum seekers heading for Australia by boat'. The tragedy of SIEV X and the government's extraordinarily inadequate response to it are crucial ingredients in the film's narrative, generating in viewers the kind of moral outrage that filmmakers like Moore understand as a key tool in politically engaged filmmaking. Like *Letters to Ali*, *Hope* occupies a position as part of a broader body of theatre and film, protest and community awareness raising in Australia that has sought to call into question the morality of government policies—and, more fundamentally, government-led narratives of nationhood, security, and belonging. These oppositional politics constitute the context in which asylum seeker and refugee stories and identities have been made recognizable in Australia.

Out of this context, it becomes necessary to ask whether these acts of representation serve their noncitizen subjects as comprehensively as they serve a certain model of Australianness. As I noted in the introduction to this book, James Goodman contends that Australia's refugee solidarity movements since 2001 have been bifurcated in terms of national and global preoccupations, the former 'geared to national policy change, effectively to remaking "the nation", and reclaiming national pride against the shame of refugee detention', and the latter more radically expansive in expressing 'anger and outrage in the name of human empathy and dignity' (270–71). Both, he maintains, are underpinned by deep emotional responses to the other, necessary for impelling cross-cultural engagement. While I would characterize the two preoccupations in terms of a layering rather than a bifurcation, it can be said that *Letters to Ali* and *Hope* share some of the global strand's cosmopolitan sensibilities and ideals, but return repeatedly to the civic reference point of the nation—its meanings and its members.

Goodman's discussion refers in particular to activism in the form of public demonstrations and volunteer programmes, but can be applied to the counter-discursive, counter-memorializing work at play in *Letters to Ali* and *Hope*. Without wishing to deny the specificity of techniques and processes employed by artists working in various genres, I would argue that the filmmakers were ideologically and affectively engaged in much the same project as Australian activists and supporters who, in recent years, have marched to the razor-wire fences of detention centres (amateur footage of which appears in *Letters to Ali*), or rallied in the nation's metropolitan spaces, or been engaged in detention centre visiting and letter-writing campaigns. These actions, like the films, unsettle the normative territoriality of nation space and normative understandings of who belongs to/in it. Both only make sense in the presence of an audience (or at least an interlocutor), whether constituted by embodied proximity or technological mediation. But in the case of documentary film as a genre, a particular kind of reflective engagement is encouraged: geographically dispersed and potentially large audiences encounter the film in the darkened silence of a cinema or the privacy of their own home. The status of the documentary film in contemporary culture supports a reflective looking: the form is arguably held to be more legitimate and trustworthy than the anarchic and unpredictable public protest, and documentary watching is often a serious, pedagogic activity. Working in concert with this seriousness are affective processes. A recent study by communication researchers Heather L. LaMarre and Kristen D. Landreville indicate that documentaries elicit stronger affective responses than fictional films on the same topic: comparing responses to films on the Rwandan genocide, they found that 'the documentary group reported higher levels of affect, as well as increased issue concern and learning', and concluded, 'as a form of political information, [documentaries] have the potential to strongly influence public opinion' (550).

Whatever this may imply in terms of the significations and intersections of truth, pedagogy, affect and community, it underscores the importance of *Letters to Ali* and *Hope* as works that, as I have argued, remake Australianness by offering audiences a moral humanitarian national identification, opposed to the exclusionary violence of detention and deterrence. Both films may represent potent tools for the 'affective embedding' that Goodman identifies as 'a precondition for sustained mobilization', or more precisely, 'cognitive reflection and action' (272). The films had the potential to achieve this affective embedding across a fairly broad sweep of Australian society (though this does not guarantee concomitant organization and action). They have been screened at cinemas across the country—*Letters to Ali*, in particular, was distributed by major Australian companies, Palace Films and Madman Entertainment—as well as abroad and have featured at film festivals locally and internationally. Both films were afforded (and legitimated by) critical attention in major media outlets. They were given largely favourable reviews on Australia's long-running film review television program, *At the Movies*, hosted by veteran critics Margaret Pomeranz and David Stratton. *Letters to Ali* was reviewed and discussed in Australia's major broadsheet newspapers, *The Australian* (national), *The Age* (Melbourne), *The Sydney Morning Herald*, *The Courier-Mail* (Brisbane) and *The West Australian* (Perth), as well as several smaller newspapers, and in *Variety* magazine. *Hope* was reviewed and discussed in several newspapers, including *The Age*, *The Daily Telegraph* (Sydney), *The Advertiser* (Adelaide), *The Canberra Times* and *The Courier-Mail*.

Both films were relatively modest in scale and budget, benefitting from pre-existing refugee support and advocacy communities in cohering their viewing audiences. Of course, such communities count among their numbers public figures, including, as I have noted, former Prime Minister Fraser in *Letters to Ali*. Insofar as the films remake Australian citizen identity, they build on existing politicized communities that form vertical as well as horizontal lines of articulation through society. Law's film was able to be produced when, as on-screen text informs us, 'People threw in their support/With 100% discount on editing, mixing, video mastering [...]/Then an editor, a composer, a sound designer, a lawyer' came on board; similarly, when Thomas was unable to secure sufficient funding via government agency or corporate routes, *Hope* was seen to completion through a grassroots fundraising campaign initiated by its producer, Sue Brooks (see 'Funding Story'), director of *Japanese Story*, the abovementioned road movie about Asian–Australian relations. In such ways, both films show how directly the presentation of irregular noncitizens as humans whose conditions of life and death are supervised by regular citizens can activate charitable action as a politicized relation of care.

This chapter has sought to trace some of the tensions and contradictions at play in documentary film as a form that is simultaneously able to lay special claim to directness or truthfulness and to retain careful control over who appears, where, and how. *Letters to Ali* and *Hope* are examples of the kinds of works that have, since 2001, sought to reflect and constitute Australian moral humanitarianism, vis-à-vis asylum, as an imagined community.

Lines of affective multicultural contact—crisscrossing between filmmakers, subjects, and audiences—are what energize both films. These offer alienated newcomers a stake in negotiating their places in Australia, even as they facilitate a performance of Australian identity by filmmakers and citizen-subjects. This identity is personal but also collective, and politicized. The epistolary fragments of an unseen Ali and Basry's own brave testimony are figured into a larger ongoing project, made to stand for a flawed asylum policy. Whether asylum seekers or refugees can make themselves recognizable to Australians on their own terms within the parameters of this project and whether, indeed, they can represent themselves outside the familiar keys of trauma, violation, and redemption are questions that trouble, to a greater or lesser extent, all accounts of noncitizenship that are presented, across the borderlines, to citizens in secure and prosperous host nations.

Chapter 4

THE PAIN OF OTHERS: PERFORMANCE, PROTEST AND INSTRUMENTAL SELF-INJURY

> …can you look at this? There is the satisfaction of being able to look at the image without flinching. There is the pleasure of flinching.
>
> —Susan Sontag, *Regarding the Pain of Others*

This chapter takes as its point of departure the idea that in and through the bodies of unauthorized Australian noncitizens, the Australian state produces a symbolic excess. The marked, managed bodies of irregular noncitizens are constructed as surplus to the nation's human requirements. Moreover, *excess* becomes coterminous with *waste* in the collective national consciousness: through the inherent indignity of incarceration, and particularly via reported acts of self-injury such as sewing lips and refusing food, asylum seeking noncitizenship comes to represent an abject corporeality, and noncitizens themselves the objects of intense responses of pity on the one hand or disgust on the other. I examine the instrumentalization of asylum seeker self-injury via an analysis of its representation in Australian performance art, theatre and protest. The case studies that form the subjects of discussion are Mike Parr's durational live art piece, *Close the Concentration Camps* (2002), in which the artist's mouth, eyes and ears were sewed together; Mireille Astore's site-responsive installation at a Sydney beach, *Tampa* (2003), which saw the artist emplaced in a cage-like structure each day for eighteen days; solidarity fasts by Australian activists and celebrities, most of them undertaken in public spaces (2002–04); and former detainee Shahin Shafaei's solo touring play about a hunger striker, *Refugitive* (2002–04). These works are framed in terms of 'instrumental' self-injury because, first, they sought broadly to amplify the effects of political self-injury by detained asylum seekers—that is, self-injury structured as protest and intent on communicating with others—thereby highlighting the way the self-injuring body puts itself to 'anti-work' in extremis; and second, because in each case, the representative or performing bodies became acutely and evidently vulnerable. In the first three works, vulnerability took the form of physical suffering or endurance, while in the fourth it took the form of a refugee, destabilized by Temporary Protection Visa status and the residue of his former detention. While presenting Australian audiences with possibilities for imaginative encounter with injured noncitizens that seem immutably other, these works also offered a more troubling context for recognition of proximity to a state-produced corporeal excess.

That the imprisonment of noncitizens generates corporeal excess is something to be understood not just conceptually but quite literally, and the biological condition of this excess is, as Australian barrister and prominent refugee advocate Julian Burnside observes, exactly as should be expected: '[t]he consequences of indefinite detention are utterly predictable. Detainees languish and lose hope. Some are driven to self-harm—hunger strikes, sewing their lips together, throwing themselves on the razor wire, hanging, swallowing poison—and entire catalogue of self-destruction. Suicide among pre-adolescent children is almost unheard of—except in Australia's detention centres' (117). Australia's systematic and totalizing implementation of immigration detention separates wasted noncitizen bodies from what might be termed 'embodied citizens', those who possess the social and juridical functions of wellness and liberty: nutrition, healthcare, belonging within a home or habitat, freedom of movement and freedom from extrajudicial detention. It should be clear, however, that not all citizens enjoy these embodied privileges. In Australia, particular disenfranchised and exploited groups have always been more vulnerable to the vicissitudes of sovereign territoriality. Most egregiously, Aboriginal people have been subjected since settlement to coercion, notoriously upheld by Australian state and federal laws that functioned until the 1970s to forcibly remove children from their families and to deny voting rights, inclusion in the census and freedom of movement. Most recently, the controversial Northern Territory National Emergency Response, more commonly known as the 'intervention' into Aboriginal communities, stands as a clear reminder of the fact that what I'm calling 'embodied citizenship' is not a necessary corollary of legal citizenship.[1] Indeed, prolonged incarceration without trial is a limit position to which, in theory, any individual may be relegated; this is attested by the recent high-profile cases of Australian citizens David Hicks and Mamdouh Habib and Australian permanent resident Cornelia Rau, as well as the handful of New Zealand citizens typically held in immigration detention in Australia.[2] Remembering Giorgio Agamben's insistence that the state of exception and the instrumentalization of bare life are characteristic functions of sovereignty rather than moments of its breakdown, embodied citizenship should be seen to be a contingent position under what Joanna Zylinska (drawing on Judith Butler) terms 'an *ethics of bodies that matter*' (85, italics in original)—a concept to which I shall return. The vulnerability of bodies to the state is in part a function of how sovereign power may innovate the method of its deployment in such a way as to erode collective oversight. As Butler notes with reference to President George W. Bush's military order on 13 November 2001 regarding the indefinite detention of suspected enemy combatants, 'the executive branch assumes the power of the judiciary' (54). As a technique of contemporary sovereignty, this is continuous with John Howard's intervention as Prime Minster into state biopolitics vis-à-vis asylum seekers in 2001; in the ABC television documentary *The Howard Years*, which aired in 2008, the former Foreign Minister Alexander Downer revealed that the Pacific Solution was devised without consultation with cabinet after Howard instructed him to 'go and find someone who'll take' the *Tampa* asylum seekers ('Whatever it Takes').

With the precariousness of human liberty in mind, as well as the uneven distribution of what Butler terms 'precarity' (being recognized as precarious), my analysis of the representation by performers and activists of asylum seekers' self-injuries is structured around how the representational body imagines and provokes imagining of the relationship between noncitizens and embodied citizens. As protest, self-injury demands, or purports to demand, that an interlocutor interrogate his or her own stake in the injury; therefore while noncitizenship-in-extremis represents a position diametrically opposed to embodied citizenship, the two are met at a mutually constitutive nexus. The aestheticized work of the citizen-performer-as-advocate in this context is complicated in terms of whom it brings close and whom it distances. The performance and activism discussed here situated performing bodies, temporally and spatially, as open to scrutiny and contemplation. Their mostly Australian citizen spectators were invited to consider relationships of proximity of a potentially intense kind. Proximity can function in several productive ways here but may not necessarily resemble a relation of care. On one level, it concerned bodily closeness between performer and spectator, which could have elicited a range of emotional responses, from pity to compassion, to horror, to indignation or even anger. The latter is more commonly elicited in response to work encountered in open public spaces, where, as Alison Jeffers notes, spectators 'are co-opted into witnessing, willingly or not', and consequently, 'the most common phrases used against it are couched in the language of physical violation' (*Refugees* 90). Proximity, then, can be experienced as personal invasion or affront on the part of a spectator. Proximity here also concerns, of course, the way lines of connection between embodied citizens and detained noncitizens are imagined, and in this capacity a performer or activist may be read as transgressing the logic of state biopolitical organization (which says that the self-injuring noncitizen exists 'out there' while legitimate, well bodies are 'here inside') in a way that suggests that injuries inflicted outside may bleed into Australia. The utopian element of the imaginative proximity generated by this kind of work is structured (as I shall discuss) along the lines of the vigil, whose ethos is the idea that *I/we will suffer so long as the other is suffering.*

Instumentalizing Pain

Bodily self-injury can be regarded, in the context at hand, as a visible sign of trauma as it is understood more holistically. The concept of the traumatic as limit-experience that is only assimilated by the psyche belatedly through involuntary repetition in dreams, hallucinations or compulsions is familiar (Cathy Caruth's *Unclaimed Experience* provides one of the clearest explanations of the concept). In the Australian context, Amanda Wise and Joseph Pugliese examine instances in which already-traumatized asylum seekers and refugees have re-traumatized or re-injured themselves and consider the psychological, social and political functions of this re-injuring. Wise employs Ghassan Hage's concept of affective intensification (which Hage theorizes in relation to Lebanese Australian communities) to characterize the psychological and political structure of the East Timorese independence movement in Sydney, which continued throughout the 1990s as the struggle for independence from Indonesia reached its apotheosis. She examines ritualized re-enactments and commemorations of trauma by East Timorese refugees, contending that the 'isolating rupture of unruly pain' was re-experienced and channelled into 'a corporeal, sensorial collective narrative' (101) and 'rendered meaningful in a very embodied way' (117). The independence movement, Wise discerns, generated for its participants bodily emotion and thus the sensation of intense connection with the suffering of absent friends and relatives. Arguing along similar lines but with reference to trauma experienced outside of the context of community, Pugliese describes the repeated self-harm with razor wire by an asylum seeker incarcerated in Australia as an act of 'corporeal poetics' that enables a paradoxical release of trauma, and a mode of communication, via repetitive wounding ('Subcutaneous' 27).

The representations of self-injury and hunger strikes in the work examined in this chapter operated as displaced indices to the first order of embodied communication that provoked them, that is, detainees' self-injuries that had been for the most part concealed behind razor wire and apprehended only via the news media, itself restricted by limited access. By referencing the most brutal manifestations of the harm caused by indefinite extrajudicial imprisonment, the artists and activists discussed here both invited spectators to contemplate the reality of lives being wasted—and furthermore, set in spatio-temporal limbo as the nation's own waste—and at the same time to consider how people living in such wastelands will put their bodies to a perverse kind of 'anti-use' or 'anti-work'. Creative and activist 'work' in this understanding is a translation of asylum seekers' part-strategic, part-symptomatic 'anti-work' in carceral spaces. This second order of self-injuries was obviously designed to be performed before an audience made up of members of the public, mostly Australians.

The artist–spectator relation upon which they were structured only reinforces and consolidates a dynamic that is already inherent in detainee self-injury. Maud Ellman argues that the hunger striking body 'is itself a text, the living dossier of its discontents' (17) and that the strike is intrinsically an act of representation that depends for its meaning upon an observer: '[s]elf-starvation is above all a performance. Like Hamlet's mouse-trap, it is staged to trick the conscience of its viewers, forcing them to recognize that they are implicated in the spectacle that they behold' (17). Pugliese also apprehends lip-sewing by asylum seekers held in Australian detention centres within a context of representation, but he understands it to be concerned as much as anything else with agency or self-recognition: 'attempts by refugees to reclaim and resignify their exilic bodies' ('Subcutaneous' 28). Such embodied reclamation, Pugliese adds, is a direct response to the mostly-incommunicado manner of the detention: '[b]y intextuating the organ of speech literally with a thread, refugees symbolically magnify the acts of censure and prohibition that reduce them to silence' ('Subcutaneous' 31). The paradox inherent in this symbolism is that it renders the body-in-pain incapable of interpellating his or her own action; the body may take on meaning, but the mind is overwhelmed by the immediacy of pain. Jeffers expresses this eloquently with reference to Elaine Scarry's theorization of pain as world-reducing: '[t]he essentially unsharable nature of the moment of pain due to its resistance to language shows how pain triumphs by separating the person expressing the pain from the one listening to that expression' (*Refugees* 103). As a protest measure, then (which is also, as I have said, a symptom of a traumatized mind), lip-sewing is tremendously vulnerable to having its subtlety shouted out by those who would amplify condemnatory or else coolly administrative readings, an important point to which I shall return.

Noncitizenship, Self-Injury and the Carceral Paradigm

Mandatory detention in Australia conditions and normalizes a cross-cultural engagement based upon professed core values which govern the work and function of federal immigration bureaucracy: order, fairness, security and control. In their application to bodies whose transnational movements and lack of adequate identity documentation mark them as irregular noncitizens, these values instantiate one version of what Zylinska calls an '*ethics of bodies that matter*' (85, italics in original). For Zylinska, that such an ethics forms the basis of hegemonic biopolitics does not mean it can't also be a framework for optimism: she makes the case that if indeed the ethics that asylum seekers activate 'both constitutes and challenges the established political discourses of the host community' (90), then 'it is precisely this *ethics of bodies that matter* that I will see as a source of political hope, as well as a guarantee of the possibility of *enacting differently* the political acts which regulate the issues of asylum, immigration and nationality' (85, italics in original). The possibilities for *enacting differently* are not, Zylinska adds, conditional upon a revised code of morality (so to oppose the core values cited above would not be the point), but rather emerge from the domain of fundamental response and responsibility, an ethics that Zylinska develops out of Emmanuel Levinas's philosophy concerning the other and one that precedes politics and morality. From this standpoint, Zylinska is able to argue that asylum seekers are 'an other whose being *precedes* the political and *makes a demand on it*. Knocking on the door of Western democracies, "bodies that matter" are ethical in the originary Levinasian sense; they are already taken account of, even if they are to be later found not to matter so much to these sovereign regimes' (95, italics in original). This last point is of more consequence, I would argue, than Zylinska seems to acknowledge.

Indeed, the conclusion Zylinska draws in her discussion is sorely tested in its application to the Australian biopolitical landscape. The claim that bodies whose appearance 'is preceded by an ethical injunction' in the form of asylum seeker legislation bring with them 'the possibility of changing the laws and acts of the *polis* and delineating some new forms of political identification and belonging' (97, italics in original) has not yet taken on any sort of recognizable form in successive policy measures since 2001; on the contrary, even the abject anti-communication that is detainee self-injury has been evacuated of most of its political traction by the tightening up of policies around access to and reporting on detention sites, the largest of which are now located offshore, combined with an increasingly circumspect approach to commentary on the issue by politicians. As I outlined in the introduction to this study, Australia's detention system has underdone various modifications since being instituted by the Migration Amendment Act 1992, developing into an apparatus of punitive deterrence from 1999, when the Temporary Protection Visa was introduced, and becoming increasingly hard-line from 2001, when the 'children overboard' affair played out and the high-profile *Tampa* incident inaugurated the Pacific Solution of offshore processing. Acts of self-injury by asylum seekers occurred regularly between 2000 and about

2004, an era when detainees would often be held for months or years without progress on their case.[3] But they never ceased, and as detainee numbers have increased since 2011, injury has increased in real terms; a request made in 2013 under the Freedom of Information Act by three news organizations, Global Mail, New Matilda and Guardian Australia, revealed an alarming increase in the frequency self-injury among detainees, the dataset showing 'operational incidents' (which include threatened and actual self-harm, self-starvation and accidents) occurring at a rate of 1.76 per person (Evershed and Laughland).

Self-injury in Australian detention centres has tended to take the form of hunger strikes and lip-sewing. In 2000, groups of asylum seekers began hunger strikes at Curtin and Woomera detention centres. In January 2002, several hundred mostly Afghan[4] asylum seekers at Woomera, around one hundred detainees at Curtin and more than twenty-five at Maribyrnong embarked upon a sixteen day hunger strike; many of these, including a number of children and teenagers, sewed their lips together, beat themselves with rocks and swallowed detergent and shampoo. Another mass hunger strike lasted for fourteen days at Woomera in June and July of the same year. In 2003, thirty-six asylum seekers embarked upon a hunger strike at Nauru detention centre. In December 2004, a group of Iranian detainees at Baxter sewed their lips together as part of a group hunger strike.[5] Hunger strikes also took place at Villawood in western Sydney over consecutive years; in October 2005 a small group of Chinese men began a strike, with two of them continuing for a month ('Detainee's Six Weeks' 26); in March 2006 up to eighty people became involved in a strike (Cubby 7) and in March and April 2007 a group of around thirty Chinese detainees launched a strike to protest against a new round of deportations, with an additional one hundred people refusing meals in solidarity (Marks 4). In November 2010, a group of detainees on Christmas Island sewed their lips shut, and reports of similar protest actions at the centre and others emerged in 2013 and 2014. These events have received varying degrees of media attention. The protests of earlier years were covered in the national and international media, earning Australia a reputation for the extremity to which its detainees went to protest their incarceration.[6] More recent strikes have been somewhat less extensively covered.

Australian detention centres are often cited in discussions of the phenomenon of asylum seeker self-injury, but they are not anomalies in this context. In May 2008, some of a group of one hundred unaccompanied minor asylum seekers detained on the island of Lesvos and seventy detained on the island of Leros (both under Greek authority) embarked upon hunger strikes in protest against poor, overcrowded conditions.[7] Self-injury and self-starvation are quite common responses to incarceration,[8] but recent protests in

Europe show that political self-injury is also a response to statelessness or the threat of deportation for asylum seekers who are comparatively at liberty. In 2010, for example, a group of Iranian asylum seekers occupied an entrance to the University of Athens to put pressure on the Greek government to grant them refugee status; eight members of the group sewed their lips together (see Khosravi). In 2011, a group of Iranian asylum seekers sewed their lips shut in protest against their deportation orders outside Lunar House immigration centre in south London and the Amnesty International Building in central London (see Taylor and Dehghan). By occupying the public sphere, asylum seekers open themselves up to all kinds of face-to-face sociality and anti-sociality; nineteen-year-old Mehran Meyari stated that as well as receiving expressions of support from members of the public, the London protest attracted antagonism:

> In the past 31 days here in Croydon we have been bullied and insulted by some people here who have asked us to end our protest and return to our countries. They don't care what has happened to us, they see us as bunch of people who want to take advantage of the UK economically, they don't want to see the reality of our situation. (qtd in Taylor and Dehghan)

In their discussion of self-injury among asylum seekers in the UK, including the well-documented lip-sewing in 2003 by an Iranian asylum seeker and a 2004 case of three Kurdish Iranian asylum seekers in Glasgow,[9] as well as actions in the Netherlands and Australia's Woomera, Jenny Edkins and Véronique Pin-Fat conclude that such self-injuries explicate the fundamental structure of sovereignty as a 'relation of violence' (1). But they are clear that this relation does not imply that sovereign power is impervious to challenge, arguing that practices of self-injury push 'beyond the impasse' in which Agamben's analysis of sovereign power 'can seem to end up' (3), and can be resistant, 'first, in a refusal to "draw the line" or make distinctions between forms of life of the type upon which sovereign power relies; and, second, in what we call *the assumption of bare life*, that is, the taking on of the very form of life that sovereign power seeks to impose (3, italics in original). The first of these refers, we might say, to bodies that by spilling their own blood insist on their consanguinity with other forms of human life, while the second point, on the 'assumption' of bare life, has much in common with what I'm conceptualizing here as detained bodies putting themselves to anti-use via their politicized self-injury. The idea of anti-use, or anti-work, can be understood as the noncitizen reflecting back on the state a grotesque vision of its normative biopolitics—the key being that 'use' and 'work' are moral terms that describe bodies rendered 'productive' under capitalism, and 'contributing' under sovereignty.

It must be said, however, that the relations of refusal and assumption Edkins and Pin-Fat identify (rightly, in my view) in self-injury as protest come under immense pressure when the spatio-temporal context for the protest is carceral, indefinite and extrajudicial; indeed, the difference between imprisonment and state coercion not 'marked by razor wire' (19) is underplayed in Edkins and Pin-Fat's comparison. In the camp, it becomes very difficult to work out how bare life, as Agamben theorizes it, can be reinstated as an agent of the role-playing volition that 'taking on' implies. For a start, prisoners have less scope to 'take' or be 'taken up'; images of the self-injuries suffered by detainees in Australian detention camps have been consistently rare, while images of the sewn lips, ears and eyes of asylum seekers protesting in public spaces, many taken in sharp close up by media photographers, have circulated widely. There are important distinctions, in terms of agency, visuality and relations of spectatorship, between the hunger-striking body occupying a public space such as a university or civic building, and the hunger-striking body that is incarcerated. But radical politics nevertheless attaches itself to imprisoned bodies, even if agency in the classical sense scarcely does. While it is the strategic occupation of public space that allows protesting asylum seekers in Athens or London to politicize their bodies-in-pain, to appear as the state's corporeal excess, bodies that have been imprisoned in the absence of judicial process or anything we might recognize as emerging from the principle of habeas corpus are always already politicized. The politicization is a consequence of the exceptionality of asylum seeker detention: it reveals, at a structural level, the vulnerability of bodies to executive power. If detainees are compelled to determine in some capacity the grammar of their politicization, their bodies can be a potent site of agency. In this way, self-harm is a limited but intense challenge to an overarching biopolitical logic that renders human lives as waste; as Adrian Parr observes with particular reference to self-harm by child detainees in Australia, '[w]hat is at stake here is the power over life' (290), meaning the power literally to lead a life.

Given that the purchase, if not the poetics, of detainees' self-injury is so fragile, it is vital to comprehend the way performance and activism have responded to this form of pain and its signification within the Australian public sphere. If ongoing Australian policy measures relegate Zylinska's hope for an ethics of bodies that matter to the domain of the utopian yet-to-come, ethical purpose can nevertheless be traced in and attached to the work discussed here. By taking up time and marking out space for embodied and symbolic encounter, artistic and activist initiatives have pitted normative moral values pertaining to the noncitizen other against what Zylinska might recognize as a pre-moral ethics of the face-to-face. As these arts and activism have been in most cases created and seen by Australians, some of them privileged, prominent individuals, we can understand them as attempts to intervene in and reorient the balance of the 'perpetual battle' for biopower of which Foucault writes: '[power] is not the "privilege", acquired or preserved, of the dominant class, but the overall effect of its strategic positions' (*Discipline* 26). Representations of injury amounted to the rejection by performers and activists of a dominant partialist politics and asked spectators to reconsider their stake in human injury, both present (in the bodies of performers) and absent (in the bodies of asylum seekers). By setting up moments of encounter in an art gallery, a beach, a major retail strip, the exterior of an administrative building and various theatres and community halls, the works registered the presence of additional interlocutors in an uneven dialogue between detainees and federal government agents.

Hegemonic Translations of Self-injury

The political leaders responsible for asylum legislation will always occupy a position as chief interpreters of detainees' abject communications. During widespread lip-sewing and hunger strikes at Woomera and elsewhere in January 2002, a widely-circulated statement by the then Minister for Immigration, Philip Ruddock, exemplified a discourse of immutable difference between Australians and unauthorized noncitizens: '[l]ip-sewing is a practice unknown in our culture [...] and it's something that offends the sensitivities of Australians' (qtd in 'Lip Sewing' 10)'. The noncitizen is framed here as lacking the finer attributes of the citizen and as demonstrating, by their recourse to self-injury, fundamental ignorance of their moral deficit. As Pugliese discerns, Ruddock's words pivot on an 'occulting logic [...] whereby the perpetrator of violence becomes the victim' ('Penal Asylum' para. 5). The statement also, of course, implies that lip-sewing is 'known' in the cultures of asylum seekers and repudiates the government's responsibility for the creation of extra-judicial carceral spaces in which politicized self-harm is enacted. In 2003, the newly appointed Minister for Immigration, Amanda Vanstone, responded to hunger strikes by asylum seekers detained at Nauru: '[i]t's not in Australian territory, it's on Nauru and being run by other people. If someone doesn't want to be there, they can go home. Nobody likes to see people who are feeling that they have to take what appear to be drastic measures in order to protest, but people will do what they want to do' (qtd in Shaw and Gregory 2). The comment espouses an almost farcical refusal to acknowledge the extra-territorial reach of the nation's asylum policy and deploys what is in all likelihood a carefully calibrated mixture of callousness and triviality, dovetailing neatly into the neoliberal fantasy that an individual's behaviour is an uncomplicated reflection of 'what they want to do'.

As a protest act, lip-sewing represents a peculiar combination of radical potency and radical instability, with the capacity to be both a profound anti-statement on the impossibility for the oppressed to be heard, and always vulnerable to hegemonic reinscription. Pugliese ventriloquizes the latter with bitter irony: '[s]ituated by government and media discourses within the topos of the abject, the refugees are framed as self-mutilating barbarians: they thus redeem our legislated violence' ('Subcutaneous' 28). Certainly, Ruddock's resolve seemed to redouble in the face of detainee self-injury: '[t]hey believe it will influence decisions. It can't and it won't' (qtd in 'Lip Sewing' 10). Rajaram notes that the Australian government's interpretation of self-injury 'as a calculated move to influence decisions or change a policy' reflects 'a continued insistence on the moral and political dichotomies of territoriality' ('Disruptive Writing' 227). Rosalyn Diprose observes that when appropriated in governmental moral discourse, the abject body of the asylum seeker can seem to offer a vivid idea with which to cohere an embodied citizenry: '[b]odies deported, incarcerated, and rejected on the basis of their foreignness only [...] have been sacrificed in the service of maintaining National unity by evoking a sense of shared and stable communal values' ('The Hand' 47). But she goes on to argue that this coherence cannot hold: 'bodies signify their uniqueness and value through community, by being exposed to other bodies. In abandoning the bodies of others in such spectacular fashion, we dissolve the limit by which this exposition takes place. In dissolving this limit we lose our exposition, and dissolve "our" community' (47). It is for this reason that Diprose characterizes lip-sewing as a 'moral implosion' (36). This reading couples national moral breakdown with self-injury as nihilism.

Political posturing can in and of itself signify a kind of moral confusion; assertions as brazenly vituperative as Ruddock's and Vanstone's are a calculated risk, and they have been ambiguous with respect to Australian national unity. The two politicians' comments quickly became notorious, intensifying convictions on both sides of the issue; they have also been widely cited in academic critiques (for example, Pugliese, Rajaram, Jeffers, Farrier, Gilbert and Lo). Tellingly, members of the same political party, under Tony Abbott's Prime Ministership, have adjusted their public lexicon on asylum seeker injury. In marked contrast to the immediate post-*Tampa* era, the language used specifically in response to self-harming by detainees has been characterized by clinical descriptions of events and corresponding security measures, as in a statement in July 2014 in the Senate by Eric Abetz, representing the Prime Minister: 'a small number of minor self-harm incidents have recently occurred [on Christmas Island] and those involved are receiving proper and appropriate medical and other support' (qtd in Davey and Farrell), or by administrative deflection, as exemplified by Minister for Immigration and Border Protection

Scott Morrison's comment on a hunger strike on Christmas Island in January 2014: '[t]his particular incident is under control, it's being managed by the service provider at the time. I get regular updates about what's happening there. It's a difficult environment when you've had [...] some people on Christmas Island now for some time' (qtd in Doyle). By framing detainee self-injury as a challenge for the outsourced multinational corporation that administers detention on Australia's behalf, Morrison sidesteps the moral stakes that Ruddock and Vanstone were all too eager to weigh in on, while projecting a seriousness that is less readily identifiable as callous or crass. Morrison's statement on detainees' suicide attempts in July 2014 adopted the language of concern: '[w]hile the government understands the concern that exists on such sensitive matters of self-harm, it is important to recognize government commentary on such issues takes into account privacy and the impact public commentary may have in encouraging such behaviour' (qtd in Davey and Farrell). But the 'occulting logic' (Pugliese, 'Penal Asylum' para. 5) that sees the nation as a moral victim has not faded altogether, as Abbott's comments the same month demonstrated; whilst he acknowledged that recent reports were 'harrowing', he maintained, 'no Australian government should be subjected to the spectacle of people saying, "unless you accept us I am going to commit self harm". And I don't believe any Australian, any *thinking* Australian, would want us to capitulate to moral blackmail' (qtd in Knott). Aside from shifts and turns in the hegemonic discursive landscape, the fact that performance and activism of the kind discussed here was relatively prominent between 2001 and 2004 and has been less so since suggests that, as state-commissioned violence charts as unrelenting a course as ever, oppositional politics has had to rethink its modes of engagement. It has had to do this in the face of what might be, grimly, a general desensitization or feelings of impotence amongst Australians in the face of what is now a familiar story of anguished detainees.

Close the Concentration Camps

Sensitization, or affective intensification in Hage's terms, has been the most prominent currency in Mike Parr's interventions into asylum politics. It manifested as brutal deliberation when the Australian performance and visual artist presented his provocatively titled durational piece, *Close the Concentration Camps* at the Monash University Museum of Art in Melbourne (15 June 2002). The work reduced the gap between representational body and its real-world referent, with Parr sitting silently on a chair from 1:00 to 6:00 p.m. with his mouth, eyes and ears sewn up and his trouser ripped open at the thigh, upon which the word 'Alien' had been branded with a hot implement just prior to the commencement of the event. Written on the wall of the gallery space, in large black lettering, were the words CLOSE THE CONCENTRATION CAMPS. The horrifying spectacle was webcast live for its duration. In another room of the gallery (not visible on the webcast) the political rationale of the work was explicated with passages from the Australian Parliamentary Joint Standing Committee on Migration's eccentrically titled report, 'Not the Hilton: Immigration Detention Centres: Inspection Report' (2000), projected on to the wall. In another room, framed maps of Melbourne and Munich drew parallels between the proximity of Maribyrnong Immigration Detention Centre to the former and Dachau Concentration Camp to the latter.

Over his more than forty-year career, Parr's performance art has tested the artist's own physical limits and threshold for pain, and in many respects his work bears similarities with that of the extreme performance artists who emerged in the 1960s and 70s, including his compatriot Stelarc, as well as Serbian-American Marina Abramovi and Americans Ron Athey and David Wojnarowicz. Durational works in Parr's late career have been directly inflected by international politics, and these include an installation at Sydney's Artspace one month before *Close the Concentration Camps*, titled, *Malevich [A Political Arm]* (3–4 May 2002), in which Parr sat with his arm nailed to the wall for thirty hours. This work protested Australia's treatment of asylum seekers, with the words CLOSE THE CONCENTRATION CAMPS written on the wall in an adjacent gallery. It also constituted a critique of Formalist visual art, exemplified by Kasimir Malevich, which Parr characterized as 'just another kind of hygiene or cleansing' (qtd in Scheer, 'Australia's Post-Olympic' 46), a view that accorded directly with his scathing assessment of Australian race relations, symbolized by the placement of a redacted copy of *The Australian National Dictionary, A Dictionary of Australianisms on Historical Principles* on a small table in the same gallery as the protest slogan on mandatory detention. On 2 May 2003, Parr underwent another process of facial suturing in protest at the Australia's involvement in the Iraq invasion. In this piece, entitled *Aussie Aussie Aussie Oi Oi Oi [Democratic Torture]*, Parr sat with his lips were sewn shut for twenty-four hours, an Australian flag attached to the stump of his left arm (the result of a birth injury) after which time electrodes were attached to his face and spectators were invited to administer electric shocks. The back wall of the gallery displayed text taken from news reports of the Iraq invasion. Two years later, Parr protested the treatment of prisoners at Guantanamo Bay detention camp in *Kingdom Come and/or Punch Holes in the Body Politic* (Artspace, Sydney, 8 April 2005), a work that also invited spectators to inflict electric shocks to the artist's body, clad in an orange boiler suit. *Close the Concentration Camps* is Parr's most complete and explicit engagement with asylum seeker self-injury.[10]

As I have noted, at the time this work was staged, reports of lip-sewing by asylum seekers in immigration detention centres had been prominent in the news media and had generated defiant responses from federal politicians, most pernicious of which was Ruddock's moral advocacy on behalf of the 'sensitivities of Australians'. Parr situated his body as a means for these sensitivities to be tested within a political and aesthetic frame and in doing so refracted the relation of surveillance that is essential for asylum seeker's injuries to take on any meaning at all in the minds of citizens. Rajaram characterizes Australia's instrumentalization of imprisoned noncitizens as a relation of spectacle and consumption: '[t]he performance of refugee identity creates a spectacle, a theatre of cruelty, inanity, absurdity and violence designed for the consumption of a public identified and cohered by the spectacle itself' ('Spectacle' 1). This comment recognizes that citizens are consumers of the nation's corporeal excess or, in other words, that two opposing publics, two collective identities, are generated via the abjection of one. Parr's intervention, then, is to construct the citizen as an abject spectacle, but even more than this, to present the citizen made abject by its very determination to hold irregular noncitizens outside the nation space. Parr can be understood as using his own body to disrupt the notional coherence of the public of which Rajaram writes.

But the meaning and ethics of the spectacle are complex. *Close the Concentration Camps* confronted some of the generalizable emotional dynamics of observing the suffering of others, but the deliberation of Parr's injury recalibrated the usual condition of the injured body in pain, that is, of being unwittingly so and as such the victim of pain. Parr's suffering is not that of a victim. Of course, the same may be said of politicized self-inflicted injury enacted by asylum seekers, except for the crucial fact that detainees do not proceed from a position of liberty, so their self-injury compounds suffering rather than creates it as art. Parr's performance was simultaneously intimate, occurring within a confined space that asked, or perhaps demanded, viewers to attend to the spectacle (the Latin *attendere*, meaning 'to stretch' one's mind toward, is instructive here), and alienating, with Parr's suturing of his face precluding any kind of responsiveness for the duration of the piece.

The use of a live webcam referenced both video surveillance in isolation cells and the mediatized glimpses of asylum seekers available to the Australian public. It also, of course, disseminated the event to a larger audience. Susan Sontag's study of the wide circulation of horrific images in contemporary life led her to observe that 'wars are now also living room sights and sounds' (16). Certainly, the live-feed vision of Parr's self-violence had to face the obstacle of 'compassion fatigue' (Scheer, 'Vast' 25) in a desensitized media age. Beyond desensitization, looking at the pain of others is a psychologically and ethically complex act; taking in the long history of visual art that preceded photography as the primary site of violent imagery, Sontag argues that as well as eliciting shame and shock from the spectator, images of suffering can also construct self-centred affects: 'the provocation: can you look at this? There is the satisfaction of being able to look at the image without flinching. There is the pleasure of flinching' (37). While we may debate whether liveness interrupts the 'pleasure of flinching' in response to visually encoded suffering, Parr's performance employed mediating tools that cast his body in flattened, photo-like projection via the live-feed as well as a large mirror on the wall facing him. The latter offered gallery attendees a mode of spectatorial indirection or distancing but at the same time reinforced the challenge of looking by making it difficult to avoid the subject; moreover, it confronted viewers with the image of themselves in the act of looking/averting. Sarah Austin notes that very few spectators walked toward Parr to look at his face directly (he was positioned sideways against the gallery wall, facing the mirrored wall): 'it was very difficult once you had entered the performance space to confront Parr's body. Faced with the back of him, there was an element of visceral fear as to what someone with their lips stitched together would look like at such close range' (Austin). Whatever the political ends of his work, Parr can (like other image-making that deals in bodily injury, such as the East Timorese protest strategy of displaying and circulating graphic photographs) be charged with exploiting a human propensity for visceral, morbid fascination.

A reviewer of *Close the Concentration Camps* considered the risk that the work might end up manipulating asylum seekers' plight, framing this as a lead question: 'Mike Parr is going to great pains to support asylum seekers—literally. Is it sensational exploitation or legitimate protest art?' (Heinrich 3). In a question and answer session at the Sydney Biennale in 2008, Parr acknowledged the inherent ethical risks associated with the piece but maintained that his suffering, while 'real' on a fundamental level, was never meant to be read as identical with that of the objects of his representation: 'it's ridiculous; you can't possibly re-represent the plight of someone in a detention centre sewing their mouth together, their lips together' (Parr, Question and Answer). Certainly, a good case can be made that *Close the Concentration Camps* contemplated this gap in subjectivity, very deliberately bringing two disparate subject-types into coalescence. For the duration Parr, a professional, successful white male—in other words, a privileged figure within the context of Australian embodied citizenship—displayed this status with his suited, professional (albeit crumpled) attire. Framed thus, Parr's endurance of the same physical injuries, the same sutured, bloodied flesh, that represent for many Australians (especially in the politically charged climate of 2002) the condition of noncitizens in detention touched on the very nexus of distinctions between the citizen and its other. Parr's self-injury brought these opposing positions into uneasy alignment. His performance suggested that the injury of asylum seekers, while occurring in an elsewhere that was geographically and experientially distant from almost all Australians, had infiltrated the supposedly healthy nation. In this way, Parr demanded that his audience members regarded the political structure of their liberty and their ethical stakes in its exceptions.

As well as this, *Close the Concentration Camps* was an act of identification on Parr's part. Injuring himself in a similar fashion to detainees as a means of abhorring their extrajudicial incarceration, Parr brought himself into alignment with the other in a kind of communion or ritual—these terms seem appropriate to account for the profound, durational investment of having a needle and thread drawn through flesh while bearing in mind the similar pain of asylum seekers. In its capacity as communion or ritual, Parr's work, like solidarity fasts by Australians, has something in common with the affective intensification of the East Timorese protest strategies described by Wise. Within the same category can be placed the ritual (re)enactments that occur each year in many parts of the Christian (particularly Catholic) world during Easter commemorations of Christ's passion and death, some of which involve self-injury. Indeed, as Wise explains, Catholic ritual and identity permeated the East Timorese protest movement, with the passion of Christ becoming woven into the project of corporal remembering of suffering: '[t]he embodied nature of Catholic ritual provides a potent ground of sensorial identification for a traumatised community, especially through the invocation of the powerful imagery of Christ's tortured body' (100).[11] The efficacy of such cultural or religious performances can be considered both in terms of external communion (with and among spectators) and in terms of a personal, internal process. Edward Scheer describes Parr's bodily installations as having the 'effect of contemporary secular ritual' ('Vast' 24), but the secular/religious distinction is perhaps collapsed in the moment of pain-infliction. What distinguishes Parr's performance most of all from religious ritual and from the protest rituals of the East Timorese in Australia is his singularity as artist; he is physically separate from the asylum seekers with whom he might be said to be in communion, and isolated from his Australian audiences as the only person in the room undergoing pain, even if his audience functions as onlooker-participants in the ritual.

The therapeutic function of protest ritual among the East Timorese analysed by Wise relates to the psychological processing of personal trauma (this psychology is apprehended in Caruth's notion of 'making known' through repetition). While Parr is not part of the traumatized community, his work nevertheless represents an intense relationship with the self; to choose to have one's flesh threaded (this is mostly performed by Parr's partner rather than himself), to sew up the orifices of speech, sight and hearing, is a concentrated act of self-possession. The combination of sensory deprivation and physical pain focuses, paradoxically, both an abject relation with the flesh and intensification of its centrality to selfhood. To a certain extent, Parr's performance in *Close the*

Concentration Camps is comparable to his decades-long exploration of corporeal limits and sensory extremism, but here he sought for his own intensity of regard to extend symbolically to others who were suffering, not in a gallery but in prison.

A core paradox of *Close the Concentration Camps* is that even as it invited viewers to attend more closely to the injuries of asylum seekers, to counteract the distancing effect produced by remote incarceration by suggesting lines of identification between asylum seekers, Parr and the audience, it also symbolized dehumanization and the failure of communication. In the abovementioned Sydney Biennale Q&A, Parr discussed the latter aspect of the work, emphasizing the production via his self-injury of what he terms an 'anti-face'. For Parr, this anti-face represents the failure of human(e) engagement that he maintains has marked European Australia's history:

> it's the response to Ruddock's claim [...] that we don't throw children overboard: that's a defining perversion of desperate refugees to this country [...] it's this cripplingly childish idea that we're exempt from the sins of our forebears, that we're all born again in this country, and that we're people of limited responsibility. So my response to this was to sort of sew my face into a knot. (Question and Answer)

Thinking of Parr's sewn face as a knot is a severe image that expresses what is, in his view, the heinous failure of Australian sociality. The emphasis on the face obviously identifies its importance in terms of human responsiveness, but Parr's anti-face seems to depart from a Levinasian insistence on the fundamental ethical demand of the face by showing, through the simultaneous metaphor and reality of bodily injury, how the face can become a site of grotesque opacity. While for Levinas, the '*self* [...] is never absolved from responsibility towards the Other' (qtd in Malka 291, italics in original), Parr's anti-face seems to contend that the face can be made impervious, can absolve itself, but only at great cost. Parr's reference to 'limited responsibility' implies that a failure to recognize fully the ethical obligation to engage compassionately—whether with indigenous Australians or with asylum seekers—produces limited human beings or a nation that has rendered its 'face' impenetrable. Of course, by identifying an infantilism at the heart of Australian ethics, Parr challenges his audiences, and himself, to begin to grow up.

Tampa

Lebanese-Australian artist Mireille Astore's *Tampa* was a durational performance work that took place in Sydney from 30 October to 16 November 2003 during the annual event, Sculpture by the Sea, which is credited as being Australia's

Fig. 5. *Tampa* by Mireille Astore. Sculpture by the Sea. Tamarama Beach, Sydney, 2003. (Photo: Fabian Astore.)

largest outdoor sculpture exhibition, attracting tens of thousands of spectators and operating in the midst of many thousands more passers-by. *Tampa* was performed at Tamarama beach (adjacent to the more famous Bondi beach). Astore utilized a cage-like structure of thin poles spaced fifteen centimetres apart, shaped as a 10:1 scaled version of the MV *Tampa*, and occupied this space for eight hours per day over the eighteen-day period. Laying her 'imprisoned' self open to observation, Astore recorded, but did not respond to, numerous comments from members of the public. Instead, she returned their gaze by taking photographs from within the structure and later uploaded spectators' comments and her own photographs onto a website. The simultaneous referencing of the Norwegian cargo ship and a detention cell in Astore's *Tampa* framed both in terms of the surveillant technologies that have cast the nation's excess bodies into stasis. In the process the installation also tested the physical reserves of its performer. Astore's corporeal investment, involving long days of self-confinement and exposure (psychological and environmental) upon the beach, was designed to suggest to spectators a coterminous relationship between unauthorized appearance at the border and imprisonment at the threshold of the nation's homely space. The artist made explicit the links between border politics, carceral politics and citizen liberty by making her performance into a geo-temporal palimpsest of all three. Interventions in space and site have been an important mode of engagement with asylum politics in Australia and elsewhere in recent years. Some, like the SIEV X memorial on the shores of Canberra's Lake Burley Griffin, perform the work of remembrance: in this case via an installation of 353 timber poles, a section of which traces the meagre outline of a smuggling boat, ghosting the sunken SIEV X; the memorial occupies a relatively secluded site and is oriented toward reflection. Other territorial interventions, like Clare Bayley's immersive play, *The Container*, performed near Edinburgh's Bristo Square (2007), outside London's Young Vic theatre (2009) and, more recently, in the Melbourne inner-city suburb of Footscray (2013), as well as Christoph Schlingensief's notorious 'game show' art experiment in central Vienna, *Ausländer raus! (Foreigners out!)* (2000), transposed the hard materiality of the container lorry and shipping container, respectively, into receptacles for unwanted human bodies, emplacing them in each instance in busy, urban zones.

Certainly, Astore's *Tampa* derived a great deal of its political, social and aesthetic resonance from its site-responsiveness. The signification of the beach in relation to issues of nation, citizenship, belonging and borders is complex and contradictory. The vast majority of Australia's population live on or proximate to the coast, and certainly the metropolitan national imaginary centres upon this space, rather than the sparsely populated interior of the continent. Neighbouring a world-famous surf beach (Bondi) and part of a hub of leisure activities centring upon the sun and sea, Tamarama epitomizes a prominent and celebrated aspect of the so-called Australian way of life, one that Astore characterizes as 'hedonistic' ('When' 240). In this regard, Astore transgressively locates her performance at the heart of a territory that is claimed and possessed by white Australia. Of course, the terms of this claim were contested on another Sydney beach, thirty kilometres south of the more wealthy Bondi and Tamarama, two years after Astore's performance, when white and Lebanese Australian youths converged in and around Cronulla beach in a series of violent, racially motivated riots; international media reports showed disturbing images of young white Australians defiantly brandishing the national flag, slogans such as 'we grew here, you flew here' and 'ethnic cleansing unit' inscribed on banners and bare chests.

The Cronulla riots exemplify the other dominant signification of the Australian beach: what Ien Ang terms the white 'psycho-geography' of invasion (129–30). Given Australia's geopolitical position as an island-continent (a position that is less a geographically evident fact, Ang argues, than a naturalized idea [129]), border consciousness and persistent invasion anxieties centre around the idea of long coastlines, and beyond, vast oceans. Katrina Schlunke articulates the border as a liminal place of entry or arrival at which one becomes illegitimate; employing the metaphor of the Australian beach, she describes the border as 'an in-between space neither land nor sea, a threshold of becoming where strangers are made rather than met' (para. 6). The coast/beach, therefore, is imagined as both safe and unsafe: simultaneously a vulnerable site of potential invasion (especially from the north) and a protective symbol of delineation that underlines notions of national territorial integrity, upon which Australians play out a central part of their leisure culture. The intervention of Astore's performance derived from the discordant emplacement of a representation of asylum and imprisonment within an affluent, heavily-populated area. If the Australian beach isn't already a heterotopia[12] (and its contradictory signification, outlined above, would suggest that it is) Astore's performance constructed Tamarama as one with its aestheticized carceral zone situated within a simultaneously natural and manicured space of bourgeois leisure.

By not responding to (but instead recording in a notebook) the comments of various members of the public for the duration of the performance, Astore implied an impasse in the possibility for conversation between Australians and detained asylum seekers. At the same time, the work produced a record of attempted dialogue via the publication on the project website of the remarks directed at Astore from passers-by. This archive of the event is still a live website that offers a fascinating visual and textual record of the performance and its impact on spectators, and at the same time documents the work's capacity as a reterritorialization or ghosting of the MV *Tampa*. The online documentation represents a diverse range of spectatorial responses, including admiration from a number of people sympathetic to the plight of detained asylum seekers, generalized concern for the artist's welfare and comfort, offers of food or drink, bemusement, antagonism, as well as frustration and hostility from people demanding Astore's recognition and a reply to their questions ('Migrant: comments').

Astore describes her position in the work as 'the personification of a refugee' ('When' 242). Her family left Lebanon for Australia upon the outbreak of civil war in 1975, though she acknowledges that their status was 'migrant', not 'refugee' ('When' 239). Seeking to stand in, then, for the unauthorized asylum seekers that were held on board the *Tampa* and by extension for all asylum seekers imprisoned in Australia's detention centres, Astore performatively places herself both inside and outside the nation, a citizen whose perspective places her in imaginative allegiance with the noncitizen. Several observers appear to have assumed that Astore was an asylum seeker or refugee; she was asked questions such as 'do you speak English?' and '[s]o when are you going to get your permanent residency visa?' ('Migrant: comments'). Her non-whiteness prompted these people to collapse the gap between performer and referent—arguably, an embodied affect Astore sought to achieve by standing as 'the personification of a refugee'

('When' 242). The verbal and photographic transactions generated by the work constituted a series of negotiations between performer and spectators, and the work's open form (occurring in public space, with no explanatory notes) accentuated the capacity of Astore's body to function, in Rajaram and Grundy-Warr's words, as an 'exemplary' site for inscription: 'exemplary bodies are often racialized or gendered (recognized or misrecognized primarily in terms of race or gender) or are migrants from particular areas' (xv).

Astore cites American artist Coco Fusco and Mexican artist Guillermo Gómez-Peña's interactive performance work, *Two Undiscovered Amerindians Visit Sydney* (1992), which satirized imperial practices of caging and display of the indigenous other, as a referent for *Tampa* ('When' 255, n. 3). She also cites Hage's concept of 'ethnic caging' (a term he deploys with reference to Australia's incarceration of asylum seekers (*White Nation* 106–07)) as an important point of departure ('When' 249). Hage considers the implications of the detention of those deemed other or external to Australian liberal democratic society in terms of the nation's internal social structure, asking, '[c]an "we" really be nice to ethnics in the internal organization of the nation and cage them in its external organization without there being any relation between the two?' (*White Nation* 107). For Hage, the ethnic caging of asylum seekers is symptomatic of the underlying sociality of 'multicultural Australia'; he apprehends it in psychoanalytic terms, as 'a phenomenon which expresses a repressed structure that constitutes and underlies all of the reality of which it is a part' (*White Nation* 108). The trope of repression can be equated with the processes of forgetting which, as I have argued, are a requisite part of narrating the unified nation. As corporeal provocation or polemic, then, Astore's work asked questions concerning the forgotten or repressed link between ethnic organization of citizenship and detention practices in Australia.

Solidarity Fasts

In her discussion of Franz Kafka's short story 'A Hunger Artist', Maud Ellman observes, '[t]he moral seems to be that it is not by food that we survive but by the gaze of others; and it is impossible to live by hunger unless we can be seen or represented doing so' (17). In Ellman's view, the receiver of the hunger strike is crucial to its efficacy; hunger striking is '[t]o hold the body up for ransom, to make mortality into a bargaining chip' (17). Being deemed exceptional to the Australian nation with which they attempt to bargain with hunger, the bodies of asylum seekers carry little capital in and of themselves; indeed, the terms 'ransom' and 'bargaining chip' suggest the possession of agency that is minimal in the face of the Australian biopower that underpins mandatory detention. But the citation of self-starved bodies in solidarity fasts seeks to alter this (im)balance.

While the Australian federal ministers maintained a strident refusal to be moved by detainee self-injury, media reports of it constructed dialogues that afforded asylum seekers some agency in terms of the interpretation of their silent acts. At the time of Parr's and Astore's works and to this day, journalistic coverage is limited by curtailed access to detainees. In January 2002, reporters outside Woomera detention centre were instructed to move 700 metres away from the centre's gates, and an hour-long stand-off ensued when the journalists refused to move. An Australian Broadcasting Corporation (ABC) radio journalist was arrested and charged with failing to leave Commonwealth land; she was later released on bail on the condition she immediately leave the area ('Woomera Crisis' 5). Despite this, journalists did access information; several Australian and international reports of the Woomera hunger strikes cited, alongside government statements, a letter by Afghan asylum seekers obtained by *The Sydney Morning Herald*: '[w]e have no hope, we see no future […] We are ready to die […] We only request the Australian people help us, otherwise we have no choice but to continue the hunger strike until the end of our life' (qtd in Debelle 6). The media also variously quoted lawyers representing detainees, advocacy and religious groups and current and former Woomera employees. In several newspaper reports, the disgust and disavowal expressed by the likes of Ruddock and Vanstone (quoted earlier) was cited alongside comments by lawyers Eric Vadarlis and Julian Burnside, as well as those by Hassan Ghulam, president of the Hazara Ethnic Society of Australia, that emphasized a necessity for humane response. Such juxtapositions show that even if sovereign biopower in its most brutal articulation is a relation of violence, it is productive of relations of resistance; indeed, part of the discontinuity that Athena Athanasiou identifies in terms of '[t]he challenge, following Foucault […] to rethink "technology" not as a singularly constituted and reified instrumentality, but rather as a plural, dispersed, and discontinuous engagement' (144) manifests as dispersed resistance to violence.

Acts of self-injury by detainees have had a strong impact upon sections of Australian society aware that governmental power is exerted in their name and who oppose this violent definition of their citizenship. For these Australians, detainee self-injury represents the extremity of Australia's human rights violations. A prominent mode of response on the part of Australian activists has been to perform their solidarity with detained asylum seekers by publicly depriving their own bodies of food. In August 2002, the Lismore Refugee Action Collective held a ten day hunger strike to protest mandatory detention policies. In November 2004, PEN Australia released statements of concern about the health of a group of Sri Lankan detainees at Baxter on hunger strike (including Sarath Amarasinghe, a writer, PEN member and creator of the newsletter *Baxter News*, excerpted in the 2007 anthology of refugee writing, *Another Country*) and on 1 December that year Rosie Scott, Denise Leith, Thomas Keneally and other PEN members fasted outside the Department of Immigration in Canberra to express solidarity with the Sri Lankans. Later that month, a number of Australians engaged in similar solidarity fasts and vigils in order to express their support for Ahwazi (Iranian Arab minority) asylum seekers who were at that time undertaking hunger strikes at Baxter detention centre. The main solidarity fast, staged for twenty-four hours from 17–18 December in Melbourne's Bourke St Mall, involved writer Arnold Zable, comedian Corinne Grant, musician Kavisha Mazella, writer Thomas Shapcott, actor Diana Greentree and artist Kate Durham, among others. Similar public fasts occurred in Launceston and Brisbane. Also in December, in an individual show of support for the Iranian hunger strikers, Democrats Senator Andrew Bartlett fasted for three days.

In these instances, the citation of injury cohered temporally with the injury being referenced; as vigils they constituted periods of conscious, sustained watchfulness or regard for the hunger strikers. As protest acts, they confronted the Australian spectator with the notional alignment of the embodied citizen with the violent existence of the detained asylum seeker. The Australian protesters utilized the bargaining power of their 'bodies that matter', under the gaze of fellow citizens, both literally and under the virtual gaze of the Internet where the fasts were publicized, using the public sphere as a forum to draw up lines of connection with the detainees, communicating the responsibility of the citizen for the carceral exclusion of the asylum seeker in corporeal terms. Such acts operate as moments of communion in which supporters and asylum seekers perform a similar (though obviously not the same) bodily protest act.

Once again, we may identify points of connection with the East Timorese independence movement. Indeed, the occupancy of public space during the independence movement is structurally very similar with the activism of Australian hunger strikers. The strategies of affective intensification applied in the East Timorese movement can be associated with the concept, explicated by Hage, of migrant guilt (see Hage, 'The Differential Intensities'); such guilt is particularly acute when those remaining in the homeland are living in a precarious and dangerous environment. In this context, the need to establish spaces of memory that 'ghost' important sites and practices of the homeland becomes important; the East Timorese movement consisted of street theatre that re-enacted torture and police brutality, as well as the public weaving of an enormous *tais* (traditional cloth) commemorating the victims of the 1991 Dili massacre, but also celebrated East Timorese culture via songs and dance and the construction of a sacred space in the form of a replica *lulik* house. Wise's reading of the affective character of the protest and commemoration strategies may be applied to the investment made by Australians who performed solidarity fasts in support of asylum seekers on hunger strikes. Indeed, to a large extent, solidarity fasts by Australians reflected a sense of citizen guilt in response to Australian noncitizenship. While not directly analogous to migrant guilt in respect of relationships to a homeland, nevertheless, the desire to pay a debt in an unequal moral economy represents a similar relation. Both migrant guilt and citizen guilt indicate a desire to bear witness corporeally to the pain of others, and to do so in the eyes of the public.

Refugitive

Iranian playwright, director and actor Shahin Shafaei (whose work in *Through the Wire* was discussed in chapter one) engages with the theme of hunger strike in his self-penned, self-directed solo play *Refugitive*. The work toured to more than forty metropolitan and rural locations across Australia from late 2002 until its final staging at the Adelaide Fringe Festival during February and March 2004. The play emerged out of Shafaei's desire for encounter and communication with Australian audiences: after his release in February 2002 from Curtin Detention Centre after twenty-two months of incarceration, Shafaei began to conceive a performance that would respond to common misconceptions held by Australians about asylum seekers. In other words, he recognized from the outset the importance of engaging lines of connection between asylum seekers and the citizens on whose behalf asylum policies are implemented. While in *Through the Wire* Shafaei undertook the painful task of enacting his own story, *Refugitive*, he insists, is not autobiographical (Cox interview). The work centres on the experiences of an unnamed man undergoing a hunger strike in detention in Australia; placed under surveillance in a small cell, the man engages in conversations with his hungry, pain-wracked belly and with different immigration authorities. Co-produced and facilitated by Australian activist, playwright and director of New Mercury Theatre Alex Broun, the premiere performance of *Refugitive* took place in Sydney in November 2002 (as part of a double-bill performance alongside Linda Jaivin's play *Halal-el-Mashakel*). Subsequently, Shafaei and Broun, in association with New Mercury Theatre, worked together to organize the extensive tour of *Refugitive* to Queensland, New South Wales, ACT (Australian Capital Territory), Victoria and South Australia.

The structure of the tour's organization highlights the importance of networks mapped by grassroots support groups; in this case, Rural Australians for Refugees and Refugee Action Collectives representing the different states visited were especially crucial in promoting the play and seeking out interest and performance sites within small towns and regional centres. As Rand

Hazou observes, by reaching a number of communities, *Refugitive* 'became a locus for a "web of discourse" [...] through which the hunger strikes could be closely examined' (184). The tour can also be seen as an important reclamation of spatio-corporeal agency on the part of Shafaei, whose previous embodied experience of Australia was carceral and agonizingly static. At the same time, Shafaei was limited by the biopolitical implications of his refugee status; while he was performing, he held a Temporary Protection Visa, under the terms of which he was not entitled to return to Australia if he travelled outside its borders.

A dynamic and physically demanding work in performative terms, *Refugitive* constructs an incisive critique of the operation of biopolitical power within the Australian detention system via its 'dialogues' with correctional and immigration authorities, wryly referred to as the 'Australian Colonisation Manager' (17) and the 'Minister of Physical Powers' (18).[13] Upon being informed that he has been 'screened out' by immigration and is 'not entitled to apply for asylum in Australia' (19), the protagonist asserts his right to request asylum and to have his case considered judicially: '[h] ow did you decide? Without any official interview in the presence of a solicitor, and hearing our reasons for seeking asylum, how did you reject us?' (19). Later, the man is told that his letter to the United Nations cannot be sent:

DIMIA MANAGER: Yes, about this letter to the UN. I read it completely.

THE MAN: But you can't read my personal letter to the UN!

DIMIA MANAGER: Who says that? You? I, as the DIMIA Manager, have the
                 authority to work as a filter for any correspondence.
                 (20)

Bringing his character into dialogue with the authorities that hold him under surveillance, Shafaei is able to locate his performance directly within the context of policy implementation; he apprehends the uncomfortable nexus of Australian legislation and international human rights obligations from a position of extremity embodied by the act of hunger striking. Moreover, Shafaei re-frames biopolitical surveillance within a performative context in which he is the author and agent of his own surveillance by an audience. While it involves some didacticism, this articulation of protest on behalf of asylum seekers is strategically important in terms of communicating the information necessary, as far as Shafaei is concerned, for an Australian audience to consider the political framework in question.

In its representation of the operation of Australian biopolitical violence, *Refugitive* incorporates satire and slapstick and utilizes the vernacular of Western popular culture. Government rhetoric is satirized in the DIMIA Manager's assertion: '[f]rom now on don't forget that you are queue jumpers, illegal immigrants [...] would you please pass me my Australian Oxford dictionary edited by Howard University, oh thanks [...] there we are, you are boat people' (16). The detainee observes that the 'Australian Colonisation Manager' sees the asylum seekers 'like gladiators. Actually, he looks at me like I'm Russell Crowe' (17). After raising the ire of this manager, the detainee is comically choked 'like Homer with Bart' (18). This aspect of the performance seems to have come as a welcome surprise to audiences. One critic observed that *Refugitive* 'surprised and delighted audiences with its lack of bitterness and disarming comedy' (Smith 22). Another noted, '[a]udiences who have seen *Refugitive* have remarked on the absence of bitterness, especially towards Australia' ('Behind the Wire' 14). Shafaei acknowledges that the incorporation of comedy enabled him to communicate with Australian audiences on terms that would be familiar: 'I started studying all the characters that would make sense [...] I knew *my* style of working was not going to make sense, it's a very different culture' (Cox interview). I discussed in chapter two the subversive potential of refugee comedy; for Shafaei, the comic elements of the performance served a very human purpose: 'to see that human face so close to you is so hard to reject [...] especially if that face hasn't tried to push you away' (Cox interview). Moreover, as Hazou has observed, the use of humour 'circumvents' (182) the valorization of trauma and suffering in stories of asylum that Julie Salverson warns against. Or as Shafaei put it in an interview: 'I am showing you that I am a human being with sorrows, with laughter [...] I would cry, I'd get hungry' (Cox interview).

Despite his description of his performance using the first-person pronoun 'I', *Refugitive* was not a mimetic or even generally naturalistic piece. It was Shafaei's position as a refugee that imbued his performance with credibility, rather than its believability. As far as the central trope of hunger strike is concerned, *Refugitive* was closer to a *translation* of self-injury than a representation of it; Shafaei's energetic performance rendered the loss of vitality consequent upon a real hunger strike as its diametric opposite—vital theatricality—for political and personal purposes. That is not to say the work wasn't drawn from personal history—certainly, three traumatized young people referred to towards the end of the play, a three year old boy who had not seen another child for several months, a thirteen year old girl who went on a hunger strike and a seventeen year old boy who sewed his lips together, are drawn directly from Shafaei's fellow detainees (Cox interview). In a review of the production, Shafaei is quoted as describing his performance in *Refugitive* as a means by which he can help 'the people who are still in detention, my friends who I am still in contact with, and I know how much pain they are going through still' (qtd in Gill 100). In a newspaper interview, he directly interprets the subjectivity and motivations of hunger strikers: '[t]he people who would go on hunger strike, they would tell you that this is a situation where you have no choice [...] People cut themselves to feel that they were still alive. They feel that they are not any more accepted as human' (qtd in Stark 2). This assumption of the role of interpreter is crucial to understanding the significance of Shafaei's work; he utilized his privileged access to the Australian public to speak for and advocate on behalf of those with whom he was incarcerated and with whom his own experience intersected, to approximate what they would have said if given the opportunity.

Just as important as what Shafaei's former fellow detainees would have said is what, in practical terms, they *could* have said. Shafaei is acutely aware of the relative empowerment that his status as an English-speaking, well-educated adult male affords him, and he maintains that the reason he did not undergo a hunger strike or sew his lips together in detention was due primarily to his understanding of English. Elaine Scarry observes that language represents a mode of being or creating in the world that unravels in the presence of physical pain: 'so long as one is speaking, the self extends out beyond the boundaries of the body, occupies a space much larger than the body' (33). Having a means of linguistic self-representation within the bureaucratic spaces of immigration detention made Shafaei, in his words, 'the fortunate one' that did not have to resort to other, desperate, means of representation (Cox interview). In *Refugitive*, bodily deprivation is framed as an attempt at communication-beyond-language with the immigration authorities: '[n]obody cared about us not eating so this was the only remaining choice to stop drinking, the only choice, the only decision that you can make around here' (15). The decision to not eat or drink gestures toward agency—even if it amounts, in Scarry's terms, to the unmaking of the world—and a challenge to recognize the precarity of exceptional bodies. The interlocutors of the hunger strike in *Refugitive*, that is, Australian immigration representatives and detention guards, determine the meaning of the strike and the value of those undergoing it, and as Shahin's character states, 'nobody cared'. The importance of the interlocutor or audience to self-injury was reinforced in the context of the play's theatrical productions. As a play, it was able to dramatize the absence of compassionate response to political starvation: the only instance of a caring interlocutor in *Refugitive* is the protagonist's gentle words to his own stomach: 'please co-operate with me for the last part, my dear stomach' (22). Here, self-starvation, whatever else it may express, is not an act of self-hatred.

Shafaei's former closeness to hunger striking bodies in detention framed his performance and protest within a context of personal and political authenticity. Even though his play is not autobiographical, Shafaei's own identity was integral to the efficacy of his performances—almost all reviews of the show provide a précis of his own story of fleeing Iran and arrival and detention in Australia. Shafaei regarded *Refugitive* as an opportunity for communication with Australians, both in terms of his identity as a refugee and as a theatre practitioner: 'it was very much an introduction of myself to Australia and Australia to myself' (Cox interview). His performances were followed by question and answer sessions that often went on for longer than the fifty-minute show; typically, Shafaei would be asked personal questions that required him to speak about his traumatic memories. In this way, Shafaei offered an intensification of the intimacy inherent in solo theatre, and his appearances before an audience were imbued with the idea of attending to (we can invoke again the Latin 'stretching toward') the noncitizen other. By constructing points of contact and dialogue, Shafaei also served as a figure by which audiences could perform their sense of obligation to asylum seekers. This manifested as an apparent willingness to operate different as a citizen; Shafaei recalls that in every question and answer session, the question would arise: 'what do you think we can do now?' For Shafaei, this was an encouraging sign of what he calls a 'social movement'. He responded by encouraging people to 'have the conversation' with each other, to attempt to contact asylum seekers in detention and to write to state and federal representatives (Cox interview). Shafaei's emphasis on conversation implies an understanding of cosmopolitan engagement as everyday practice. As well as encouraging social engagement, Shafaei's suggestions to his audiences highlight the interdependent relation between Australians and asylum seekers: democratically elected state and federal politicians enact the detention system in the latter's name.

Contaminating Citizenship

Judith Butler's discussion, in *Precarious Life*, of the United States' sovereign or executive authority in the context of the Guantanamo Bay prison camp for 'suspected enemy combatants' represents an important component of her broader mapping of sovereignty's decentralization, and her concomitant assertion that states of exception recur across time and place:

> It is crucial to ask under what conditions some human lives cease to become eligible for basic, if not universal, human rights [...] to what extent is there a racial and ethnic frame through which these imprisoned lives are viewed and judged such that they are deemed less than human, or as having departed from the recognizable human community? (57)

Butler's questions are critical for foregrounding ways human rights are attenuated by state coercion and for highlighting how noncitizen, non-white bodies are more liable to be captured outside the terrain of recognizable belonging. In this context, it seems necessary to remember the limitations of the performance and activism discussed here. The political act of placing one's performing body on the line and asking spectators to consider the meanings that attach to self-injury as a limit-form of communication across culture and the law is fraught with risk—especially in outdoor public spaces, where spectators may not have consented to see injury represented. There is the risk that the performer overrides its referent, his or her debasement becoming unhelpfully ironic in its artificiality, and there is the risk that audiences will be repulsed or affronted by the spectacle.

Despite this, the interventions into public space enacted by Parr, Astore, various Australian activist hunger strikers and Shafaei registered that their bodies, situated at various positions along a bureaucratized, racialized and gendered spectrum from belonging to non-belonging, had been affected and indeed infected by the injuries of detained asylum seekers. They also interpellated the desperation of incarcerated asylum seekers, permitted recourse only to set themselves to a wretched form of 'anti-use' or 'anti-work', as signalling an ethical malaise at the national level. Rajaram's image of an 'intercontamination of identity' ('Disruptive Writing' 220) between asylum seekers and Australian citizens (which he invokes with reference to poetry by asylum seekers) is apt here. The works that I have examined in this chapter engineered a demasking of the state's ability to inoculate those it purports to serve, to prevent citizens from being altered by the abjection of outsiders. Foucault's observation that 'power is tolerable only on condition that it mask a substantial part of itself' (*History* 86) is borne out by Australia's immigration detention system, with its strategies of geographical (via camps placed in remote and offshore locations) and discursive (via strict limitations on contact with members of the public) masking. Unmasking is also in part about a process of investment and endurance by performers, which complicate orders of seen and unseen power, seen and unseen human beings, as well as bodies in pain and bodies not in pain. To represent or reproduce the injuries of others is to instrumentalize pain as a public condition, drawing attention to a common human vulnerability to injury, and thereby up the stakes of a community's knowledge, which is always already there at the margins of consciousness, of how pain comes to reside in the bodies of those it excludes. The instrumental performance of injury can show that when 'the advent of the refugee' is accompanied by the 'brutal mark of sovereignty' (Rajaram, 'Disruptive Writing' 220), the bodies of citizens will also be marked.

Chapter 5

WELCOME TO COUNTRY?
ABORIGINAL ACTIVISM
AND ONTOLOGIES OF SOVEREIGNTY

We can't separate ourselves from other human beings—it's a duty.

—Wadjularbinna Nulyarimma

At the opening of the Australian parliament on 12 February 2008, Prime Minister Kevin Rudd acknowledged the traditional owners of the land after being Welcomed to Country in a ceremony performed by Aboriginal people from around Australia. Similar welcomes and acknowledgements of country are common at many types of events and gatherings (with State and Territory guidelines devised on their implementation), but they had never been part of the opening of the federal parliament prior to 2008. The landmark welcome ostensibly enacted the idea that the Australian government's authority is somehow granted by—and not imposed upon—Aboriginal people. That this symbolism is conspicuously at odds with historico-political reality has underpinned public debate in Australia over the efficacy of the Welcome to Country and acknowledgement of traditional owners. In March 2010 the suggestion by the then opposition leader Tony Abbott that the discursive acknowledgement of traditional owners is often 'out-of-place tokenism' (qtd in Maiden 1) prompted a brief flurry of discussion on the role of symbolic thought and action in organizing human affairs generally, and specifically, on whether Australians should be explicitly reminded of the unceded, unresolved sovereignty of Aboriginal people—in other words, of unfinished business.[1]

Setting aside for a moment debates over intention, efficacy and symbolism, it is undeniable that whatever form of Aboriginal sovereignty the Welcome to Country and acknowledgement of country signify or articulate, its structural difference from executive, legislative and judicial powers—the bulwarks of what Aboriginal scholar Aileen Moreton-Robinson terms 'patriarchal white sovereignty' (87)—is profound in a nation that only recently saw the first Aboriginal person elected to the federal House of Representatives. Moreton-Robinson pinpoints the ambivalence of ceremonial recognition, arguing that it is 'simultaneously a reminder and a denial of the existence of Indigenous sovereignty. The reminder is evidenced by the presence of Indigenous bodies, but its denial is contained in the words "traditional lands", which transports ownership back into the past not the continuing present' ('Writing' 98). In October 2009, less than two years after the inaugural federal Welcome to Country, Rudd telephoned the Indonesian president, Susilo Bambang Yudhoyono, to request that a boat carrying 255 Sri Lankan Tamils heading for Australia's Christmas Island be intercepted and escorted to the port of Merak, on the north-western tip of Java. The Indonesians obliged, but a six-month long stand-off ensued when the asylum seekers refused to disembark at Merak until they had been assured passage to Australia. At a refugee support rally in the city of Melbourne on 1 May 2010, Aboriginal Australian activists responded to the stand-off by producing Original Nation Passports for the Merak asylum seekers. This was a defiant rejoinder to the Australian government's decision a fortnight prior to freeze all Afghan and Sri Lankan refugee claims until further notice. Aboriginal activist Robbie Thorpe (who also identifies himself by his adopted tribal name, Djuran Bunjileenee), flanked by other activists publicly signing stacks of passports outside the neo-classical façade of Melbourne's Trades Hall, announced: 'we want to make it clear that the Aboriginal people, the true sovereigns of this land, are offering them a passport to enter into our territorial waters, and our land', adding, 'we're the colonised refugees' (qtd in 'Aboriginal Passports').

Aboriginal jurisdiction over and responsibilities toward newcomers are, then, negotiated under the spotlight of mainstream cultural and political life as well as in fringe activism. Considered side-by-side, indigenous activism via the production of passports or visas (a reterritorialization of valorized documents of state power) and indigenous welcome protocols and ceremonies (which publicly enact the idea of an unextinguished indigenous territorial authority) suggest something of the contradictory cultural conditions under which Aboriginal status claims exist in Australia today. The juxtaposition draws attention, ultimately, to contested ontologies of sovereignty. As far as governmental power is concerned, the non-status of indigenous territorial sovereignty is thrown into sharp relief by John Howard's pronouncement at the launch of his 2001 election campaign: '[w]e will decide who comes to this country and the circumstances in which they come' (qtd in Marr and Wilkinson 324). What, then, might be the value of taking indigenous protocols as a provocation in the context of unauthorized asylum seekers? What might

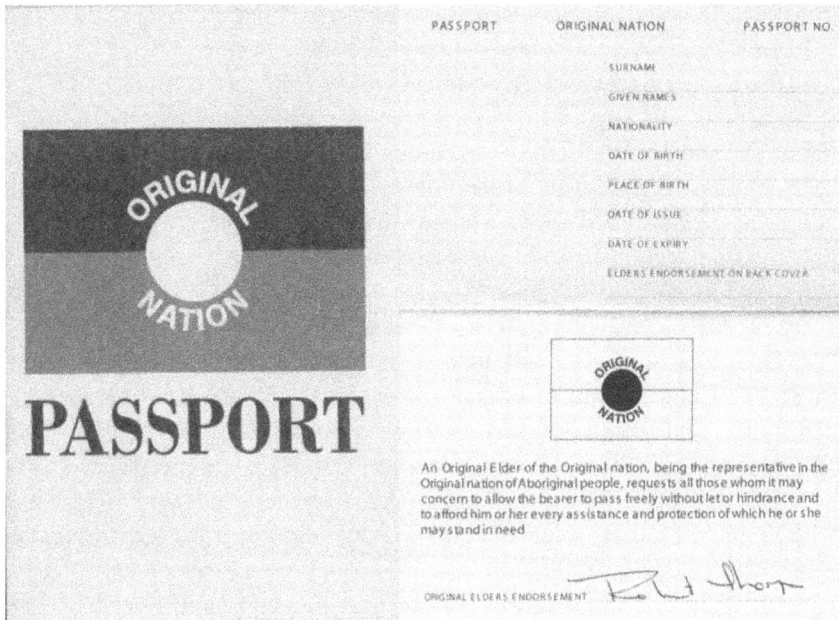

Fig. 6. Scan of *Original Nation Passport*, created by Robbie Thorpe, 2010.

derive from a structurally marginalized but ceremonially, performatively acknowledged Aboriginal territorial claim (inhering in the right to welcome, or presumably reject, the stranger) in the context of determinations of belonging and non-belonging, citizen and alien, audacious boat-person and deserving offshore refugee?

In this chapter I want to examine what happens when we take indigenous rights and responsibilities regarding newcomers/strangers as an analytical framework or point of departure for understanding transnational positionalities (asylum seekers and refugees) and local positionalities (Aboriginal Australian), and for perceiving a synthesis of the two. I trace contexts of social engagement, including activism (including interventions in space as well as written statements) and interpersonal contact, that represent certain contingent spaces for belonging (and less frequently, non-belonging) for people who are barred from both political and imagined community. These engagements are understood, by way of an integrated performance and discourse analysis, in their capacity as practices that reconfigure power relationships and affective atmospheres in public and private spaces. They offer a picture of Aboriginality as a complex and ambivalent contemporary identification, explicating some of the conflicted allegiances aroused by the citizen–noncitizen dichotomy, while foregrounding indigenous authority and knowledge as lived practice, and perhaps, alternative sovereignty. The term alternative sovereignty is a hazy one that affixes to juridico-political, philosophical and affective meanings that can be contiguous or at odds; to be sure, the term implies a paradoxical condition: that is, two absolute authorities co-existing in one political community. But it has to be understood in the context of how, as Moreton-Robinson explains, indigenous rights are indexed to the ways that their inverse, 'White possession', functions as a 'regime of truth' ('Towards' 389). Moreton-Robinson makes the point, via Foucault, that 'rights should not be understood as the establishment of legitimacy but rather the method by which subjugation is carried out' ('Towards' 390). One way of understanding these methods is to look at the ways in which indigenous peoples influence, or do not influence, mechanisms of belonging, for themselves and others.

While projects such as Aboriginal-Asian theatre practitioner Jimmy Chi's acclaimed musical theatre work *Bran Nue Dae* (premiered 1990) and Vietnamese Australian (and former refugee) Hung Le and Aboriginal Australian Ningali Lawford's comedy collaboration *Black and Tran* (premiered 2000) represent important creative intersections between Aboriginal and non-European migrant perspectives and cultural contexts,[2] it is fair to say that in theatrical and cinematic responses to asylum in post-*Tampa* Australia, Aboriginal figures seldom appear in any significant capacity. As far as the stranger–citizen dyad central to so many refugee narratives is concerned, Aboriginality, Australia's 'citizen other' category, has tended to be sidelined in the project of representing the plight of disenfranchised noncitizens. Michael James Rowland's feature film *Lucky Miles* (2007) is one fairly prominent exception to this tendency, offering reflections on how Aboriginality connects with asylum and related issues of sovereignty, territory, biopower and citizenship (see Cox, 'Welcome'). It must, of course, be noted that arguments for comparison or alignment between indigenous Australians and asylum seekers run the risk of recapitulating well-traversed theorizations of postcolonial power relations, or worse, of corralling Aboriginality and asylum as twin paradigms of victimhood and marginalization. But in its attempt to position indigenous sovereignty and draw out its implications in terms of the reception of unauthorized asylum seekers, the following discussion represents a crucial development of this book's concern with how noncitizenship has come to function in Australian identity formation. The way Aboriginal Australian identity is strategically politicized by the Aboriginal activists, scholars and elders cited in this chapter opens up a space that complicates the role noncitizenship has in constituting and legitimizing belonging.

Hegemonic Australian nationalism is most explicitly problematic in relation to Aboriginal Australians, the people against whom the founding violence of settler sovereignty was acted. In Australia, the assumption of ownership and authority by the British was not achieved via any of the routes laid out under common and international law: conquest (by force of arms), cession (under treaty) or settlement (of uninhabited land).[3] This originary colonial failure— anchored by the doctrine of *terra nullius* (land belonging to no one)—to engage with indigenous peoples under common or international (not to mention indigenous) law continues to represent an intractable problem. Some progress has been made in reconciling indigenous land title claims under Australian law, but these are often in remote geographical spaces that settler Australia does not use or occupy. The Aboriginal Land Rights (Northern Territory) Act 1976 provided the basis upon which indigenous people in the Northern Territory could claim land rights based on traditional occupation; currently forty-nine percent of the land in the state is indigenous-owned. In 1992 the High Court's landmark ruling in Mabo v Queensland (No. 2) overturned terra nullius with respect to land (giving way to the concept of Aboriginal native title) but maintained that Aboriginal title to some land had been validly extinguished. The court also ruled that indigenous Australians remained subject to Australian sovereignty; in effect, reiterating the axiom that state sovereignty is self-authorizing.[4]

The Mabo decision prompted the Native Title Act 1993, which while certainly not guaranteeing native title to indigenous people, provides a mechanism for dealing with claims. In 1996, the High Court's ruling in another landmark case, Wik Peoples v Queensland, stated that native title rights could continue on lands held under certain statutory pastoral leases; in other words, that the two titles could co-exist. However, the High Court rulings and the Native Title Act (along with a 1998 Amendment) do not simply promote indigenous land title (much less sovereignty); indeed, the Act retrospectively validates forms of settler land title that were arguably made improperly, particularly vis-à-vis the Racial Discrimination Act 1975.[5] The Australian state has not found a way to reconcile juridically the issue of native title, much less that of indigenous sovereignty; as historian Henry Reynolds observes, 'Australian jurisprudence makes sense only if the Aboriginal people were traditionally so primitive as to be almost without law, politics or authority—a conclusion at odds with modern anthropological knowledge and with principles of human rights upheld by the High Court in the Mabo judgement' ('Sovereignty' 210). It is from this paradigm of non-sense that alternative articulations of sovereignty or territoriality manifest.

The establishment of sovereignty in Australia without conquest, cession or settlement (of empty land) places it in a singularly problematic position in comparison to other former European colonies. But in terms of the collision between state sovereignty and indigenous rights, Australia is not alone in its dilemma; in September 2007, when the United Nations Declaration on the Rights of Indigenous Peoples was adopted by the United Nations General Assembly, four member states voted against it: Australia, Canada, New Zealand and the United States. Representatives of these four countries variously expressed concerns about how key provisions of the Declaration relating to sovereign authority—including the right to self-determination and the upholding of customary legal systems, access to land and resources—could be practically implemented. These objections were not merely the domain of non-indigenous representatives; New Zealand's Minister of Maori Affairs under the Helen Clark Labour government, Parekura Horomia, stated:

> [T]he declaration [is] fundamentally incompatible with New Zealand's constitutional and legal arrangements and established Treaty [of Waitangi] settlement policy. Article 26 of the Declaration states that indigenous peoples have the right to the lands, territories and resources they have traditionally owned, occupied or otherwise used or acquired. For New Zealand this covers potentially the entire country. It appears to require recognition of rights to lands now lawfully owned by other citizens, both indigenous and non-indigenous. This ignores contemporary reality and would be impossible to implement. (Horomia)

In this situation global thinking on sovereignty presents local difficulties; the UN-constructed pronouncement on indigenous people's rights comes into conflict in fundamental ways with the political and territorial structures of several nations. Nonetheless, on 3 April 2009, the Australian government endorsed the Declaration (Canada, New Zealand and the United States have also done so). While of certain symbolic significance, the practical effects of this endorsement in terms of political recognition of Aboriginal sovereignty are uncertain, especially since a Declaration is not legally binding. The complex relationship between activism (or sociality) and practical, material power is a dialectic that lies at the heart of this chapter.

Constructing Australian Sovereignty

In legitimating the British claim to sovereignty over the continent of Australia outside the mechanisms of established common and international law (conquest, cession or settlement of uninhabited land), the determination of Australia as terra nullius was crucial: the territory was held to be uninhabited according to the terms of European international law. More specifically, this meant that the indigenous peoples were not recognized as having any social or political organization and that the territory was, as such, without sovereign claim. As I noted in the introduction to this book and in chapter three, indigenous Australians were demarcated from non-indigenous Australians until the latter half of the twentieth century by limited voting rights, exclusion in the census and biopolitical coercion (the removal of children from their families, institutionalization in missions and residential facilities, town boundary zones operating on a curfew basis and restricted travel/movement rights).

In territorial or spatial terms, the imprecision of sovereign control belies the totalizing presumption of its founding authorization. The latter is the so-called paradox of political founding, mentioned in the introduction to this study: the problem of sovereignty, as Anthony Burke observes, 'presuming itself to authorise and precede the very act of its coming into existence' (para. 16). Henry Reynolds argues that territorial control by colonial authorities in Australia was in fact gradual and incomplete; he distinguishes three (simplified) 'zones of territory' whereby control was exercised directly (such territory was small), intermittently, or not at all ('Sovereignty' 211). The 'politics of forgetting' (Connolly 138)—facilitated by a common acceptance of unifying narratives of national identity, pride and security—necessary for the maintenance of the Australian nation subsequent to its paradoxical (and violent) founding is of the same nature as the effacement of liberal principles necessary for widespread public acceptance of the coercive marginalization of asylum seekers, their relegation to border spaces that are effectively excised from the dominant idea of nation. The extrajudicial incarceration of asylum seekers, especially mandatory, indefinite detention, can occur because the sovereign authority and much of the population have entered into something akin to a politics of forgetting, in which the violence detention is subsumed ideologically as realpolitik, a necessary biopolitical organization operating in the interests of sovereign and territorial integrity.

The year 2001 was an important one for Aboriginal Australia. While the *Tampa* stand-off in late August precipitated the radical Pacific Solution and terrorist attacks in the United States produced a vociferous nationalism and militarism articulated around perceived imminent security threats, an official 2001 deadline for national reconciliation between Aboriginal and non-Aboriginal Australians, set with bipartisan support in the federal parliament a decade earlier, passed by without being met. This was in spite of an apparent groundswell of public support for reconciliation, expressed in large-scale symbolic actions such as national people's bridge walks, marches, 'sorry' books and cultural performances (perhaps most notably, the Festival of the Dreaming in 1997, part of the Cultural Olympiad that preceded the Sydney 2000 Olympics) in the years leading up to the deadline. Suvendrini Perera pinpoints the year 2001 in Australia as marking a 'shift in focus from the pivotal question of internal or domestic sovereignty and the relationship between the state and its Indigenous subjects to the exercise of sovereignty at the extremities of the national geo-body over its oceans and neighbouring regions, as well as upon enemies imaginatively located at the limits of the nation' ('Acting Sovereign' 4–5). In the aggressive repudiation of people seeking refuge in Australia without documentation, widely applauded in the hawkish period of 2001 and after, national interests moved away from indigenous Australia.

Taken together, two significant events of more recent years exemplify the duality between material power and social action that underlies the ambivalent and continually re-negotiated relationship between Aboriginal people and Australian sovereignty. The tenuous basis upon which Aboriginal self-determination stands was illustrated in late June 2007, when the Howard government sent six hundred Australian Defence Force personnel into Northern Territory indigenous communities in response to an alleged epidemic of child sexual abuse. This controversial Northern Territory National Emergency Response or 'Intervention', which saw the government acquire Aboriginal lands under temporary lease, was enabled via a 'special measures' exemption from the Racial Discrimination Act 1975. The Intervention was replaced in 2012 by a similar set of policy provisions, the Stronger Futures Policy. Such initiatives reaffirm Australian sovereignty by exerting exceptional powers and underline Giorgio Agamben's assertion, 'the sovereign [...] is the one who marks the point of indistinction between violence and right by proclaiming the state of exception and suspending the validity of the law' (*Means* 104). On 13 February 2008, as the first item of business at the opening of parliament for the year, Rudd apologized on behalf of the parliament to Aboriginal Australians forcibly removed from their families (the Stolen Generations) and their descendants. This act was of great importance to many indigenous people, who had requested in vain for several years that Howard issue a statement of apology. While it emphasized unity and reconciliation and not an alternative or parallel indigenous claim to sovereignty, Rudd's words acknowledged the damage inflicted as a direct result of the power wielded by the Australian state: '[w]e apologise for the hurt, the pain and suffering we, the parliament, have caused you by the laws that previous parliaments have enacted. We apologise for the indignity, the degradation and the humiliation these laws embodied' (Rudd). Even as these two events indicate a renewed federal interest in indigenous Australia, they offer a profoundly contradictory engagement, whereby coercion, in the form of the suspension of racial discrimination legislation and the temporary acquisition of Aboriginal lands, sits alongside what many regarded as a significant expression of recognition and respect.

Several hundred indigenous people from across Australia converged upon Canberra for the official apology; it and the indigenous Welcome to Country that had opened parliament the preceding day were well-received by many. Ngambri (Canberra region) elder Matilda House-Williams, who led the Welcome to Country, described it as '[t]he best time in the history of the Australian Parliament [...] A Prime Minister has honoured us, the first people of this land, the Ngambri people by seeking a welcome to country. In doing this, the Prime Minister shows what we call proper respect' (qtd in 'MPs "Welcomed to Country"'). Yankunytjatjara (north-west South Australia) elder and former public administrator Lowitja O'Donoghue described the apology in affective terms as 'a healing process for many of the stolen generation' (qtd in Coorey and Peatling 1). However, other Aboriginal commentators expressed disappointment over the fact that the Prime Minister and opposition leader's speeches were not accompanied by a speech from a national Aboriginal representative, and that meetings between government and Aboriginal representatives were not held at the time of the apology. Sam Watson, a Birri Gubba (central Queensland) activist, writer and filmmaker, notes that in Canberra 'there wasn't a sustained engagement between the Rudd government and the Aboriginal community leaders; there needs to be a lot of work done there' (qtd in 'Sam Watson'). Without discounting the point that the formal apology, like the ceremonies of the previous day, did not produce Aboriginal authority—territorial, structural or otherwise— it is my purpose here to map some of the more minoritarian, and indeed intimate, ways in which cultural work operates in Aboriginal activism and interpersonal sociality.

Activist Work

The remote Northern Territory Aboriginal community of Ampilatwatja, home to the Alyawarra people, is one of the prescribed townships that was acquired by the federal government in 2007 for a five-year lease under the terms of the Northern Territory Intervention. In August 2009 Alyawarra members, represented by spokesperson Richard Downs, lodged a formal request with James Anaya, United Nations Special Rapporteur on the Situation of Human Rights and Fundamental Freedoms of Indigenous Peoples, that they be classified as refugees. Downs's letter to Anaya reads: '[t] he current status of Aboriginal people is that we are refugees in a Country we have called our own since time immemorial' and requests that the United Nations '[e]nsure[s] that the Australian government is aware of, and fulfils, its obligations under the International Refugee Convention, the UN Charter for Human Rights, the Declaration on the Rights of Indigenous Peoples, and other international human rights covenants' (Downs). This followed a protest that began a month earlier, when thirty community elders walked off the dilapidated Ampilatwatja and established a camp outside the government-controlled boundary.[6] The activism is a response to a lack of improvement in living conditions despite promises made at the time of the Intervention. The submission to the United Nations serves the potent political function of contextualizing the Alyawarra's position—forced relinquishment of leasehold and scant provision for basic housing and infrastructure—in terms of an internationally recognized political status. For Downs, the walk-off constitutes a simultaneous exile and return, with the camp situated on his mother's country; in other words, even as it embodies the abjection of the townspeople, the protest is a rejection of government determination and an attempt to, as Downs explains, 'create a sustainable community for ourselves' (qtd in 'Aboriginal Community'). In Sydney in April 2010 a documentary charting the construction of a protest house at the camp (with the support of trade unions and community organizations), *The Ampilatwatja Walk-off Protest vs the NT Intervention*, was presented by Actively Radical TV.

While the Ampilatwatja people's invocation of the international discourse of asylum is intended to situate their own position—and dispossession—it also articulates a generalized connection with refugees based upon similar disenfranchisement and displacement. The reactions of a number of other Aboriginal activists, elders and scholars to asylum seekers and refugees constitute quite a cohesive statement of responsibility for and hospitality toward the dispossessed other. But like the Ampilatwatja action, these responses also seem to be propelled by an expressed understanding of experiences of displacement and oppression, and in this capacity they strategically underscore a politicized Aboriginal identity, even as they communicate a humanitarian concern for the noncitizen stranger.

The Aboriginal Tent Embassy, which has stood on the lawn of Old Parliament House in Canberra intermittently since 1972 and continuously since 1992, is an important nexus of Aboriginal activism, especially regarding sovereignty and land rights.[7] Current and former representatives of the Tent Embassy have publicly expressed support for asylum seekers and refugees. At an event organized by the Refugee Action Committee in 2000 to welcome refugees who had been resettled in Canberra, Gunilaroi/Kamilaroi (north-central New South Wales) member Robert Craigie invoked a connection between them and Aboriginal people who, he asserted, had become refugees within their own country. On behalf of Isabelle Coe, a Wiradjuri/Ngunnawal (Canberra region) elder and Tent Embassy founding activist, and other embassy members, Craigie offered Canberra as a 'safe haven' (qtd in Griffiths). Sam Watson, who was a founding member of the Tent Embassy in 1972, has been

Fig. 7. The Aboriginal Tent Embassy on its 30th Anniversary. Canberra, 26 January 2002. National Library of Australia, vn3507110. (Photo: Loui Seselja.)

a vocal advocate for asylum seekers and refugees for several years. In 2001, in response to the infamous *Tampa* stand-off, Watson expressed identification with the desperation of the asylum seekers: 'why [...] would they be risking their lives, and the lives of their children, on the open seas. They need medical treatment and deserve a safe haven' (qtd in Mason). Watson's support formulates a mutually-constitutive solidarity: '[t]he government is scapegoating refugees in the same way as they scapegoat indigenous people' (qtd in Mason). In 2002, in response to mass hunger strikes and self-harm taking place at the remote Woomera detention centre, Pat Eatock extended an offer of asylum to detainees on behalf of the Tent Embassy. Although a symbolic gesture that was never going to directly influence policy decisions, the offer (which was reported by the national and international media) denounced the 'callous and inhumane' (qtd in Barkham 18) treatment of asylum seekers at the same time as it explicated the sovereign claim that is central to the Embassy's continuing activism. The following year, a representative from the Tent Embassy joined elders from the Bungala (Port Augusta), Kokatha (northern South Australia), and Adnyamathanya (Flinders Ranges) nations at a large rally at the (now closed) Baxter detention centre, near Port Augusta (Murphy).

Emerging at a time when asylum was one of the most inflammatory and emotive issues in Australia (propelled by tense situations such as *Tampa* and detainee hunger strikes), these statements essentially answered affective discourse with affective discourse; while they could not intervene materially in the politics they decried, they enabled the circulation of alternative ideas— of welcome and hope—legitimized by Aboriginal territorial authority. More recently, in November 2009 Watson, Eatock and Natasha Moore released a statement on behalf of the Socialist Alliance Indigenous Rights collective, asserting, '[w]hile Prime Minister Kevin Rudd increasingly resembles previous Coalition PM John Howard—the arrogantly inflexible and hard-line political "leader" who could never admit to an error of judgment or say sorry—he forgets that 98% of Australians are "boat people", the descendants of boat people or, more recently, "plane people"' (qtd in 'Aboriginal Leaders').

Aboriginal activists Noeleen Ryan-Lester and Linda Dare have articulated the same line of connection at rallies and in media interviews. Noeleen Ryan-Lester, an Adnyamathana (the Flinders Ranges of South Australia) woman and social justice campaigner, invokes a connection between indigenous people and asylum seekers in terms of biopolitical coercion under Australian sovereign power; in an interview, she notes, 'Baxter is not the first detention centre in Port Augusta. The first one was the Davenport mission, where they put Aboriginal people. It had a fence around it too, to stop the Aboriginal people from coming to Port Augusta. Port Augusta was just for the whites' (qtd in Taylor). Like Ryan-Lester, Linda Dare of the Bungala people (South Australia) identifies a continuity between successive histories of exclusion, coupled with what is effectively, in Connolly's terms, a 'politics of forgetting' (138); in the same interview, she asserts: 'John Howard [...] and everyone in Parliament have got to realise that we are the first people of this country [...] what right have they got to lock up other people? They got off a bloody boat, or their ancestors did' (qtd in Taylor). In 2003, Dare (along with Bungala, Kokatha and Adnyamathana community members) joined a gathering of several hundred refugee activists outside Baxter detention centre (Murphy). In 2005, Ryan-Lester and Dare were part of an anti-racism protest by the Port Augusta indigenous community, an act they linked to simultaneous protest activities at nearby Baxter, thereby drawing lines of embodied connection between two of the nation's spaces of exception, or in Foucauldian terms, its heterotopias of deviation.

Wading into the contentious waters of asylum politics in post-2001 Australia, members of the Aboriginal Tent Embassy and activists such as

Ryan-Lester and Dare might be seen to be addressing what Ghassan Hage insists is a key inequality of hope in contemporary Australia. Hage argues that hope is not a vague or whimsical idea but is vital to social success; he observes, 'once one has hope within one's field of vision, one discovers the astounding degree to which the constellations of feelings, discourses and practices articulated to hope permeate social life' (9). From this, he claims that 'societies are mechanisms for the distribution of hope, and [...] the kind of affective attachment (worrying or caring) that a society creates among its citizens is intimately connected to its capacity to distribute hope' (*Against* 3). We can, then, see that what Aboriginal refugee activists offer is 'care' in place of a dominant affect of 'worry', and thereby begin to respond to inequality in the 'distribution of hope' (*Against* 17). Given that Aboriginal supporters of asylum seekers and refugees frequently cite a sense of affinity with those suffering oppression and that this reinforces a politicized self-identification, their activism is intermeshed with Aboriginal interests as well those of the newcomers. Of course, a redistribution of hope can seem a distant aspiration in the sobering light of the Australian Indigenous Doctors' Association 2010 Health Impact Assessment of the Northern Territory Emergency Response, which reported that Aboriginal Australians suffer 'a deep sense of alienation and a collective existential despair' (Health Impact)—in another word, hopelessness. Nevertheless, that the nature of engagement between Aboriginal people and refugees is small-scale, its political impact undramatic, does not, I argue, diminish its significance for those it affects.

Gungalidda (Gulf of Carpentaria) elder and Aboriginal Tent Embassy member Wadjularbinna Nulyarimma elaborates in an essay the activist perspectives I have described with reference to spiritual and ecological values. Likening the Australian government's control of discourse on unauthorized asylum seekers to a similar control of discourse on Aborigines, she writes, 'we know that what the Government says about Aboriginal Peoples is wrong, so we are not going to believe' pejorative rhetoric on asylum seekers (Wadjularbinna para. 2). Central to Nulyarimma's argument is a humanist duty of responsibility: '[b]efore Europeans came here, (illegally), in the Aboriginal world, we were all different, speaking different languages, but we all had the same kinship system for all human beings . . . everyone is part of us and we should care about them. We can't separate ourselves from other human beings—it's a duty' (Wadjularbinna para. 6). In an essay that scathingly unravels the concept of the 'un-Australian', re-deploying it with reference to the Australian government's treatment of Aborigines and asylum seekers, Tony Birch articulates a similar view of duty to the stranger, asserting that Aboriginal people 'must [...] assert more moral authority and *ownership* of this country. Our legitimacy does not lie within the legal system and is not dependent on state recognition [...] we need to claim and legitimate our authority by speaking out for, and protecting the rights of others, who live in, or visit *our* country' (20–21, italics in original). The notion of ethical inseparability between asylum seekers and Australians challenges the dichotomies of citizen and alien, legitimate and illegitimate, that rationalize mandatory detention. Nulyarimma's and Birch's perspectives are founded upon concepts of indigenous sovereignty defined in part by a right and responsibility to offer hospitality to newcomers. These are expressed as community perspectives: Nulyarimma writes on behalf of Gungalidda elders who, she asserts, were distressed by the *Tampa* incident and subsequent legislative amendments, while Birch writes in part as a call to activism, concluding his essay with an affective rally to Aboriginal people 'to speak, to write, to march, to protest, to be angry and put that anger into expression and action' (22).

Seeking to elucidate the question, '[w]hat can Indigenous people offer to thinking about refugee issues?', Mark Minchinton invokes (after Dinesh Wadiwel) Achille Mbembe's concept of *necropower* (the ultimate, defining power of the sovereign to kill) to align the oppression of Aboriginal Australians and asylum seekers. He considers carceral spaces that construct 'death worlds' and confer bodies the (non-)status of 'living dead', concepts taken from Mbembe that engage Agamben's idea of *homo sacer* or bare life (crucially, however, Agamben argues that modern biopower inheres in the production of infinitely surviving bare life, rather than death (*Remnants* 155)). Minchinton describes Palm Island's carceral history to illustrate his point: 'Palm Island was a site of beatings, humiliations, and arbitrary imprisonment; a place where Indigenous people's right to movement, food, health care, and freedom of association was denied' (2). He continues: '[l]ike refugees, Indigenous people are exiles. But exiled in their own country. Both groups have much to offer each other: much to learn in terms of resistance, of perseverance, of working together to make Australia a place that welcomes difference and diversity' (3). If Minchinton's identification of certain carceral histories occludes other (for example, convict) histories, this serves the strategic, affective purpose of formulating cross-cultural solidarity in the present.

The trope of affinity as a result of comparable experiences under sovereign power is, as I have sought to show, a recurring and productive one in activist and academic contexts. In spite of this coherence of perspective, it is important to resist homogenizing Aboriginal responses to asylum seekers and refugees. The former ATSIC (Aboriginal and Torres Strait Islander Commission) family policy and health commissioner Marion Hansen has identified unauthorized asylum seekers as competing figures of oppression and marginalization that detract from social, political and economic focus on Aborigines. At a National Press Club of Australia seminar on 21 September 2001, Hansen (in opposition to whom Nulyarimma positions her article) expressed support for the Howard government's policies and voiced concerns that the economic cost of detaining asylum seekers and subsequently assisting their resettlement in Australia threatens the employment prospects of Aboriginal people and comes at the expense of funds for Aboriginal support and benefit programs (Wright 3). Professing to speak on behalf of indigenous people around Australia with whom she had spoken on the issue of illegal immigrants, Hansen called into question the hardship of people who seek to arrive by boat: 'We have to protect our shores. Questions have been put to me that if they are really refugees, how come they can afford to pay literally thousands of dollars to these smugglers or people who are actually getting these boats to come across here?' (qtd in Wright 3).

Indigenous law specialist and Tanganekald and Meintangk (south-east South Australia) member Irene Watson argues that the opposition expressed by a number of Australians to the prolonged, indefinite detention of asylum seekers redirects public attention away from human rights issues concerning indigenous Australians. While she does not support the mandatory detention of asylum seekers, she notes, 'it is the detention of Aboriginal peoples in this country that we have turned our gaze away from; a much more deserving victim has emerged, along with another human rights struggle, the refugee' (42). Watson is referring specifically to the high rates of juvenile detention of Aborigines in the Northern Territory, a comparison that identifies a similar instrumentalization of vulnerable lives, even if it risks obscuring the differences between two forms of incarceration, particularly in terms of judicial process. While Watson is more sympathetic towards asylum seekers, her view is, like Hansen's, underpinned by a sense that asylum seekers represent a competing oppressed minority in Australia and as such threaten the fragile social, political and economic standing of indigenous Australians. In Watson's formulation, affective human rights responses (to the deserving victim) that might prompt social change are in limited supply; or to put it another way, attention has an all-too-protean relationship with immediate politicization.

Intimate Work

Activist practices within the public sphere such as those I have discussed often articulate to and are sustained by personal contact and intimate engagement. It is the demand inhering in the face-to-face encounter that structures what I'm calling 'intimate work' in this context; Levinas emphasizes recognition and response that are epitomized in the human(e), naked encounter 'face-to-face with the Other' ('Time' 45), a relation that embodies a fundamental ethical demand and a primordial condition of being in the world. Anecdotal evidence derived from my interviews with refugees underscores the ethical and affective work of face-to-face contact in activating a redistribution of hope. Iranian artist and refugee Ardeshir Gholipour proudly recalls being welcomed to Australia by occupants of the Canberra Aboriginal Tent Embassy; this welcome was deeply significant for Gholipour, whose detention for five years and prolonged battle to avoid deportation took a psychological toll, communicating to him that he was not welcome under the terms of sovereign Australia (Cox interview). By making contact with Tent Embassy members, Gholipour can be seen, paradoxically enough, to be framing his sense of belonging in terms of a communal, politicized otherness; the Canberra Tent Embassy (like other protest sites that have stood for shorter periods in Sydney and Melbourne in recent years) occupies a manicured civic space that is invulnerable to native title legal claims and as such constitutes a highly visible confrontation, or what Paul Dwyer terms a 'counter-memorialising' (199), of the displacement that has occurred in order for the space to become a state possession. The alternative authority of Aboriginal sovereignty offered a similar feeling of belonging in Australia for Shahin Shafaei when following his release from detention he was, in his words, 'adopted' by an indigenous community in North Queensland, and gifted a carved pendant by community members (Cox interview). In these instances, an intimate experience of Aboriginal welcome was a crucial aspect of the personal and politicized work of belonging in a new country.

The potential of face-to-face welcome and support is understood by Lowitja O'Donoghue, whose association with refugee issues encompasses involvement with the United Nations and local humanitarian and refugee support organizations, including the Refugee Advocacy Service, A Just Australia and the National Council of Churches in Australia. In public statements, the former chairwoman of ATSIC has articulated a politicized link between Aboriginal people and unauthorized asylum seekers; in an address to the National Council of Churches on 11 July 2004, she commented, 'when asylum seekers—boat people—are dismissed as queue jumpers or "illegals", I want to remind Prime Minister Howard and Ministers Ruddock and Vanstone, that my people had to deal with boat people over 200 years ago!' (Address). O'Donoghue expresses a particular sense of affinity with Afghan asylum seekers, citing the Afghan heritage of many of the indigenous people of her Oodnadatta (South Australia) region as a result of colonial-era contact with cameleers (Speech). This articulation of kinship intervenes in unitary discourses of Australian nationhood by (re)claiming a national history that is sidelined in celebratory narratives of British settlement and convict heritage.[8] Identification with Afghans in O'Donoghue's state capital of Adelaide is strong; the city's Aboriginal Catholic Ministry has forged particularly close ties with the Afghan refugee community and in 2003 its Aboriginal Otherway

Centre (a drop-in community centre) was partially converted into a makeshift mosque (Australian Catholic 4).

In recent years, O'Donoghue's key affective work has been as an advocate, teacher and mother figure to young Afghan refugees living in Adelaide on Temporary Protection Visas. She became involved in the lives of the young people when she gave English classes at an Adelaide Baptist church and subsequently became a support figure to them and a regular presence at the so-called Afghan room established by her friend, broadcaster Stephen Watkins, in his home. The young refugees, who had spent various periods in immigration detention centres, appear to have responded to the support with a sense of belonging; as one declares of the Afghan room, '[t]his is our territory' (qtd in Jopson 33). For O'Donoghue, the act of welcoming refugees must be performed in a personal (as intimate practice) as well as political capacity; in a speech she comments that she has 'welcomed them. They are here. They are part of us. They are grafted into my ancestry and my country' ('Return'). The 'us' that O'Donoghue invokes is not the imagined community for whom the Australian government claims to act, but an alternative community founded upon kinship connections and continuing indigenous sovereignty. O'Donoghue's public explanation of intergenerational, communal and territorially located grafting combines with her private role as 'a mother figure' (qtd in Jopson 33) to young individuals. The image of grafting is a striking one, invoking an irreversible blood link; it performs precisely the opposite function of another biological metaphor for unauthorized migration, that of contamination. Indeed, it speaks to an active cultivation of the 'intercontamination of identity' that Prem Kumar Rajaram notes is a consequence of Australia's relationship of disavowal with undocumented asylum seekers ('Disruptive Writing' 220). For O'Donoghue, intercontamination or grafting has historical, political, biological and emotional dimensions, all of which are imbricated with her Aboriginality.

Of course, the consequences of encounter between Aboriginal people and asylum seekers should not be characterized simplistically in terms of solidarity, hospitality and support; certainly, other face-to-face encounters have manifested quite differently. The ambivalence that can underpin interpersonal contact is illustrated well by the indigenous Tiwi Islanders' relationship with uninvited boat arrivals to their territory in recent years. The Tiwi Islands (comprising Melville Island and Bathurst Island) are situated eighty kilometres from the Northern Territory's capital city, Darwin, and within the regulated zone of the Australian Defence Force Border Protection activities in the Arafura and Timor Seas. On 4 November 2003 a group of fourteen Turkish Kurds and four Indonesian crew members landed at

Melville Island. Suvendrini Perera describes the encounter between the Tiwi people and the boat arrivals:

> The Islanders [...] were surprised to come across obviously foreign men on the beach who asked them, 'Is this Australia?' Perhaps the arrivals were confused by the large number of black faces and the general third world look of the place. The Islanders' answer marked a subtle distinction: You are on Melville Island. Yes, it is Australia. *In but not of.* Did the arrivals register any qualification? [...] They requested water, indicated they were from Turkey, and asked for asylum. Only a few weeks earlier, the Islanders had been instructed by visiting officials what to do in such an eventuality. The men were provisioned, quickly dispatched back to their boat, and the authorities notified. ('Pacific' 201–02)

That same day, the government applied a retrospective excision of the island (and thousands of other islands proximate to the continent) from the migration zone, promptly towed the boat into international waters and directed it back to Indonesia. The Tiwi people's submission to Australian authority resulted in the politically cynical exclusion of their island from the national community and from Australian legal obligations pertaining to migration. While the excision was later rejected in the senate (but re-implemented in 2005), and although some outraged Melville Islanders reportedly resolved to disobey future government directives (Hodson), the government's extraordinary action nonetheless reveals its capacity to control spaces in which it holds scant influence in terms of local social and cultural organization—places that retain, in local terms, indigenous sovereignty.

Perera's narrative of Tiwi obedience to and subsequent instrumentalization by the government is complicated by recent developments in the Islanders' response to arrivals from the north. In April 2009 Tiwi Land Council executive and ranger Andrew Tipungwuti made a request to the government for greater powers to patrol the coastline, stating, 'Our marine rangers don't have adequate powers to help and secure these people until the right authorities arrive' (qtd in Toohey, 'Tiwi Islanders' 2). Head marine ranger on the Tiwis Jack Long articulated how a fear of contagion can exist alongside a sense of kinship: 'I'm Stolen Generation—my mother was full-blood and my father was an Afghan, so of course I've got some sympathy for them. [...] The real question is about disease. We don't know what's coming in on these boats' (qtd in Toohey, 'Save us'). In November 2009, Tiwi Land Council Chairman Robert Tipungwuti made an offer to the government for Bathurst Island to become a site for a new immigration detention centre ('Seeking Asylum' 16). The Tiwi community's position at the maritime vanguard of unauthorized arrivals offers an alternative perspective on indigenous and asylum seeker engagement, reminding us that indigenous sovereignty can articulate as readily to defence of country as to solidarity and welcome.

'Aboriginal Laws Live'

The activism and social practices that I have discussed in this final chapter of the book are in many ways marginal; they remind us that the implications and meanings of the explicitly global or transnational phenomenon of asylum are negotiated and contested within communities and between individuals as much as through legislation and state biopolitics. At the same time, they instantiate indigenous concerns and interests as global, and not just local, concerns and interests. But what might it mean for Aboriginal Australians to articulate, if and when they choose to do so, support for asylum seeking noncitizens? What is the structure of this activist support and how does it construct or configure Aboriginal identities? I have already identified the purchase of James Goodman's argument that Australia's refugee support movements have a dual orientation to national and global universalist preoccupations. But I would argue that Aboriginal activist support for asylum seekers and refugees functions in a way that is distinct from either of these modes. Aboriginal support for asylum seekers tends not to attempt to reclaim national identity, to reassert Australianness as a compassionate and hospitable identity; nor does it seek to advocate for asylum seekers on the basis of values of global interconnection or cosmopolitanism—on the contrary, indigenous activists identify themselves very much in localized, territorialized terms, strategically maintaining their essential difference from other Australians. Their outrage on behalf of asylum seekers is, I want to suggest, subtly but crucially different to the outrage expressed by other activists; it is the difference between saying *these are not Australian values* and *Australian values are not our values*.

Henry Reynolds's characterization of colonial authority in what became the nation of Australia in terms of spheres of influence, that is, the gradual but incomplete encroachment of British territorial control, is instructive for remembering the incommensurability of discourse and practice in the context of sovereignty: '[b]ecause of the vast size of the continent and the slow expansion of British settlement there were many systems of law and many sovereignties in nineteenth century Australia' ('Sovereignty' 211). Reynolds maintains that indigenous sovereignty must be linked logically to land title: 'If, as the High Court declared in Mabo, native title was extinguished in a piecemeal fashion over a long period of time, the same clearly happened with sovereignty. If native title survives in some places then remnant sovereignty must also still exist among communities that still recognise, exercise and accept their traditional law' (211).

Irene Watson observes that '[i]n the struggle for Aboriginal sovereignty [...] the prevailing "reality" is that the sovereignty of Aboriginal laws is an impossibility' (24). State sovereignty is, in terms of this prevailing reality, exclusive and inviolable. And undoubtedly, in the context of unauthorized asylum seekers, the Australian government's biopolitical power does not permit structural challenge from Aboriginal laws or authorities. Yet Watson articulates the paradoxical reality that in spite of their impossibility, 'Aboriginal laws live'; they stand 'elsewhere' to Australian sovereignty and law (24). This concept—which recalls Birch's assertion that Aboriginal 'legitimacy does not lie within the legal system and is not dependent on state recognition' (20)—expresses something of the *aliveness* that I have sought to trace by foregrounding activist and social engagements and representations. James Thompson's identification in his book *Performance Affects* of 'a certain power of affect that is *more than the moment*' (120, italics in original) seems to explicate Watson's and Birch's convictions regarding the reality of lives and laws 'elsewhere', and indeed, underlines my argument that the engagements and representations discussed here offer more than momentary frisson; they are the continuing, cumulative basis of cross-cultural understandings and knowledges, producing, in however minor and incomplete a capacity, alternative landscapes of identity, belonging and community across Australia. And where they are enacted publicly, these engagements invite spectators to think through practical, affective and even ethical understandings of amorphous citizenships—and sovereignties—in the twenty-first century.

CONCLUSION: A GLOBAL POLITICS OF NONCITIZENSHIP

Some of the most high-profile indignities suffered by the world's displaced noncitizens in recent times offer a picture of how human lives are coerced and disavowed against a background of profoundly inequitable economic organization in a globalized world. In July 2014, the Australian government donated two patrol boats to the Sri Lankan government so that this developing nation could assist one of the world's most wealthy in implementing Operation Sovereign Borders. This military-economic transaction, commissioned during a state visit to Sri Lanka by the Minister for Immigration and Border Protection, Scott Morrison, coincided directly with Australia's interception at sea, outside Australian territorial waters, of an asylum seeker vessel and the government's subsequent *Tampa* moment, whereby the 157 Sri Lankan asylum seekers were detained on a customs vessel in an undisclosed location outside Australian waters whilst their fate was wrangled in the High Court and in diplomatic discussions with Sri Lanka and India. Australian human rights lawyer Hugh de Kretser explained during the episode:

> It's a zone that is outside of Australian territorial waters but in which Australia […] can exercise power to prevent the entry of vessels. The Australian government is effectively arguing, 'we can exercise power in that zone but we don't have responsibility for the exercise of that power'. […] It's very difficult to predict what will happen. […] It's extraordinary what's happening; it's taking the 'stop the boats' mantra to a whole new level. (qtd in Morris)

When asked in a television interview to confirm that the asylum seekers would not be returned to Sri Lanka, Prime Minister Tony Abbott declared, 'I will confirm today, as I always will, that we will operate in accordance with our legal obligations, and we will operate in accordance with safety at sea' (qtd in Morris). The prominent Australian barrister and human rights activist Julian Burnside stated that the interception may amount legally to piracy (qtd in Borello). Echoing this assessment was former conservative Prime Minister Malcolm Fraser, speaking at Sydney's Lowy Institute for International Policy, where he described Australia's actions as 'piracy on the high seas' and 'in breach of international law' (qtd in Snow). But unless Australia is made to answer charges of piracy under international law, which is of course tremendously remote, the event will demonstrate the simultaneous reach and impunity of sovereign power beyond its territorial borders.

When the Australian government announced at the end of July 2014 that the 157 asylum seekers being held on the customs vessel would be temporarily brought onshore to an undisclosed location, but would not remain nor be permitted to apply for asylum in Australia, we saw a clear example of how Agamben's concept of exclusion as a condition of being '*captured outside*, that is, it is included by virtue of its very exclusion' (*Means* 40, italics in original) need not have a consistent relationship with territorial logic. Australia's zones of exclusion, where noncitizen bodies are held beyond the reach of sovereign law and yet instrumentalized by it, are wherever the government geographically designates them to be. In this particular case, Australia's biopolitical manoeuvring involved international negotiations with India, resulting in Morrison's announcement upon his return from discussions there that in 'a significant and generous extension of Indian government policy on these matters', the Indian government had agreed to 'consider the return of non-Indian citizen residents who may be Sri Lankan nationals' ('Sri Lankan'). In the end, the Indian solution sought by the Australian government fell through, and the asylum seekers were transported to detention centres on Nauru. But because the people-smuggling vessel was intercepted in a 'contiguous zone', where the Migration Act 1958 doesn't apply, the 157 individuals will not be resettled in Australia. For its part, India is not a signatory to the UN Refugee Convention, but its protection, as of 2014, of some 200,000 refugees from neighbouring countries (UNHCR Regional Operations Profile—South Asia), far in excess of Australia's refugee population, attests not only to the gross asymmetry of global humanitarian burden sharing but also of the extent to which the liberal and humanitarian principles of economically developed nations are incommensurate with their practices (and attempted practices).

As far as covert and overt maritime interventions are concerned, there are some stark similarities between Australian government-sanctioned actions and those of Thai authorities, some confirmed by the Thai government, who have in recent years set adrift unprovisioned boats carrying Rohingya asylum seekers (Allard 11; Bhaumik). The crucial difference is the economic, legislative and also linguistic architecture of the respective sea expulsions. Abbott's and Morrison's performances of obscurantist leadership exemplify Agamben's observation (via Guy Debord) that 'the complete triumph of the spectacle', by which an allegiant state and economy organizes contemporary social life, manifests not just in relations of production, or even relations of violence, but in 'the alienation of language itself, of the very linguistic and communicative nature of humans' expropriating 'the very possibility of a common good' (*Coming* 79). Such an expropriation of the concept of common good has been evident in Morrison's administrative as well as international diplomatic interventions. In October 2014, it was confirmed that Morrison took the extraordinary step of personally issuing a 'Conclusive Certificate', activating a rarely used clause in the Migration Act 1958 in order to block the permanent protection of at least one asylum seeker, preventing access to appeal via the Refugee Review Tribunal (according to unconfirmed reports, the cases of several individuals have been dealt with in this way). The document reads:

I, SCOTT MORRISON, Minister for Immigration and Border Protection, acting under section 411(3)(b) of the *Migration Act 1958*, believing that it would be contrary to the national interest for my decision to refuse to grant a Protection (Class XA) (Subclass 866) visa to [name redacted] to be changed or reviewed, hereby issue a conclusive certificate in relation to that decision. (Conclusive)

The Conclusive Certificate is a powerful demonstration of the alienation of which Agamben writes: the instrumental language of the executive here forecloses the scope of the judiciary on the basis of a nebulous declaration of a confidential 'national interest'. The unilateralism that Morrison engineered, in a fell swoop of some sixty words, was merely a further erosion of the principle of separation of executive and legislative powers in this context. Unauthorized maritime arrivals are already prevented from appealing their cases in Australia's Refugee Review Tribunal: section 411(2) of the Migration Act 1958 states, 'decisions made in relation to a non-citizen who is not physically present in the migration zone when the decision is made' are 'not RRT-reviewable' (Migration Act 1958—Sect 411), and the linguistic and ontological contortions of the Migration Amendment (Unauthorised Maritime Arrivals and Other Measures) Act 2013 mean that it has become impossible for maritime arrivals to find themselves 'physically present in the migration zone'. Successive Australian governments' dizzyingly convoluted constructions of executive jurisdiction, in tandem with militarized incursions outside national borders in the exercise of power to exclude, powered by robust economic means, show just how far a state of exception can stretch. The nation's elected representatives have demonstrated, especially since 2001 but also before, an audacious willingness to use geopolitical limbo and the language of national interest to create precedents of exceptionality vis-à-vis irregular noncitizens.

The vast expenditure of time, resources and intellectual energy on this category of unauthorized human being is remarkable. At a UNHCR consultation meeting with NGOs in June 2014, the United Nations High Commissioner for Refugees, António Guterres, commented on Australia's 'very strange' and disproportionate response to irregular boat arrivals, contextualizing this alongside the nation's responses to other modes of regular and irregular migrant arrival, and to Australia's relatively generous offshore humanitarian programme; as he put it, if migrants 'come in a boat it is like something strange happens to their [Australians'] minds' ('UN High'). The following month, the *New York Times* editorial picked up on Guterres's comment, echoing his bewilderment and similarly condemning what it called Australia's 'draconian' policy innovations (Editorial Board). Guterres was right to diagnose the issue of unauthorized maritime arrival as presenting a 'collective sociological and psychological question' for all Australians, but Australia is not completely out of step with a global neoliberal politics of noncitizenship. July 2014 saw a series of large and at times frenzied protest actions in the United States calling for the deportation of tens of thousands of unaccompanied minors who had crossed the border with Mexico in recent months (Dart); these were visceral reflections of a desire amongst some (though by no means all) US citizens to fuse the idea of expulsion with the idea of the illegal noncitizen, whatever human form the latter may take. Meanwhile, Spain, Italy and Greece continue to be at the maritime vanguard of boat arrivals from Africa, hundreds of whom do not survive the voyage, while those who do arrive encounter nations increasingly hostile to 'illegals'. The movement of asylum seekers into Europe and Turkey also continues to stem from the Middle East; the 2013 UNHCR report on Asylum Trends in Industrialized Countries attributed, for instance, the tripling of asylum applications in Italy in 2011 to the Arab Spring ('Asylum Trends' 13). In October 2014 the UK government announced its withdrawal of funds for migrant boat rescue operations in the Mediterranean, on the grounds that provisions for maritime rescue encourage people to attempt the dangerous sea voyage; this announcement coincided with the termination of Italy's official maritime rescue operation, Mare Nostrum (Travis). Discourse on asylum globally is dominated by a language of crisis and enumeration, even when it is, as in UNHCR reports, expressed in terms of a humane imperative to assist asylum seekers. It is not difficult, therefore, to see how easily crises *for* asylum seekers are discursively rendered as crises *of* asylum seekers, and for fixations to develop on the unauthorized noncitizen as an assailant or contaminant. As Sophie Nield observes, '[t]he discourse surrounding borders and their policing speaks to the profound anxiety that meets the recognition that the supposedly concrete and visible entity, the border itself, is vulnerable. The prevalence of terms such as "porous" and "permeable" in describing borders, and the threats of "flooding", "swamping" and "overrunning" all reflect a particular spatial imaginary' (68). The stringent biopolitics of asylum that is established in Australia functions, quite clearly, as an ideological sticking point, its stakes galvanized anew by confected traumas of events such as *Tampa* or SIEV 36 or the idea of a ghost ship of asylum seekers being held at bay somewhere outside Australian waters by those who implement Operation Sovereign Borders.

The challenge for representation in theatre, film and activism is to meet the urgency of countering dominant pejorative narratives that are applied generically to all undocumented noncitizens, without (as I argued in chapter one) inserting asylum seeker or refugee characters into a collectivity whose innocence is instantiated by their radical vulnerability to power and contingency. It is not just Australian practitioners that are susceptible to this pitfall in the representation of history, identity and contemporary politics. When the famed intercultural theatre practitioner, Ariane Mnouchkine, presented her five-hour epic *Le Dérnier Caravansérail (Odyssées)* around the world, it reproduced many of the tropes of rightless innocence that Arendt foresaw so clearly as the refugee's 'greatest misfortune' (*Origins* 295). The work premiered at Théâtre du Soleil's La Cartoucherie in Paris in 2003 and toured to Quimper, Bochum, Lyon, Berlin, New York, Melbourne and Athens between 2004 and 2006. Broken into two parts, *Le fleuve cruel* (the cruel river) and *Origines et destins* (origins and destinies), its numerous vignettes drew on interviews and correspondence with asylum seekers and other displaced people. With its vast assortment of characters, its preoccupation with victimization and its repetitive focus on acute pain, *Le Dérnier Caravansérail* was, as I have argued elsewhere, 'a kind of mythopoetics of the dispossessed' (Cox, *Theatre & Migration* 18). Helena Grehan reflects on the philosophical framing of the production by Mnouchkine's colleague Hélène Cixous, particularly Cixous's reservations about the use of 'spectacle to "seduce", "clothe" and to reveal the difficult and painful experiences of refugees', into a productive discussion of 'the limits of emotional responsiveness or empathy' (118). What is most troubling to me about this production—troubling especially because none of the production's almost uniformly rapturous reviews noted it—was its fudging of Australian history. One of the scenes enacted a terrifying retreat order issued to a flimsy people-smuggling vessel by Australian Special Air Service (SAS) personnel aboard a helicopter. This was, as the production's programme outlined, a representation of the *Tampa* affair (which is the only occasion where the elite SAS has ever been deployed in the context of Australian border protection operations). But in fact, the SAS did not intercept a flimsy smuggling vessel at all; they were deployed to intercept the massive Norwegian cargo ship from which the *Tampa* incident gets its name. The spectacular scene in *Le Dérnier Caravansérail*, then, constructed a dangerous conflation of events, whose purpose seems to have been to evacuate the cowering asylum seekers of any shred of agency or political identity. The dubious truths of Mnouchkine's work were devised for the purpose of engendering highly emotional responses to the innocent noncitizen other, but the result was to take noncitizens out of politics and out of history, flattening both.

The theatre, film and activist work that I have examined in this book emerged to a significant extent in a responsive relation to the same political and ethical contexts that Mnouchkine and her collaborators were concerned with, chiefly, differential categorizations of human legitimacy in the contemporary world and the abuses to which they give rise. The five chapters of this work share a common concern with the capacity of performance to construct engagements and dialogues, both practical and imaginative, between individuals and across communities and cultures. The need for such work is underscored by Ghassan Hage's clear-sighted analysis of the disarticulation that has accomplished mandatory extrajudicial detention in a democratic Australia:

> At first sight, this idea of a non-social space inhabited by non-people does not seem like a credible idea, but the message the government intends to convey is implicitly quite efficient and credible: dealing with the illegal refuge seekers in this way does not reflect in any way on the values Australians hold regarding how their society should be internally structured. (*White* 106–07)

But as Hage knows, the biopolitics of exceptionality generates dissent within the body politic. One of the key contentions of this book has been that the crisis of dissent vis-à-vis asylum is a crisis of contemporary Australianness as much as anything else. By explicating, practicing and modelling contexts for cross-cultural contact, theatre, film and activism can offer insights into how dealings with Australian noncitizens both reflect and generate Australian identity. That is not to say that such practice reinforces, by default, binary categories of citizen and noncitizen; nevertheless, the work makes meaning within the terms of the binary.

One way of negotiating the binary may be in the terms of the true hospitable encounter; Jeffers conceptualizes this in terms of risk and change: 'there can be no hospitality without risk. That risk is taken on both sides because, in the truly hospitable encounter, both host and guest must be prepared to be changed' (*Refugees* 162). All of the work I have discussed made meaning, to greater or lesser extents, in the context of host communities. While members of these communities may not have been prepared to be 'changed' in quite the way Jeffers describes, they did change the terms of what Australianness can mean.

In doing so, we may ask how far they simply reified the self-identification of an ill-defined imaginative community, 'the already converted'. The question of preaching to the converted is often raised in evaluations of contemporary asylum seeker and refugee representation, but the diversity and complexity of the work I have discussed in this book, and of work that I have not been able to include here, suggests to me that the 'converted' may be a straw figure. Efficacy or cultural work seems to be less akin to a self-reinforcing hall of political mirrors or a unidirectional conversion of the so-called unconverted from one political commitment to another, than with complex, subtle, partial, ambivalent ways in which, in Baz Kershaw's terms, 'ideological business' (29) is transacted.

Performing Noncitizenship has incorporated work that reflected a high level of artistic expertise or economic and institutional investment, as well non-professional work by people with limited opportunities for self-representation or participation. However they are organized, arts projects dealing with asylum seekers and refugees are inflected at successive moments of process and circulation by power, social status, professional experience and economic resource, such that appropriation and imagination, business and friendship, are inevitably intertwined. The value of creative practice by asylum seekers and refugees can relate as much to the affective textures of communication as to politicized protest. Some of the practice I have discussed in this book has led indirectly or directly to other projects. In 2008–10, for instance, a group of teenage refugees from the Horn of Africa embarked on a community arts project led by Shahin Shafaei (whose work as a theatre practitioner in Australia has been discussed here in relation to *Through the Wire* and *Refugitive*, and who subsequent to these projects became an Australian permanent resident) and supported by the Horn of Africa Communities Network Association in partnership with the Victorian College of the Arts. The aim of the Melbourne-based project was to produce a number of theatre pieces and short films based upon the young people's life stories, interwoven around the theme of journeys to Australia. Shafaei's approach as director/facilitator/collaborator combined artistic and therapeutic imperatives. He observes that the development of communication skills, personal confidence, friendship and resettlement among the young refugees, encouraged within workshops and rehearsals over several months, was as significant as the work presented on stage or screen (Cox interview). Investing over an extended period of time in the lives of young people whose backgrounds are similar to yet different from his own, Shafaei has mobilized a heterogeneous refugee community for the professional purpose of performing arts training and the affective purpose of assisting young people in becoming at home in Australia. Shafaei's career upon his release from immigration detention highlights the value of creative arts work in terms of both self-representation and community cultural development and indeed situates him as an exemplary figure of cosmopolitan belonging in Australia.

The afterlives of five of the theatrical productions examined here include their publication in an anthology of plays that I edited in 2013, *Staging Asylum: Contemporary Australian Plays about Refugees*. These are *CMI (A Certain Maritime Incident)*, *Nothing But Nothing*, *Journey of Asylum—Waiting*, *The Rainbow Dark* and *The Pacific Solution* (the collection also includes Linda Jaivin's *Halal-el-Mashakel*). The rendering of these works as published scripts transposed them from the event context with which this discussion has been most concerned to that of the textual archive. If nothing else, this transposition (which in some respects must constitute a reduction) registers the fact that each of the plays, some written by Australians and some by refugees, was implicitly part of something bigger, that they signified and resonated in the context of one another as well as with some of the most troubling political and social realities facing Australian citizens and Australian noncitizens. If the purpose of political theatre is sometimes assumed to be broadly akin to activism—and my alignment of theatre and activism in this book is a way of suggesting that their respective purposes *do* overlap—then the publication of these plays is in part an attempt to ensure their transition from activism to theatre history.

Irregular noncitizenship continues to be absolutely central to the negotiation of social and political life in twenty-first century Australia. The works examined in *Performing Noncitizenship* did not shift this centrality, but instead they sought ways in which new habits of thought, belief and action might be structured in response to it. At the same time, performance practices that seek to unsettle dominant constructions of noncitizenship are informed at a very deep level by the political discourses and the structures of power against which they push. These discourses and structures are continually reconfiguring themselves and their moral rationale. The theatre, film and activism discussed in this book occupy a geo-historical moment but do not encompass it, even though they are defined by and generative of it; they are among the transactions within and across Australian communities that continue to remember the fact that as long as the completeness of certain human lives is refused by their being cast into a politics outside the law of citizens, there is much that remains to be done.

NOTES

Introduction: Framing Noncitizenship

1 SIEV is an operational acronym used by Australian maritime defence personnel that stands for 'Suspected Illegal Entry Vessel', or more recently, 'Suspected Irregular Entry Vessel'.

2 For further discussion of the legal implications of the SIEV 36 incident, see Vincent 2009.

3 In July 2008 it was announced that the policy of mandatory detention of asylum seekers would be abandoned in most cases, in order to address the 'worst excesses' of the Howard era ('New Directions'), but in practice this announcement essentially came to naught.

4 As of 30 April 2013, a total of 8,797 people were being detained in a range of facilities, 5,178 of these in immigration detention centres (Christmas Island, Curtin, Maribyrnong, Northern, Perth, Scherger, Villawood, Wickham Point and Yongah Hill) (Immigration Detention Statistics Summary 3). The government's statistics summary does not include detainees held at recently reopened facilities on the island nation of Nauru and Manus Island in Papua New Guinea.

5 In July 2014, a High Court injunction on the government's interception and return policy forced its admission that a group of 157 Sri Lankan Tamil asylum seekers were being held on a customs vessel outside Australian territorial waters; barrister and human rights activist Julian Burnside stated that the government's action may amount to piracy (Borrello; see Conclusion).

6 Agamben develops his ideas on sovereign power and biopolitics in several works. Chief among them, and key referents in this book, are *Homo Sacer: Sovereign Power and Bare Life*, *Means Without End: Notes on Politics*, *Remnants of Auschwitz: The Witness and the Archive*, and *State of Exception*.

7 The United States has several hundred detention sites, which hold more than thirty thousand immigrants and asylum seekers at any one time (for an in-depth analysis, see Amnesty International's 2009 report *Jailed Without Justice*). Meanwhile, member states of the European Union (EU) voted in 2008 to limit the detention of noncitizens in its detention centres to eighteen months (Brothers); the United Kingdom utilizes 'Removal Centres' mainly for the detention of failed asylum seekers (see 'Immigration Removal Centres').

8 This definition is upheld in the 1967 United Nations Protocol Relating to the Status of Refugees, which removed the 1951 Convention's geographical and temporal limitations.

9 One of the worst and most high-profile maritime tragedies since SIEV X was the SIEV 221 disaster in December 2010, in which an asylum seeker vessel was wrecked off the coast of Christmas Island, resulting in the deaths of 48 people.

10 As Prime Minister, John Howard employed the term in statements and in writing. In an article published in several Australian newspapers in 2001, he wrote, 'For every queue jumper seeking to enter Australia through the back door there is another genuine refugee whose prospects of a better life either in Australia or elsewhere are put on hold' ('Messages' 19; 'A Clear Message' 5). A leading Australian educational resource, Making Multicultural Australia, lists the term 'queue-jumper' as a 'hotword' ('Queue-Jumper').

11 This quote is a line from the second verse of the Australian national anthem, 'Advance Australia Fair'.

12 In a settler colonial context, 'white' may not correlate clearly to ancestry; I use the term here discursively to refer to Australia's dominant Anglo-Celtic ethnicity, but it can also incorporate Australians of western, eastern and southern European ancestry and is as such a strategically imprecise, but nonetheless 'core', invisible norm.

13 In October 2013, the Tony Abbott government announced the reinstatement of the Temporary Protection Visa category and in December of that year lost a Senate vote on the issue. In March 2014, the Minister for Immigration and Border Protection, Scott Morrison, imposed a freeze on the granting of permanent protection visas. In June 2014, the Australian High Court ruled against the Abbott government's attempt to reinstate the TPV. At the time of writing, a reinstatement attempt is continuing in the form of the Migration and Maritime Powers Legislation Amendment (Resolving the Asylum Legacy Caseload) Bill 2014.

14 The United States has recourse to the immigration statuses, Temporary Protected Status and Deferred Enforced Departure for citizens of designated countries who have not been found to be refugees but whose safety would be at risk upon return to their homeland (see Temporary Protected Status). In the UK, there is provision for a Temporary Protection directive 'in the event of a mass influx of displaced people' (see Immigration Rules Part 11A). In 2003, a Human Rights Watch report argued that temporary protection status is inappropriate for fully adjudicated refugees, stating: 'Australia is the *only* country to grant temporary status to refugees who have been through a full asylum determination system and who have been recognized as genuinely in need of protection for 1951 Refugee Convention reasons' ('Human Rights Watch Commentary on Australia's Temporary Protection Visas for Refugees').

15 There has to date been no further official investigation into the SIEV X tragedy. The events of 2001 concerning asylum seekers and the Australian government's and opposition's responses to them are examined in detail by journalists David Marr and Marian Wilkinson in *Dark Victory*.

16 The legislation includes: the Migration Amendment (Excision from Migration Zone) Act 2001; the Migration Amendment (Excision from Migration Zone) (Consequential Provisions) Act 2001; the Border Protection (Validation and Enforcement Powers) Act 2001; the Migration Legislation Amendment (Judicial Review) Act 2001; the Migration Legislation Amendment Act (No. 1) 2001; the Migration Legislation Amendment Act (No. 5) 2001; the Migration Legislation Amendment Act (No. 6) 2001.

Chapter 1: The Politics of Innocence in Theatres of Reality

1 See, for example, Jay Fletcher, 'Theatrical Mockery of Refugees', as well as the introduction to a collection of academic analyses of history, media representation and policy, *Does History Matter? Making and Debating Citizenship, Immigration and Refugee Policy in*

Australia and New Zealand, in which the authors avoid attributing clear volition to asylum seekers implicated in the SIEV 36 tragedy: '[t]he explosion was apparently caused when fuel that had been poured onto the deck, possibly to compel the Navy to take the boat's passengers to Australia, was accidentally ignited' (1).

2 A 2012 report by the Migrant Smuggling Working Group at the University of Queensland's TC Beirne School of Law explains that while numerous captains and crew of SIEVs have been convicted of smuggling offences, far fewer convictions have been possible with respect to the directors and organizers of the vessels. Moreover, the report states that as of 2012, there are 'no known cases involving high-profile organisers of migrant smuggling by air to Australia'. See Migrant Smugglers: Profiles and Prosecutions.

3 The New South Wales state government's Ministry for the Arts assisted the interstate tour after federal funding was unexpectedly withdrawn. For discussion of the funding controversy, see Caroline Wake, 'To Witness Mimesis', 119.

4 Iranians Farshid Kheirollahpoor, Shahin Shafaei and Mohsen Soltany Zand were detained together for certain periods in Western Australia and were already acquainted with one another, while Iraqi man Rami was detained at Villawood in Sydney.

5 At the time of production, Soltany Zand, Kheirollahpoor and Rami had been granted permanent protection in Australia. Shafaei held a Temporary Protection Visa.

6 For a discussion of *I've Got Something to Show You*, see Alison Jeffers, 'Looking for Estrafil', 91–106.

7 Verbatim works by Actors for Human Rights (a constituent strand of Ice and Fire Theatre Company) include their flagship production, *Asylum Monologues* (2006–), and *Asylum Dialogues* (2008–), both scripted by Sonja Linden.

Chapter 2: Domestic Comedy and Theatrical Heterotopias

1 See, for example, Book I, sec. 13 of Arthur Schopenhauer's *The World as Will and Idea*. As I discuss later in this chapter, Henri Bergson developed the idea of incongruity in terms of the living and the mechanical in *Laughter: An Essay on the Meaning of the Comic*.

2 Thomas Hobbes is the best-known proponent of the superiority theory of comedy. For further discussion of incongruity and superiority theories in the context of comedy and horror, see John Mullarkey, 'Bergson and the Comedy of Horrors', 243–255, esp. 247–49.

3 In the following analysis, accounts of staging draw upon the Metro Arts Theatre productions of *The Rainbow Dark* and *The Pacific Solution*, directed by Kat Henry and Marcel Dorney, respectively. All citations from the texts are taken from the published versions of the plays in *Staging Asylum: Contemporary Australian Plays About Refugees*, edited by Emma Cox.

4 'Of Other Spaces' was not reviewed for publication by Michel Foucault and as such is not part of the official corpus of his work.

5 Interestingly, of the four examples of crisis heterotopia that Foucault cites, two are oriented toward female sexuality: 'adolescents, menstruating women, pregnant women, the elderly' (24).

6 This is an improvised cannabis bong made from a plastic Orchy juice bottle (Orchy is an Australian fruit juice brand that has been sold for more than fifty years in Australia and markets itself as the nation's first chilled juice).

Chapter 3: Territories of Contact in Documentary Film

1 Ali is not his real name; the boy's identity was protected owing to fears that the film's explicit criticism of government policy might jeopardize his asylum claim.

2 The Port Hedland immigration detention centre opened in 1991, was privatized by the Howard government in the late 1990s, and closed in 2004. It has since been transformed into Beachfront Village, an accommodation facility to support the town's booming commodities industry.

Chapter 4: The Pain of Others: Performance, Protest and Instrumental Self-Injury

1 The intervention was facilitated in 2007 via a 'special measures' exemption from the *Racial Discrimination Act 1975*; it represented a state of exception with the chief rationales of reducing the gap (in terms of physical and social health) between Aborigines and other Australians, and of addressing child sexual abuse in Aboriginal communities, although no prosecutions were made with respect to the latter. The intervention was replaced in 2012 by a similar set of policy provisions, the Stronger Futures Policy. See chapter 5 for further discussion.

2 For further information on the composition of the detention population see Immigration Detention Statistics Summary.

3 A 2001 Australian Human Rights and Equal Opportunity Commission report on Australia's onshore immigration detention facilities expressed serious concerns about the living conditions in the centres (*HREOC* 2001). A 2008 Commission report (also of onshore facilities) found that while there has been some improvement in conditions, detainees are still held for too long (*HREOC* 2008).

4 The detainees were responding to the department's decision to halt the processing of visas for Afghan asylum seekers.

5 For details on self-injury and protests in Australian detention centres during the period 2000–2004, see Mary Crock, Ben Saul and Azadeh Dastyari 201–02.

6 The 2002 Woomera, Curtin and Maribyrnong hunger strikes and self-harm were reported by *The New York Times*, Reuters, the BBC, *The Guardian*, the UK *Independent*, the *Birmingham Post*, the *Agence France-Presse*, and the *South China Morning Post*, among other outlets.

7 These hunger strikes by unaccompanied minors had a direct political impact that Australian strikes did not: the detained children were visited by Giorgos Costandopoulos, the Greek deputy health minister, who stated they would be transferred to better accommodation on the mainland. See Brabant, and 'Left to Survive Systematic Failure to Protect Unaccompanied Migrant Children in Greece', 69–70.

8 Even the simulation of incarceration for a finite period can result in self-inflicted injury, as Philip Zimbardo's notorious Stanford Prison Experiment in 1971 revealed. See Sherrer.

9 For more information on the Glasgow protest, see Doherty.

10 For detailed analysis of these works, see Edward Scheer, 'Australia's Post-Olympic Apocalypse?'

11 Amanda Wise observes that the proportion of East Timorese (within East Timor) identifying as Catholic rose from less than thirty per cent prior to 1975 to more than ninety per cent during Indonesian occupation. She attributes this, and the centrality of Catholicism to the protest movement in Australia, to several factors: the role of the

Catholic Church in East Timor as a place of sanctuary from violence, the church's active promotion of East Timorese cultural traditions and the function of Catholicism as a means of cultural resistance to and differentiation from the predominantly Muslim Indonesia (97–9).

12 See chapter two, Domestic Comedy and Theatrical Heterotopias, for a fuller discussion of Foucault's concept and its implications for performance and asylum.

13 All quotes from *Refugitive* are taken from its published version in *Another Country: Writers in Detention* (2007).

Chapter 5: Welcome to Country? Aboriginal Activism and Ontologies of Sovereignty

1 I employ the terms 'Aboriginal' and 'indigenous' interchangeably to refer to Australians of Aboriginal and Torres Strait Island heritage.

2 Peta Stephenson's *The Outsiders Within: Telling Australia's Indigenous–Asian Story* offers an insightful analysis of Aboriginal, Asian and white Australian cultural, artistic, literary and performative engagements over the last 100 years. Helen Gilbert and Jacqueline Lo's *Performance and Cosmopolitics: Cross-Cultural Transactions in Australasia* examines Aboriginal and Asian influences on Australasian theatre practice from the colonial era to the present.

3 It should be acknowledged that lawful modes of claiming sovereignty contain their own problems: in Aotearoa–New Zealand, a fundamental contention in relation to the Treaty of Waitangi (1840) is its guarantee that Maori retain *tino rangatiratanga*, which translates to 'self-determination', or arguably, 'absolute sovereignty'. The Maori version of the Treaty states that *kawanatanga*, or governorship, is to be ceded to the British, while in the English version, the term *sovereignty* is used. For in-depth analysis, see Claudia Orange's comprehensive *The Treaty of Waitangi*.

4 For further discussion on the 'non-justiciability' of sovereignty and its implications in relation to indigenous Australians see Maria Giannacopoulos; Henry Reynolds, 'Sovereignty'.

5 For further discussion on the issue of indigenous Native Title and the implications of the High Court decisions and legislation, with links to court decisions and relevant legislation, see Rod Hagen.

6 The protest echoes earlier actions, most famously the Gurindji/Wave Hill cattle station walk-off of 1966–75 (to which I referred briefly in chapter three), led by Vincent Lingiari, which mobilized the land rights movement and led to the Aboriginal Land Rights (Northern Territory) Act 1976.

7 The Embassy consists of a brightly painted shed and a small collection of tents and communal living spaces occupying part of the lawn in front of the Old Parliament House, within the current parliamentary precinct. The site displays the Aboriginal flag, several protest banners and murals bearing messages on indigenous rights and maintains a sacred fire representing peace, justice and sovereignty. Both an activist and living space, the embassy was a point of convergence, social interaction and emotional connection at the time of the official apology in 2008.

8 For a discussion of the history Aboriginal and Muslim relations, see Peta Stephenson, '*Islam in Indigenous Australia:* Historic Relic or Contemporary Reality?'

BIBLIOGRAPHY

'Aboriginal Community Returns to Country: Ampilatwatja Walkoff vs NT Intervention'. The Juice Media (video). *Intervention Walkoff's Blog*. http://interventionwalkoff.wordpress. com/video/. Accessed 23 April 2010.

'Aboriginal Leaders: "Rudd Must Change Refugee Policy"'. *Green Left Online* 817: 11 November 2009. http://www.greenleft.org.au/node/42721. Accessed 9 November 2010.

'Aboriginal Passports Issued to Asylum Seekers Prevented from Entering Australia'. *The Juice Media* 25 May 2010. http://www.youtube.com/watch?v=XkjJpz7nxWM. Accessed 4 November 2010.

Agamben, Giorgio. *The Coming Community*. Trans. Michael Hardt. Minneapolis and London: University of Minnesota Press, 2009. [Italian 1990]

———. *Homo Sacer: Sovereign Power and Bare Life*. Trans. Daniel Heller-Roazen. Stanford: Stanford University Press, 1998. [Italian 1995]

———. *Means Without End: Notes on Politics*. Trans. Vincenzo Binetti and Cesare Casarino. Minneapolis and London: University of Minnesota Press, 2000. [Italian 1996]

———. *Remnants of Auschwitz: The Witness and the Archive*. Trans. Daniel Heller-Roazen. New York: Zone Books, 1999. [epigraph: 155] [Italian 1998]

———. *State of Exception*. Trans. Kevin Attell. Chicago: University of Chicago Press, 2005. [Italian 2003]

Ahmed, Sara. *Strange Encounters: Embodied Others in Post-Coloniality*. London and New York: Routledge, 2000.

Allard, Tom. 'Boat People Cast Adrift, Admits PM'. *The Sydney Morning Herald* 14 February 2009: 11.

Al-Qady, Towfiq. *Nothing But Nothing: One Refugee's Story*. Dir. Assistant Leah Mercer. Metro Arts Theatre, Brisbane, 10–19 April 2005.

———. *Nothing But Nothing: One Refugee's Story*. *Staging Asylum: Contemporary Australian Plays about Refugees*. Ed. Emma Cox. Sydney: Currency Press, 2013. 185–202.

Anderson, Benedict. *Imagined Communities: Reflections on the Origin and Spread of Nationalism*. Revised edition. London and New York: Verso: 1991.

Andrew, Neal. 'Foucault in Guantanamo: National, Sovereign, Disciplinary Exceptionalism'. *Challenge: Liberty and Security*. 12 April 2005. http://www.libertysecurity.org/article199. html. Accessed 23 April 2013.

Ang, Ien. *On Not Speaking Chinese: Living Between Asia and the West*. London and New York: Routledge, 2001.

Appiah, Kwame Anthony. *Cosmopolitanism: Ethics in a World of Strangers*. New York and London: Norton, 2006.

Arendt, Hannah. *The Human Condition*. Chicago: University of Chicago Press, 1998 [1958].

————. *The Origins of Totalitarianism*. Cleveland and New York: Meridian Books, 1958 [1951].

Astore, Mireille. 'When the Artwork Takes the Pictures'. *Law Text Culture* 10 (2006): 239–58.

————. 'Tampa'. 2003. http://mireille.astore.id.au/tampa/. Accessed 25 January 2015.

————. 'Migrant: comments'. 2003. http://mireille.astore.id.au/Migrant/Comments. htm. Accessed 13 May 2009. [Website no longer accessible]

————. *Tampa*. Sculpture by the Sea, Tamarama beach, Sydney. 30 October—16 November 2003.

'Asylum Trends in Industrialized Countries, 2013'. UNHCR, 26 March 2014. http://www.unhcr.org/5329b15a9.html. Accessed 24 July 2014.

Asylum Monologues. Promotional DVD. London: Actors for Refugees, 2006.

Athanasiou, Athena. 'Technologies of Humanness, Aporias of Biopolitics, and the Cut Body of Humanity'. *Differences: A Journal of Feminist Cultural Studies* 14.1 (2003): 125–62.

Austin, Sarah. 'Mike Parr and the discursive rupture: the condemned and punished body as a political strategy in *Close the Concentration Camps*'. *Double Dialogues* 6 (2005). www.doubledialogues.com/archive/issue_six/austin.html. Accessed 28 June 2014.

Australian Catholic Social Justice Council (ACSJC) Briefing 34, April 2003: 4.

Australian Citizenship Test: Snapshot Report. Department of Immigration and Citizenship, Australian Government. April 2009. http://www.citizenship.gov.au/_pdf/cit-test-snapshot-apr-09. pdf. Accessed 11 May 2009.

Australian Human Rights and Equal Opportunity Commission (HREOC). 'A Report on Visits to Immigration Detention Facilities by the Human Rights Commissioner 2001'. December 2001. https://www.humanrights.gov.au/publications/report-visits-immigration-detention-facilities-human-rights-commissioner-2001. Accessed 25 January 2015.

————— '2008 Immigration Detention Report—Summary of Observations following the Inspection of Mainland Immigration Detention Facilities'. January 2009. https://www.humanrights.gov.au/publications/2008-immigration-detention-report-summary-observations-following-inspection-mainland. Accessed 25 January 2015.

Australians Against Racism. 'Australia IS Refugees!' Competition guidelines, 2002. http://www.australiansagainstracism.org/content/schools10-12project.pdf. Accessed 22 April 2008. [Website no longer accessible]

'Awash Among the Acronyms'. Rev. of *CMI (A Certain Maritime Incident)* by version 1.0. *The Canberra Times* 16 October 2004: 23.

Bachelard, Gaston. *The Poetics of Space*. Trans. Maria Jolas. Boston, MA: Beacon Press, 1969. [French 1957]

Balfour, Michael, ed. *Refugee Performance: Practical Encounters*. Bristol and Chicago: Intellect, 2013.

Barkham, Patrick. 'PM Calls Asylum Protest Blackmail—Aborigines Throw Their Weight behind Afghan Hunger Strikers'. *The Guardian* 26 January 2002: 18.

Barwell, Graham, and Kate Bowles. 'Border Crossings: The Internet and the Dislocation of Citizenship'. *Not on Any Map: Essays on Postcoloniality and Cultural Nationalism*. Ed. Stuart Murray. Exeter: University of Exeter Press, 1997. 135–52.

'Behind the Wire'. Rev. of *Refugitive* by Shahin Shafaei. *Geelong News* 12 November 2003: 14.

Bergson, Henri. *Laughter: An Essay on the Meaning of the Comic*. Trans. Cloudesley Brereton and Fred Rothwell. New York: Macmillan, 1914 [1900].

Bhaumik, Subir. 'Burmese Rohingya Refugees Rescued in India's Andamans'. *BBC News* 10 February 2011. www.bbc.co.uk/news/world-south-asia-12413528. Accessed 24 July 2014.

Birch, Tony. 'The Last Refuge of the "Un-Australian"'. *UTS Review* 7.1 (2001): 17–22.

Blythe, Alecky. *Do We Look like Refugees?!* Dir. Alecky Blythe. Produced with Rustaveli Theatre. UK tour, 2010-2011.

———. 'Introduction' to *Come Out Eli. The Methuen Drama Anthology of Testimonial Plays*. Ed. Alison Forsyth. London: Methuen, 2013. 125.

Bonney, Jo. 'Preface'. *Extreme Exposure: An Anthology of Solo Performance Texts from the Twentieth Century*. Ed. Jo Bonney. New York: Theatre Communications Group, 2000. xi–xvi.

Borello, Eliza. 'Julian Burnside says Government could be guilty of piracy for holding 153 asylum seekers at sea'. *ABC News* 9 July 2014. www.abc.net.au/news/2014-07-09/government-accused-of-piracy-by-lawyer-julian-burnside/5586084. Accessed 9 July 2014.

Botham, Paola. 'Witnesses in the Public Sphere: *Bloody Sunday* and the Redefinition of Political Theatre'. *Political Performances: Theory and Practice*. Ed. Susan C. Haedicke, Deirdre Heddon, Avraham Oz, and E. J. Westlake. Amsterdam and New York: Rodopi, 2009. 35–53.

Bourke, Latika. 'Manus Island riot: Independent report by Robert Cornall details deadly detention centre violence'. *ABC News* 26 May 2014. www.abc.net.au/news/2014-05-26/scott-morrison-releases-review-into-manus-island-riot/5478170. Accessed 5 July 2014.

Brabant, Malcolm. 'Victory for Greek Hunger Strikers'. *BBC News* 25 May 2008. http://news.bbc.co.uk/2/hi/europe/7419667.stm. Accessed 3 November 2008.

Brion, Denis J. 'The Criminal Trial as Theater: The Semiotic Power of the Image'. *Law, Culture and Visual Studies* 2014: 329–59.

Brennan, Bernadette. 'Travelling Towards Ourselves: Rights and Recognition in Clara Law's *Letters to Ali*'. *Studies in Australasian Cinema* 3.1 (2009): 15–28.

Brothers, Caroline. 'EU Votes to Allow Member States to Detain Illegal Immigrants for 18 Months'. *The New York Times* 18 June 2008. http://www.nytimes.com/2008/06/18/world/europe/18iht-migrant.4.13810524.html. Accessed 6 July 2009.

'Brutal Look at Reality'. *Canberra Times* 31 March 2005: 9.

Burke, Anthony. 'The Perverse Perseverance of Sovereignty'. *Borderlands e-journal* 1.2 (2002). http://www.borderlands.net.au/vol1no2_2002/burke_perverse.html. Accessed 8 July 2009.

Burnside, Julian. *Watching Brief: Reflections on Human Rights, Law, and Justice*. Melbourne: Scribe, 2007.

Butler, Judith. *Bodies That Matter: On the Discursive Limits of 'Sex'*. New York and London: Routledge, 1993.

———. *Precarious Life: The Powers of Mourning and Violence*. London and New York: Verso, 2004.

Cambis, Tahir, and Helen Newman. *Anthem: An Act of Sedition*. Carlton, Victoria: Media World Pictures, 2004.

Carless, Victoria. *The Rainbow Dark*. Dir. Kat Henry. Metro Arts Theatre, Brisbane, 25 October–4 November 2006.

———. *The Rainbow Dark. Staging Asylum: Contemporary Australian Plays about Refugees*. Ed. Emma Cox. Sydney: Currency Press, 2013. 43–66.

Caruth, Cathy. *Unclaimed Experience: Trauma, Narrative, and History*. Baltimore and London: Johns Hopkins University Press, 1996.

Cavanagh, Greg. *Inquest into the Death of Mohammed Hassan Ayubi, Muzafar Ali Sefarali, Mohammed Amen Zamen, Awar Nadar, Baquer Husani*. Darwin Coroner's Court, 17 March 2010. http://www.defence.gov.au/siev36/inquest.htm. Accessed 22 May 2014.

Chi, Jimmy, and Kuckles. *Bran Nue Dae*. Dir. Andrew Ross. Octagon Theatre, Festival of Perth, 22 February–17 March 1990.

Clark, Chelsea. 'Numbers, Not Names: Play Tells the Story of Detainees'. Prev. of *Through the Wire* by Ros Horin. *Daily Telegraph* 23 January 2004: 18.

Conclusive Certificate Under Subsection 411(3). Commonwealth of Australia. [Redacted.] 2014. static.guim.co.uk/ni/1413861954063/Conclusive-Certificate-reda. pdf?guni=Article:in%20body%20link. Accessed 31 October 2014.

Connolly, William E. *The Ethos of Pluralization*. Minneapolis and London: University of Minnesota Press, 1995.

Convention Relating to the Status of Refugees. United Nations: Office of the High Commissioner for Human Rights. Adopted 28 July 1951. http://www.unhchr.ch/html/menu3/b/o_c_ref.htm. Accessed 19 July 2014.

Coorey, Phillip, and Stephanie Peatling. 'For the Pain, Suffering and Hurt, We Say Sorry'. *The Sydney Morning Herald* 13 February 2008: 1.

Cox, Emma. Interview with Ardeshir Gholipour. Canberra, 24 July 2008. Unpublished.

———. Interview with Christine Bacon. Toynbee Hall, London, 7 June 2007. Unpublished.

———. Interview with Shahin Shafaei. Melbourne, 19 July 2008. Unpublished.

———. Personal correspondence with Leah Mercer. 20 June 2007.

———. Personal correspondence with Towfiq Al-Qady. 1 August 2007.

———, ed. *Staging Asylum: Contemporary Australian Plays about Refugees*. Sydney: Currency Press, 2013.

———. *Theatre & Migration*. Houndmills, Basingstoke: Palgrave, 2014.

———. 'Victimhood, Hope and the Refugee Narrative: Affective Dialectics in Magnet Theatre's *Every Year, Every Day, I am Walking*', *Theatre Research International* 37.2 (2012): 118–133.

———. 'Welcome to Country? Aboriginal Sovereignties and Asylum Seekers', *Australian Studies* 3 (2011). http://www.nla.gov.au/openpublish/index.php/australian-studies Accessed 24 July 2014.

Cox, Eva, and Terry Priest. *Women in Immigration Detention: More Questions than Answers*. The Pamela Denoon Trust for the Women's Electoral Lobby, Australia, August 2005.

Crock, Mary, Ben Saul, and Azadeh Dastyari. *Future Seekers II: Refugees and Irregular Migration in Australia*. Leichhardt, New South Wales: Federation Press, 2006.

Crothers, Lauren, and Ben Doherty. 'Australia Signs Controversial Refugee Transfer Deal with Cambodia'. *The Guardian* 26 September 2014. www.theguardian.com/world/2014/sep/26/australia-signs-refugee-deal-cambodia. Accessed 1 November 2014.

Cubby, Ben. 'Protest at Villawood'. *The Sydney Morning Herald*. 21 March 2006: 7.

Dalton, Trent. 'New Horizons'. *Brisbane News* 15 June 2005: 1, 6.

Darling, Jonathan. 'Another Letter from the Home Office: Reading the Material Politics of Asylum'. *Environment and Planning D: Society and Space* 32 (2014): 484–500.

Dart, Tom. 'Communities Polarised by Influx of Unaccompanied Child Migrants'. *The Guardian* 19 July 2014. www.theguardian.com/world/2014/jul/19/communities-polarised-unaccompanied-child-migrants. Accessed 23 July 2014.

Davey, Melissa and Paul Farrell, 'Immigration department "meets over detention self-harm"'. *The Guardian* 9 July 2014. www.theguardian.com/world/2014/jul/09/immigration-department-crisis-meeting-self-harm-gillian-triggs. Accessed 9 July 2014.

Dean, Bentley. *A Well-Founded Fear*. Prod. Anne Delaney. November Films, 2008.

Dean, Joan F. 'Joe Orton and the Redefinition of Farce'. *Theatre Journal* 34.4 (1982): 481–92.

Debelle, Penelope. 'Afghan Hunger Strikers 'Ready To Die''. *The Sydney Morning Herald* 22 January 2002: 6.

Delbo, Charlotte. *Auschwitz and After*. Trans. Rosette C. Lamont. New Haven and London: Yale University Press, 1995. [French 1970]

———. *Days and Memory*. Trans. and preface Rosette Lamont. Evanston, Illinois: Northwestern University Press, 2001. [French 1985]

'Detainee's Six Weeks Without Food'. *Daily Telegraph* 1 December 2005: 26.

Diprose, Rosalyn. 'The Hand that Writes Community in Blood'. *Cultural Studies Review* 9.1 (2003): 35–50.

Doherty, James. 'Kurds in hunger protest said to be close to death'. *The Scotsman* 5 March 2004. http://news.scotsman.com/asylumseekerdeaths/Kurds-in-hunger-protest-said.2509018.jp. Accessed 6 July 2009.

Downs, Richard. Letter to Professor James Anaya, 20 August 2009. *Intervention Walkoff's Blog*: http://interventionwalkoff.wordpress.com/statements/. Accessed 23 April 2010.

Doyle, Julie. 'Immigration Minister Scott Morrison suggests Operation Sovereign Borders has reduced asylum seeker arrivals in Indonesia'. *ABC News* 4 February 2014. www.abc.net.au/news/2014-01-15/morrison-says-asylum-seeker-boat-arrivals-dropping/5201116. Accessed 5 July 2014.

Dunne, Stephen. 'Hard Times Behind Barrier Of Bureaucracy'. Rev. of *Through the Wire* by Ros Horin. *The Sydney Morning Herald* 24 January 2004: 19.

Dwyer, Paul. 'Re-embodying the Public Sphere: The Arts of Protest'. *Unstable Ground: Performance and the Politics of Place*. Gay McAuley, ed. Brussels and Oxford: Peter Lang, 2006. 187–204.

Dyrenfurth, Nick. 'Battlers, Refugees and the Republic: John Howard's Language of Citizenship'. *Journal of Australian Studies* 84 (2005): 183–96, 259–61.

Editorial Board. 'Australia's Refugee Problem'. *The New York Times* 4 July 2014. www.nytimes.com/2014/07/05/opinion/australias-refugee-problem.html?_r=0. Accessed 24 July 2014.

Edkins, Jenny, and Véronique Pin-Fat. 'Through the Wire: Relations of Power and Relations of Violence'. *Millennium: Journal of International Studies* 34.1 (2005): 1–24.

Edkins, Jenny. *Trauma and the Memory of Politics*. Cambridge: Cambridge University Press, 2003.

Elliot, Stephan. *The Adventures of Priscilla, Queen of the Desert*. Dir. Stephan Elliot. PolyGram Filmed Entertainment, 1994.

Ellis, Ben. *These People*. Sydney: Currency Press, 2004.

Ellman, Maud. *The Hunger Artists: Starving, Writing, and Imprisonment*. Cambridge, MA: Harvard University Press, 1993.

Eltham, Ben. *The Pacific Solution*. Dir. Marcel Dorney. Metro Arts Theatre, Brisbane, 25–29 July 2006.

———. *The Pacific Solution*. *Staging Asylum: Contemporary Australian Plays about Refugees*. Ed. Emma Cox. Sydney: Currency Press, 2013. 67–112.

Enough Rope with Andrew Denton. Episode 69: Interview with Gaby Schultz and Shahin Shafaei. *ABC television* 21 March 2005. Transcript: http://www.abc.net.au/tv/enoughrope/transcripts/s1328996.htm. Accessed 23 July 2014.

Evans, Chris. 'New Directions in Detention, Restoring Integrity to Australia's Immigration System'. 29 July 2008. http://www.chrisevans.alp.org.au/news/0708/immispeeches29-01.php. Accessed 23 April 2009.

Evershed, Nick and Oliver Laughland. 'Rise in hunger strikes and self-harm in Australian immigration centres'. *The Guardian* 20 June 2013. www.theguardian.com/world/2013/jun/10/hunger-strikes-self-harm-australian-immigration-detention. Accessed 5 July 2014.

Farrier, David and Patricia Tuitt. 'Beyond Biopolitics: Agamben, Asylum, and Postcolonial Critique'. *The Oxford Handbook of Postcolonial Studies*. Ed. Graham Huggan. Oxford: Oxford University Press, 2013. 253–70.

Farrier, David. *Postcolonial Asylum: Seeking Sanctuary Before the Law*. Liverpool: Liverpool University Press, 2011.

FitzGerald, Stephen. *Immigration—A Commitment to Australia: Executive Summary*. Canberra: Australian Government Publishing Service, 1988. www.multiculturalaustralia.edu.au/doc/fitzgerald_2.pdf. Accessed 1 November 2014.

FitzSimons, Trish, Pat Laughren and Dugald Williamson. *Australian Documentary: History, Practices and Genres*. Melbourne: Cambridge University Press, 2011.

Fletcher, Jay. 'Theatrical Mockery of Refugees'. *Green Left Weekly* 10 October 2009. https://www.greenleft.org.au/node/42550 . Accessed 14 October 2014.

Foucault, Michel. *Discipline and Punish: The Birth of the Prison*. Trans. Alan Sheridan. New York: Pantheon, 1977. [French 1975]

———. 'Of Other Spaces'. Trans Jay Miskowiec. *Diacritics* 16.1 (1986): 22–27. [French 1984]

———. *The History of Sexuality: An Introduction, Volume 1*. Trans. Robert Hurley. New York: Vintage, 1990. [French 1976]

'Funding Story: Interview with the Director—Steve Thomas'. http://www.hopedocumentary.com.au/hope/about-funding.htm. Accessed 14 June 2011.

Galetta, Antonella. 'The Changing Nature of the Presumption of Innocence in Today's Surveillance Societies: Rewrite Human Rights or Regulate the Use of Surveillance Technologies?' *European Journal of Law and Technology* 4.2 (2013). ejlt.org/article/view/221/377#_edn1. Accessed 20 July 2014.

Giannacopoulos, Maria. '*Mabo, Tampa* and the Non-Justiciability of Sovereignty'. *Our Patch: Enacting Australian Sovereignty Post-2001*. Ed. Suvendrini Perera. Perth: Network Books, 2007. 45–60.

Gibney, Matthew J. *The Ethics and Politics of Asylum: Liberal Democracy and the Response to Refugees*. Cambridge: Cambridge University Press, 2004.

Gilbert, Helen, and Jacqueline Lo. *Performance and Cosmopolitics: Cross-cultural Transactions in Australasia*. Houndmills, Basingstoke: Palgrave Macmillan, 2007.

Gill, Harbant. 'Wired for Sound'. Rev. of *Through the Wire* by Ros Horin. *Herald-Sun* 2 May 2005: 100.

Goodman, James. 'Refugee Solidarity: Between National Shame and Global Outrage'. *Theorizing Emotions: Sociological Explorations and Applications*. Ed. Debra Hopkins, Jochen Kleres, Helena Flam and Helmut Kuzmics. Frankfurt and New York: Campus Verlag, 2009. 269–89.

Grace, Helen. "Small-fry': Suburban Decline and the Global Outback in Recent Asian Australian Cinema'. *Studies in Australasian Cinema* 2.3 (2008): 195–212.

Grant, Bruce. 'After the Exodus'. *Inside Story: Current Affairs and Culture.* 29 January 2009. http://inside.org.au/after-the-exodus/. Accessed 19 April 2009.

Grehan, Helena. *Performance, Ethics and Spectatorship in a Global Age.* Houndmills, Basingstoke: Palgrave, 2009.

Griffiths, Phil. 'LL: Art: Canberra Welcomes Refugees'. 30 August 2000. http://www.mail-archive.com/leftlink@vicnet.net.au/msg03494.html. Accessed 6 February 2009.

Groves, Abigail. 'Blood on the Walls: Self-mutilation in Prisons'. *The Australian and New Zealand Journal of Criminology* 37.1 (2004): 49–64.

Gurr, Michael. *Something to Declare: True Stories of Asylum Seekers in Australia.* Dir. Aubrey Mellor. Beckett Theatre, Malthouse, Melbourne, 21 June 2003; subsequent national tour.

Hage, Ghassan. *Against Paranoid Nationalism: Searching for Hope in a Shrinking Society.* Sydney: Pluto Press, 2003.

———. 'The Differential Intensities of Social Reality: Migration, Participation and Guilt'. *Arab-Australians Today: Citizenship and Belonging.* Ed. Ghassan Hage. Melbourne: Melbourne University Press, 2002. 192–205.

———. *White Nation: Fantasies of White Supremacy in a Multicultural Society.* New York: Routledge, 2000.

Hagen, Rod. 'Native Title'. 1998, 1999. http://rodhagen.customer.netspace.net.au/nativetitle.html#Mabo. Accessed 14 January 2009.

Hazou, Rand. '*Refugitive* and the Theatre of Dys-Appearance'. *RIDE: Research in Drama Education* 13.2 (2008): 181–86.

Health Impact Assessment of the Northern Territory Emergency Response. Canberra: Australian Indigenous Doctors' Association, 2010. 8.

Heinrich, Karen. 'The Culture—Flinch Art'. Rev. of *Close the Concentration Camps* by Mike Parr. *The Age* 12 June 2002: 3.

Henderson, Ian. 'Tampa, Terror Boost Howard—National Barometer'. *The Australian* 26 September 2001: 12.

Hodson, Michael. 'Tiwi Islanders: 'We're all Non-Australians''. *Green Left Online* 562: 19 November 2003. http://www.greenleft.org.au/2003/562/29197. Accessed 20 May 2009.

Hoffstaedter, Gerard. 'Rudd's PNG deal is a co-dependency, not a "regional solution"'. *The Conversation* 21 July 2013. https://theconversation.com/rudds-png-deal-is-a-co-dependency-not-a-regional-solution-16251. Accessed 5 July 2014.

Horin, Ros. *Through the Wire.* Dir. Ros Horin. Sydney Opera House studio, 14–23 October 2004; regional tour March-May 2005.

Horomia, Parekura. 'Maori Party's Head in the Clouds over Non-binding UN Declaration'. Press Release, New Zealand Government, 14 September 2007. http://beehive.govt.nz/release/m%C3%A2ori+party%E2%80%99s+head+clouds+over+non-binding+un+declaration. Accessed 12 February 2009.

Howard, John. 'A Clear Message Sent to the World'. *Herald-Sun* 4 September 2001: 5.

———. 'Messages to the World'. *The Courier-Mail* 5 September 2001: 19.

Howard, Ruth. *Bridge of One Hair.* Dir. Faye Dupras. Jumblies Theatre, Harbourfront Centre, World Stage, 25–29 April 2007.

'Human Rights Watch Commentary on Australia's Temporary Protection Visas for Refugees'. *Human Rights Watch* 13 May 2003. http://www.hrw.org/legacy/backgrounder/refugees/australia051303.pdf. Accessed 19 April 2009.

Humphries, Glen. 'Inspiration from the Inside'. Rev. of *Through the Wire* by Ros Horin. *Illawarra Mercury* 31 March 2005: 38.

Hunter, Mary Ann. 'A Life Between Yes and No'. Rev. of *Nothing But Nothing: One Refugee's Story* by Towfiq Al-Qady. *RealTime* 67 (June-July 2005): 30.

Immigration Detention Statistics Summary. Department of Immigration and Citizenship. Australian Government. 30 April 2013. http://www.immi.gov.au/managing-australias-borders/detention/_pdf/immigration-detention-statistics-apr2013.pdf. Accessed 29 May 2013.

'Immigration Removal Centres'. Home Office: United Kingdom Border Agency. http://www.ukba.homeoffice.gov.uk/managingborders/immigrationremovalcentres/. Accessed 6 July 2009.

Immigration Rules Part 11A: Temporary Protection. UK Government. 13 February 2014. https://www.gov.uk/government/publications/immigration-rules-part-11a. Accessed 31 October 2014.

Jailed Without Justice: Immigration Detention in the USA. Amnesty International. 25 March 2009. http://www.amnestyusa.org/uploads/JailedWithoutJustice.pdf. Accessed 6 July 2009.

Jaivin, Linda. *Halal-el-Mashakel*. *Staging Asylum: Contemporary Australian Plays about Refugees*. Ed. Emma Cox. Sydney: Currency Press, 2013. 113–33.

———. *Seeking Djira*. Fortyfivedownstairs, Sydney, 7–17 August 2003.

Jeffers, Alison. 'Looking for Estrafil: Witnessing "Refugitive" Bodies in *I've Got Something to Show You*'. *Get Real: Documentary Theatre Past and Present*. Ed. Alison Forsyth and Chris Megson. Houndmills, Basingstoke: Palgrave Macmillan, 2009. 91–106.

———. *Refugees, Theatre and Crisis: Performing Global Identities*. Houndmills, Basingstoke: Palgrave Macmillan, 2012.

Johnston, Meg. 'Unsettling Whiteness: The Slippage of Race and Nation in Clara Law's *Letters to Ali*'. *Studies in Australasian Cinema* 2.2 (2008): 103–19.

Joint Standing Committee on Migration. *Immigration Detention in Australia: Facilities, Services and Transparency*. Third Report of the Enquiry into Immigration Detention in Australia. Canberra, August 2009. http://www.aph.gov.au/House/committee/mig/detention/report3/fullreport.pdf. Accessed 1 September 2009.

Jopson, Debra. 'The Barefoot Regent in her Afghan Court'. *Sydney Morning Herald* 8 March 2003: 33.

Jupp, James, ed. *The Australian People: An Encyclopedia of the Nation, Its People and Their Origins*. Second edition. Cambridge: Cambridge University Press, 2001.

Journey of Asylum—Waiting. Dir. Catherine Simmonds. 16—21 March 2010, Bella Union Theatre, Melbourne.

Journey of Asylum—Waiting. Programme note. Asylum Seeker Resource Centre, 2010.

Keneally, Thomas, and Rosie Scott, eds. *Another Country: Writers in Detention*. Expanded edition. Broadway, New South Wales: Sydney PEN and Halstead Press, 2007.

Kennedy, Rosanne. 'Stolen Generations Testimony: Trauma, Historiography, and the Question of 'Truth''. *Aboriginal History* 25 (2001): 116–31.

Kershaw, Baz. *The Politics of Performance: Radical Theatre as Cultural Intervention*. London and New York: Routledge, 1992.

Khoo, Olivia, Belinda Smaill, Audrey Yue. *Transnational Australian Cinema: Ethics in the Asian Diasporas*. Plymouth: Lexington Books, 2013.

Khosravi, Massoud Faramarzi, 'Iranian asylum seekers sew mouths shut to protest Greek mistreatment'. *France 24*, 25 October 2010. <observers.france24.com/content/20101025-iranian-sew-mouths-shut-athens-protest-greece-asylum-human-rights. Accessed 4 July 2014.

Kleres, Jochen. 'Preface: Notes on the Sociology of Emotions in Europe'. *Theorizing Emotions: Sociological Explorations and Applications*. Ed. Debra Hopkins, Jochen Kleres, Helena Flam and Helmut Kuzmics. Frankfurt and New York: Campus Verlag, 2009. 7–27.

Knott, Matthew. 'Tony Abbott says government will not give in to "moral blackmail" over asylum seeker suicide attempts', *Sydney Morning Herald* 9 July 2014. http://tinyurl.com/oemdjh5. Accessed 9 July 2014.

Krauth, Kirsten. 'Refugees: Between Reality and Performance'. *RealTime* 67 June-July 2005: 28.

LaMarre, Heather L. and Kristen D. Landreville. 'When Is Fiction as Good as Fact? Comparing the Influence of Documentary and Historical Reenactment Films on Engagement, Affect, Issue Interest, and Learning'. *Mass Communication and Society* 12.4 (2009): 537–55.

Laub, Dori. 'Truth and Testimony: The Process and the Struggle'. *Trauma: Explorations in Memory*. Ed. and introductions Cathy Caruth. Baltimore and London: Johns Hopkins University Press, 1995. 61–75.

Law, Clara, and Eddie L. C. Fong. *Letters to Ali*. Fitzroy, Victoria: Lunar Films, 2004.

Lawler, Ray. *Summer of the Seventeenth Doll*. London: Angus and Robertson, 1957.

'Left to Survive: Systematic Failure to Protect Unaccompanied Migrant Children in Greece'. Human Rights Watch, 2008. www.hrw.org/sites/default/files/reports/greece1208web_0.pdf . Accessed 4 July 2014.

Le, Hung, and Ningali Lawford. *Black and Tran*. Melbourne International Comedy Festival, 1–23 April 2000.

Levinas, Emmanuel. 'Afterword: The Author's Answers to His Readers' Questions'. Trans. Ruth Feldman. *If This is a Man* and *The Truce*. Trans. Stuart Woolf. London: Abacus, 1987. 381–98.

———. 'Ethics as First Philosophy'. Trans. Seán Hand and Michael Temple. *The Levinas Reader*. Ed. Seán Hand. Oxford: Basil Blackwell, 1989. 75–87. [French 1984]

———. 'Time and the Other'. Trans. Richard A. Cohen. *The Levinas Reader*. Ed. Seán Hand. Oxford: Basil Blackwell, 1989. 37–58. [French 1947]

Levi, Primo. *If This Is a Man* and *The Truce*. Trans. Stuart Woolf. London: Abacus, 1987. [Italian 1947; 1963]

———. *The Drowned and the Saved*. Trans. Raymond Rosenthal. New York: Vintage International, 1989. [Italian 1986]

'Lip Sewing'. *The Sydney Morning Herald* 21 January 2002: 10.

Longworth, Ken. 'Inside Story on Detainees'. Prev. of *Through the Wire* by Ros Horin. *The Newcastle Herald* 11 April 2005: 50.

Maiden, Samantha. 'Abbott Reopens Culture Wars Over Nods to Aborigines'. *The Australian*. 15 March 2010: 1.

Malka, Shlomo. 'Ethics and Politics'. Interview with Emmanuel Levinas and Alain Finkielkraut. Trans. Jonathan Romney. *The Levinas Reader*. Ed. Seán Hand. Oxford: Basil Blackwell, 1989. 289–97.

'Managing Australia's Borders'. Department of Immigration and Citizenship, Australian Government. http://www.immi.gov.au/managing-australias-borders/detention/facilities/about/. Accessed 12 May 2009.

Mansouri, Fethi, and Melek Bagdas. *Politics of Social Exclusion: Refugees on Temporary Protection Visa in Victoria*. Burwood, VIC: The Centre for Citizenship and Human Rights, Deakin University, 2002.

Marks, Benjamin. 'Support for Hunger Strikers'. *The Australian*. 9 April 2007: 4.

Marr, David, and Marian Wilkinson. *Dark Victory*. Crows Nest, New South Wales: Allen & Unwin, 2003.

Mason, Bill. 'Treatment of Refugees 'Heartless''. *Green Left Online* 463: 5 September 2001. http://www.greenleft.org.au/2001/463/25312. Accessed 6 February 2009.

McCallum, John. 'CMI (A Certain Maritime Incident): Introduction'. *Australasian Drama Studies* 48 (2006): 136–42.

McKay, Jim, Geoffrey Lawrence, Toby Miller and David Rowe. 'Gender Equity, Hegemonic Masculinity and the Governmentalisation of Australian Amateur Sport'. *Culture in Australia: Policies, Publics and Programs*. Ed. Tony Bennett and David Carter. Cambridge: Cambridge University Press, 2001. 233–51.

Migrant Smugglers: Profiles and Prosecutions. University of Queensland TC Beirne School of Law, 2012. www.law.uq.edu.au/ms-organisers. Accessed 21 July 2014.

Migration Act 1958—Sect 411. www.austlii.edu.au/au/legis/cth/consol_act/ma1958118/s411.html. Accessed 31 October 2014.

Migration and Maritime Powers Legislation Amendment (Resolving the Asylum Legacy Caseload) Bill 2014. The Parliament of the Commonwealth of Australia. parlinfo. aph.gov.au/parlInfo/download/legislation/bills/r5346_first-reps/toc_pdf/14209b01. pdf;fileType=application%2Fpdf. Accessed 1 November 2014.

Minchinton, Mark. 'The Living Dead: Asylum Seekers and Indigenous Australians'. Context paper for launch of report: *Relocation of Refugees from Melbourne to Regional Victoria: A Comparative Evaluation in Swan Hill and Waarnambool*. Institute for Community, Ethnicity and Policy Alternatives and Sudanese Australian Integrate Learning Program. 20 June 2007.

Mitchell, Tony. 'Three Australian Films by Clara Law'. *Hong Kong Film, Hollywood and New Global Cinema: No Film is An Island*. Ed. Gina Marchetti and Tan See Kam. Oxford and New York: Routledge, 2007. 91–106.

Mnouchkine, Ariane. *Le Dérnier Caravansérail*. Théâtre du Soleil. La Cartoucherie, Paris, 2003.

Monks, Aoife. '"This Painful Chapter": Performing the Law in *Bloody Sunday: Scenes from the Saville Inquiry*'. *Contemporary Theatre Review* 23.3 (2013): 345–56.

Moreton-Robinson, Aileen. 'Towards a New Research Agenda? Foucault, Whiteness and Indigenous Sovereignty'. *Journal of Sociology* 42 (2006): 383–95.

———. 'Writing off Indigenous Sovereignty: The Discourse of Security and Patriarchal White Sovereignty'. *Sovereign Subjects: Indigenous Sovereignty Matters*. Ed. Aileen Moreton-Robinson. Crows Nest, New South Wales: Allen & Unwin, 2007. 86–102.

Morgan, Joyce. 'Acting to Fathom the Truth'. Rev. of *Through the Wire* by Ros Horin. *The Sydney Morning Herald* 15 January 2004: 14.

Morris, Madeleine. 'Government's Operation Sovereign Borders faces legal and moral challenges', *7.30*, ABC video report, 9 July 2014. http://www.abc.net.au/7.30/content/2014/s4042825.htm. Accessed 10 July 2014.

'MPs 'Welcomed to Country''. *ABC News* 12 February 2008: http://www.abc.net.au/news/stories/2008/02/12/2160117.htm. Accessed 14 January 2009.

Mullarkey, John. 'Bergson and the Comedy of Horrors'. *Understanding Bergson, Understanding Modernism*. Ed. Gontarski, S. E., Paul Ardoin, Laci Mattison. London and New York: Bloomsbury, 2013. 243–255.

Murphy, Emma. 'Solidarity and Defiance in the Desert'. *Green Left Online* 535: 23 April 2003. http://www.greenleft.org.au/2003/535/30437. Accessed 9 July 2009.

Neill, Rosemary. 'Love, Laughs and Loss behind the Razor Wire'. *The Australian*, Review section. 22 April 2006: 1.

Neumann, Klaus, and Gwenda Tavan, eds. *Does History Matter? Making and Debating Citizenship, Immigration and Refugee Policy in Australia and New Zealand*. Canberra: ANU E Press, 2009.

Nicholson, Helen. *Applied Drama: The Gift of Theatre*. Houndmills, Basingstoke: Palgrave Macmillan, 2005.

Nield, Sophie. 'On the Border as Theatrical Space: Appearance, Dis-location and the Production of the Refugee'. *Contemporary Theatres in Europe: A Critical Companion*. Ed. Joe Kelleher and Nicholas Ridout. London and New York: Routledge, 2006. 61–72.

'Norforce'. *Message Stick, ABC television* 22 October 2004, 6:00pm. Transcript: http://www.abc.net.au/tv/messagestick/stories/s1222121.htm. Accessed 25 January 2015.

Norrie, Justin. 'Rock the Boat, Baby'. Rev. of *CMI (A Certain Maritime Incident)* by version 1.0. *The Sydney Morning Herald* 26 March 2004: 15.

O'Donoghue, Lowitja. Address to the National Council of Churches in Australia (NCCA) Triennial Forum: 'At the Cross Roads: Living is a World of Change'. 11 July 2004. http://www.ncca.org.au/special_projects/decade_to_overcome_violence/resources/theological_reflections/lowitja_odonoghue_ncca_forum_address. Accessed 10 February 2009.

———. 'Return to Afghanistan: Resettlement or Refoulment?' Speech, Adelaide, 27 February 2003. http://www.safecom.org.au/lowitja.htm. Accessed 10 February 2009.

———. Speech delivered at a fundraising event for the Refugee Advocacy Service of South Australia. 17 April 2003.

Orange, Claudia. *The Treaty of Waitangi*. Wellington: Allen & Unwin / Port Nicholson Press, 1987.

Parr, Adrian. 'The Deterritorializing Language of Child Detainees: Self-harm or Embodied Graffiti?' *Childhood* 12.3 (2005): 281–99.

Parr, Mike. *Close the Concentration Camps*. Monash University Museum of Art, Melbourne, 15 June 2002.

———. Question and Answer Session. Sydney Biennale, Cockatoo Island, Sydney, 22 June 2008.

Perera, Suvendrini. 'Acting Sovereign'. *Our Patch: Enacting Australian Sovereignty Post-2001*. Ed. Suvendrini Perera. Perth: Network Books, 2007.

———. 'A Pacific Zone? (In)Security, Sovereignty, and Stories of the Pacific Borderscape'. *Borderscapes: Hidden Geographies and Politics at Territory's Edge*. Ed. Prem Kumar Rajaram and Carl Grundy-Warr. Minneapolis: University of Minnesota Press, 2008. 201–27.

Peters, Julie Stone. 'Legal Performance Good and Bad'. *Law, Culture and the Humanities* 4.2 (2008): 179–200.

Phelan, Peggy. 'Marina Abramovic: Witnessing Shadows'. *Theatre Journal* 56.4 (2004): 569–77.

'PM Tells People Smugglers to "Rot in Hell"'. *Lateline, ABC television* 18 April 2009. http://www.abc.net.au/lateline/content/2008/s2546319.htm. Accessed 25 January 2015.

Pomeranz, Margaret. Review of *Letters to Ali. At the Movies, ABC television* 2005. http://www.abc.net.au/atthemovies/txt/s1203207.htm. Accessed 12 June 2011.

Popkin, Jeremy D. 'Ka-Tzetnik 135633: The Survivor as Pseudonym'. *New Literary History* 33.2 (2002): 343–55.

'Press Conference with Senator Chris Evans, Minister for Immigration and Citizenship and António Guterres, United Nations High Commissioner for Refugees' Chris Evans, Australian Labor Party website, 24 February 2009. http://www.chrisevans.alp.org.au/news/0209/immiinterviewtranscripts24-02.php. Accessed 8 April 2009.

Protocol Against the Smuggling of Migrants by Land, Sea and Air. Supplementing the United Nations Convention Against Transnational Organized Crime. United Nations, 2000. www.uncjin.org/Documents/Conventions/dcatoc/final_documents_2/convention_smug_eng.pdf. Accessed 23 July 2014.

Pugliese, Joseph. 'Migrant Heritage in an Indigenous Context: For a Decolonising Migrant Historiography'. *Journal of Intercultural Studies* 23.1 (2002): 5–18.

———. 'Penal Asylum: Refugees, Ethics, Hospitality'. *Borderlands e-journal* 1.1 (2002). http://www.borderlands.net.au/vol1no1_2002/pugliese.html. Accessed 8 July 2008.

———. 'Subcutaneous Law: Embodying the *Migration Amendment Act 1992*'. *The Australian Feminist Law Journal* 21 (2004): 23–34.

'Queue-Jumper'. Making Multicultural Australia: Hotwords. http://www.multiculturalaustralia.edu.au/hotwords/unpack/Queue-jumper. Accessed 2 July 2009.

Rajaram, Prem Kumar, and Carl Grundy-Warr. 'Introduction'. *Borderscapes: Hidden Geographies and Politics at Territory's Edge*. Ed. Prem Kumar Rajaram and Carl Grundy-Warr. Minneapolis: University of Minnesota Press, 2008. ix-xl.

Rajaram, Prem Kumar. 'Disruptive Writing and a Critique of Territoriality'. *Review of International Studies* 30 (2004): 201–28.

———. '"Making Place": The "Pacific Solution" and Australian Emplacement in the Pacific and on Refugee Bodies'. *Singapore Journal of Tropical Geography* 24.3 (2003): 290–306.

———. 'The Spectacle of Detention: Theatre, Poetry and Imagery in the Contest over Identity, Security and Responsibility in Contemporary Australia'. *Asia Research Institute: Working Paper Series* 7 (2003): 1–24.

Reynolds, Henry. *North of Capricorn: The Untold Story of the People of Australia's North*. Crows Nest, New South Wales: Allen & Unwin, 2005.

———. 'Sovereignty'. *Citizenship and Indigenous Australians: Changing Conceptions and Possibilities*. Ed. Nicolas Peterson and Will Sanders. Cambridge: Cambridge University Press, 1998. 208–15.

Rodan, Debbie. 'Testimony, Narrative, and a Lived Life'. *Balayi: Culture, Law and Colonialism Journal* 1.1 (2000): 55–75.

Rogers, Dave. *They Get Free Mobiles... Don't They?* Dir. Stuart Brown. Banner Theatre. The Forum, Manchester, 14 June 2007; subsequent national tour.

Rose, Colin. 'Refugee Tale Is Harrowing Indeed, but Where Do We Fit In?' Rev. of *Through the Wire* by Ros Horin. *Sun Herald* 17 October 2004: 29.

Rowland, Michael James, and Helen Barnes. *Lucky Miles*. Dir. Michael James Rowland. Puncture, 2007.

Rudd, Kevin. 'Apology to Australia's Indigenous Peoples'. House of Representatives, Parliament House, Canberra, 13 February 2008. http://www.australia.gov.au/about-australia/our-country/our-people/apology-to-australias-indigenous-peoples. Accessed 25 January 2015.

Salverson, Julie. 'Change on Whose Terms? Testimony and an Erotics of Injury'. *Theater* 31.3 (2001): 119–25.

———. 'Transgressive Storytelling or an Aesthetic of Injury: Performance, Pedagogy and Ethics'. *Theatre Research in Canada* 20.1 (1999): 35–51.

'Sam Watson on the 'Sorry' Speech'. *MurriBlog*. Audio from 4ZZZ radio. 22 February 2008. http://murriblog.blogspot.com/2008/02/sam-watson-on-sorry-speech.html. Accessed 6 February 2009. [Website no longer accessible]

Scarry, Elaine. *The Body in Pain: The Making and Unmaking of the World*. Oxford: Oxford University Press, 1985.

Scheer, Edward. 'Australia's Post-Olympic Apocalypse?' *PAJ: A Journal of Performance and Art 88* 30.1 (2008): 42–56.

———. 'A Vast Field of Lyrical Aggression: Politics and Ethical Spectatorship in Recent Durational Art by Mike Parr'. *Broadsheet* 33.2 (June–August 2004): 23–26.

Schloenhardt, Andreas, and Hadley Hickson. 'Non-Criminalization of Smuggled Migrants: Rights, Obligations, and Australian Practice under Article 5 of the Protocol Against the Smuggling of Migrants by Land, Sea, and Air'. *International Journal of Refugee Law* 25.1 (2013): 39–64.

Schlunke, Katrina. 'Sovereign Hospitalities?' *Borderlands e-journal* 1.2 (2002). http://www.borderlands.net.au/vol1no2_2002/schlunke_hospitalities.html. Accessed 8 July 2009.

Schopenhauer, Arthur. *The World as Will and Idea* [*Die Welt als Wille und Vorstellung*], trans. R. B. Haldane and J. Kemp, 6th ed., London: Routledge & Kegan Paul, 1907 [German 1818/1844].

'Seeking Asylum in Tiwis'. *Northern Territory News / Sunday Territorian* 17 January 2010: 16.

Senate Select Committee on a Certain Maritime Incident. Canberra: Commonwealth of Australia, 2002. http://www.aph.gov.au/binaries/senate/committee/maritime_incident_ctte/report/report.pdf . Accessed 23 July 2014.

Shafaei, Shahin. 'Refugitive: A One-Man Theatre Work'. *Another Country: Writers in Detention*. Expanded edition. Ed. Thomas Keneally and Rosie Scott. Broadway, New South Wales: Sydney PEN and Halstead Press, 2007: 15–22.

———. *Refugitive: A One-Man Theatre Work*. Prod. and dir. Shahin Shafaei and Alex Broun. New Mercury Theatre; subsequent tour of Queensland, New South Wales, ACT, Victoria and South Australia, 2002–2004.

Shaw, Meaghan, and Peter Gregory. 'Hunger Strikers 'Not Our Problem''. *The Age* 18 December 2003: 2.

Shen, Shiao-Ying. 'Finding One's Way Home: Clara Law's Letters to Oz'. *Chinese Women's Cinema: Transnational Contexts*. Ed. Lingzhen Wang. New York and Chichester: Columbia University Press, 2011. 347–68.

Sherrer, Hans. 'Quiet Rage: The Stanford Prison Experiment'. *Prison Legal News* 9 July 2003. http://www.prisonexp.org/legnews.htm. Accessed 6 July 2009.

Siegal, Matt. 'Crisis in tiny Nauru puts spotlight on Australia's asylum seeker policy'. *Reuters* 18 February 2014: www.reuters.com/article/2014/02/18/us-australia-nauru-insight-idUSBREA1H20U20140218. Accessed 5 July 2014.

Simmonds, Catherine, with asylum seekers and refugees from the ASRC. *Journey of Asylum—Waiting*. *Staging Asylum: Contemporary Australian Plays about Refugees*. Ed. Emma Cox. Sydney: Currency Press, 2013. 135–84.

Simmonds, Diana. 'Arts'. *Sunday Telegraph* 10 October 2004: 124.

Smith, Rochelle. 'Iran Playwright to Perform One-Man Show in Geelong'. Prev. of *Refugitive* by Shahin Shafaei. *Geelong Advertiser* 12 November 2003: 22.

Snow, Deborah. '"Piracy on the High Seas": Malcolm Fraser', *The Sydney Morning Herald* 9 July 2014. www.smh.com.au/federal-politics/political-news/piracy-on-the-high-seas-malcolm-fraser-20140709-zt1eq.html. Accessed 10 July 2014.

Soltany Zand, Mohsen. *Inside Out*. Armidale, NSW: Kardoorair Press, 2010.

Sontag, Susan. *Regarding the Pain of Others*. London: Penguin, 2003.

Spivak, Gayatri. 'Three Women's Texts and Circumfession'. *Postcolonialism and Autobiography*. Ed. Alfred Hornung and Ernstpeter Ruhe. Amsterdam: Rodopi, 1998, 7–22.

'Sri Lankan Asylum Seekers to be Transferred from Customs Ship to Onshore Detention Centre'. *ABC News* 25 July 2014. http://www.abc.net.au/news/2014-07-25/asylum-seekers-to-be-transeferred-to-onshore-detention-centre/5624350. Accessed 25 July 2014.

Stanley, Liz, Andrea Salter, and Helen Dampier. 'The Epistolary Pact, Letterness, and the Schreiner Epistolarium'. *Auto/Biography Studies* 27.2 (2012): 262–93.

Stark, Jill. 'Inside Story'. *The Age* 10 May 2005: 2.

Stephenson, Peta. 'Islam in Indigenous Australia: Historic Relic or Contemporary Reality?' *Politics and Culture* 4 (2004). http://aspen.conncoll.edu/politicsandculture/arts.cfm?id=55. Accessed 14 April 2010.

———. *The Outsiders Within: Telling Australia's Indigenous–Asian Story*. Sydney: University of New South Wales Press, 2007.

Stratton, David. Review of *Hope, At the Movies, ABC television* 2008. http://www.abc.net.au/atthemovies/txt/s2259589.htm. Accessed 12 June 2011.

Taylor, Fleur. 'Interview: Refugee Activists Support Aboriginal Rights'. Interview with Noeleen Ryan-Lester and Linda Dare. *Socialist Alternative* 90 (April-May 2005).

Taylor, Matthew, and Saeed Kamali Dehghan. 'Iranians on hunger strike protest against deportation'. *The Guardian* 6 May 2011. www.theguardian.com/uk/2011/may/06/iranians-hunger-strike-protest-deportation. Accessed 4 July 2014.

Temporary Protected Status. U.S. Citizenship and Immigration Services. 16 October 2014. http://www.uscis.gov/humanitarian/temporary-protected-status-deferred-enforced-departure/temporary-protected-status Accessed 31 October 2014.

Thomas, Steve. *Hope*. Melbourne, Flying Carpet Films, 2007.

Thompson, Helen. 'Alrekabi's Music Makes Art of Asylum Stories'. Rev. of *Through the Wire* by Ros Horin. *The Age*, 16 May 2005: 9.

Thompson, James. *Performance Affects: Applied Theatre and the End of Effect*. Houndmills, Basingstoke, Palgrave Macmillan, 2009.

Through the Wire. Information Pack. Redfern, New South Wales: Performing Lines, January 2006.

Tompkins, Joanne. *Unsettling Space: Contestations in Contemporary Australian Theatre*. Houndmills, Basingstoke: Palgrave Macmillan, 2006.

Toohey, Paul. 'Save us from Boatpeople, say Tiwi Islanders'. *The Australian* 13 May 2009. http://www.theaustralian.com.au/news/save-us-from-boatpeople-tiwis/story-e6frg6po-1225711584007. Accessed 28 January 2013.

———. 'Tiwi Islanders want more Power to Stop Boatpeople'. *The Australian* 1 May 2009: 2.

Travis, Alan. 'UK Axes Support for Mediterranean Migrant Rescue Operation'. *Guardian* 27 October 2014. www.theguardian.com/politics/2014/oct/27/uk-mediterranean-migrant-rescue-plan. Accessed 31 October 2014.

Trezise, Bryoni. 'Version 1.0 Shares the Shame'. *RealTime* 61 June-July 2004: 6.

UNHCR Regional Operations Profile—South Asia. UNHCR, 2014. www.unhcr.org/pages/49e4876d6.html Accessed 25 July 2014.

'UN High Commissioner Criticises Australia's "Strange" Obsession with Boats'. Refugee Council of Australia, 18 June 2014. refugeecouncil.org.au/n/mr/140618_UNHCRNGO.pdf. Accessed 24 July 2014.

version 1.0. *CMI (A Certain Maritime Incident)*. Performance Space, Sydney, 26 March–11 April and 13–17 October 2004; The Street Theatre, Canberra, 19–23 October 2004.

version 1.0. *CMI (A Certain Maritime Incident)*. *Staging Asylum: Contemporary Australian Plays about Refugees*. Ed. Emma Cox. Sydney: Currency Press, 2013. 1–42.

Vincent, Michael. 'Oil Rig Asylum Seekers' Status Uncertain'. *ABC News* 22 April 2009. http://www.abc.net.au/news/stories/2009/04/22/2549236.htm. Accessed 22 April 2009.

Wadjularbinna [Nulyarimma]. 'A Gungalidda Grassroots Perspective on Refugees and the Recent Events in the US'. *Borderlands e-journal* 1.1 (2002). http://www.borderlands.net. au/vol1no1_2002/wadjularbinna.html. Accessed 8 July 2009.

Wake, Caroline. 'To Witness Mimesis: the Politics, Ethics and Aesthetics of Testimonial Theatre in *Through the Wire*'. *Modern Drama* 56.1 (2013): 102–25.

Watson, Irene. 'Aboriginal Sovereignties: Past, Present and Future (Im)Possiblities'. *Our Patch: Enacting Australian Sovereignty Post-2001*. Ed. Suvendrini Perera. Perth: Network Books, 2007. 23–43.

Waugh, Thomas. *The Right to Play Oneself: Looking Back on Documentary Film*. Minneapolis: University of Minnesota Press, 2011.

'Whatever it Takes'. *The Howard Years*. ABC television. Episode 2, 24 November 2008.

Whitlock, Gillian. 'Letters from Nauru'. *Life Writing* 5.2 (2008): 203–17.

Wiles, David. *Theatre and Citizenship: The History of a Practice*. Cambridge: Cambridge University Press, 2011.

Willey, David. 'Roman Police find Sewer Children'. *BBC News* 4 April 2009. http://news.bbc.co.uk/2/hi/europe/7983880.stm. Accessed 1 July 2009.

Williams, David A. 'Political Theatrics in the 'Fog of War''. *Australasian Drama Studies* 48 (2006): 115–29.

Wise, Amanda. *Exile and Return Among the East Timorese*. Philadelphia: University of Pennsylvania Press, 2006.

Woolley, Agnes. *Contemporary Asylum Narratives: Representing Refugees in the Twenty-First Century*. Houndmills, Basingstoke: Palgrave Macmillan, 2014.

'Woomera Crisis Hunger Strike: All Media Forced 700m from Compound'. *Adelaide Advertiser* 28 January 2002: 5.

Wright, Lincoln. 'Asylum-seekers 'Affect Aborigines' Prospects''. *The Canberra Times* 22 September 2001: 3.

Zubrycki, Tom. *Molly and Mobarak*. Leichhardt, New South Wales: Jotz Productions, 2003.

Zylinska, Joanna. *The Ethics of Cultural Studies*. London and New York: Continuum, 2005.

INDEX

www.ingramcontent.com/pod-product-compliance
Lightning Source LLC
Chambersburg PA
CBHW022358280326
41935CB00007B/236